The Catholic Revival in English Literature, 1845–1961

THE CATHOLIC REVIVAL IN ENGLISH LITERATURE, 1845–1961

Newman, Hopkins, Belloc, Chesterton, Greene, Waugh

IAN KER

UNIVERSITY OF NOTRE DAME PRESS · *Notre Dame, Indiana*

Manufactured in the United States of America

Library of Congress Cataloging-in-Publication Data
Ker, I. T. (Ian Turnbull)
The Catholic revival in English literature, 1845–1961 : Newman, Hopkins, Belloc, Chesterton, Greene, Waugh / Ian Ker.
p. cm.
Includes index.
ISBN 0-268-03879-1 (cloth : alk. paper)
ISBN 0-268-03880-5 (pbk. : alk. paper)
1. English literature—Catholic authors—History and criticism.   2.
Christianity and literature—England—History—19th century.   3. English
literature—19th century—History and criticism.   4. Catholics—England—
History—19th century.   5. Catholic literature—History and criticism.
6. Catholic Church—In literature.   7. Catholics in literature.   I. Title.
PR468.C3 K47   2003
820.9'9222—dc21
2003012366

∞This book is printed on acid-free paper.

For William Oddie

CONTENTS

ACKNOWLEDGMENTS

I am grateful to Professor William Myers of Leicester University for reading most of the typescript and for his helpful comments. Dr. Robert Carver of Durham University and Rev. Dr. Anthony Meredith, S.J., of Heythrop College, London University, gave me valuable information which I have made use of in, respectively, the introduction and chapter 2. To the Rev. Professor James Reidy of the University of St. Thomas, Minnesota, I am indebted for guiding me in my reading many years ago of Belloc and Chesterton; he has also kindly read all the typescript.

I thank the publisher for permission to reprint under a different title and with some modifications my chapter entitled "Newman's Postconversion Discovery of Catholicism" in *Newman and Conversion,* ed. Ian Ker (Edinburgh: T & T Clark, 1997). Parts or versions of all but one of the other chapters were given as lectures to various institutions and universities, and I must thank those whose comments helped me complete this book.

The Catholic Revival in English Literature, 1845–1961

INTRODUCTION

John Henry Newman's *The Idea of a University* (1873) consists not only of the famous *Discourses on the Scope and Nature of University Education* (1852) but also of the lesser known *University Subjects Discussed in Occasional Lectures and Essays,* originally published as *Lectures and Essays on University Subjects* (1859), which in many ways forms a practical application of the theory of the first half of the book. Amongst these essays and lectures is "Catholic Literature in the English Tongue, 1854–8," which is not a piece that has ever attracted any attention, even from Newman scholars. It is a curiously self-falsifying essay, the thesis of which was anyway to be decisively disproved within a few years and during the course of the next hundred years.

The burden of Newman's argument is that English literature—and he means modern or postmedieval literature, as he doesn't refer even to Chaucer—is essentially Protestant literature and there is nothing that Catholics can hope to do to change the situation: a Catholic literature is simply an impossibility in the context of English culture. Discussing the nature of a literary classic—in the course of which he strikingly anticipates T. S. Eliot's "What Is a Classic?" (1944)[1]—he maintains, as though it were an obvious fact: "In no case can we, strictly speaking, form an English Literature; for by the Literature of a Nation is meant its Classics, and its Classics have been given to England, and have been recognized as such, long since." Newman doubts anyway whether there will be any more "classical authors" as such, as English literature has probably passed its hour of glory: "[T]his is not a day for great writers, but for good writing." This is especially true, he adds, of periodical literature: "There never was a time when men wrote so much and so well, and that, without being of any great account themselves." But while the articles in contemporary periodicals may evince a superior style to that even of the classic English prose writers, the fact that they are anonymous is a serious deficiency, since "the

1

personal" element is so important in great writers. And so Newman concludes that Catholic writers can aspire only to produce ephemeral work, not likely "to last much beyond themselves."[2]

These are remarkable words, considering that they are taken from one of the Victorian prose classics comparable to such works as Matthew Arnold's *Culture and Anarchy,* Carlyle's *Past and Present,* and Ruskin's *Stones of Venice.* It is an even more extraordinary assertion when one considers that the Victorian period, the richest apart from the Elizabethan in English literature, was less than halfway through. George Eliot had not yet published a single novel, Dickens was still at the height of his powers, Trollope was only just beginning his Barchester novels, Hardy had not yet written a single novel. Newman himself had no idea when he wrote this essay that six years after its completion he himself would be publishing one of the great autobiographies in English, the *Apologia pro Vita Sua* (1864). Nor could he possibly have conceived that two years after its publication he would be receiving into the Roman Catholic Church a young Oxford undergraduate called Gerard Manley Hopkins, who was destined to become one of the major or "classic" English poets. If Newman's essay was so happily lacking in prescience about both the future prospects of English literature and the possibility of any significant Catholic contribution, what of his unhesitating assertion that "[w]e have . . . a Protestant literature"? In fact, he is rather more equivocal than that bald statement suggests, admitting in the very next sentence that "the most illustrious amongst English writers has so little of a Protestant about him that Catholics have been able, without extravagance, to claim him as their own, and that enemies to our creed have allowed that he is only not a Catholic, because, and as far as, his times forbade it."[3]

Here Newman is much more prescient in his anticipation of a subject which has attracted growing attention from scholars. The first published study, *The Religion of Shakespeare* (1899), in fact, was by Henry Sebastian Bowden, an Oratorian priest like Newman (who had introduced the institute to England after his conversion) and the son of Newman's close friend from undergraduate days, John William Bowden. Bowden moreover was drawing upon papers left by the Shakespearian scholar Richard Simpson, who was also a convert well known to Newman. Since then a good deal has been written both about Shakespeare's Catholic "recusant" background and about the evidence from his writings.[4] Writing cautiously and not from a Catholic point of view, a modern biographer concludes from the available evidence that Shakespeare's parents "appear to have been Catholics who conformed" to the Church of England, "as thousands of similar conviction did, and they raised a son who conformed: Shakespeare would show a close familiarity with Catholic practices, and at least as much intimacy and sympathy with the 'old faith,' as any Protestant writer of his time."[5]

Apart from Shakespeare, Newman strangely mentions only Pope and Johnson. He ignores two major poets, Crashaw and Dryden, both of whom were converts to Catholicism, as well as Robert Southwell. It is true that Dryden's Catholicism is of interest only in one (long) poem, and Newman can be forgiven for ignoring Southwell and Crashaw when the same neglect persisted through the twentieth century. One obvious reason for this was the huge influence of the Anglo-Catholic T. S. Eliot's view of metaphysical poetry, a view which definitely excluded a baroque poet like Crashaw as foreign and alien to the English tradition. A recent study by Alison Shell (*Catholicism, Controversy and the English Literary Imagination, 1558–1660*), appearing in the last year of the last century and hopefully inaugurating a fresh approach, has pointed out the inconsistency and unfairness of on the one hand praising the Protestant Spenser for enriching English poetry by importing an Italian style, and on the other hand dismissing the Catholic Crashaw as an un-English minor poet for doing exactly the same thing. In other words, it is religious prejudice rather than literary considerations which has prevented Crashaw from being even considered as an important English metaphysical poet like Donne and Herbert.

In her revisionist study, which she clearly sees as a literary counterpart to the revisionist critique of the history of the English Reformation mounted most notably by J. J. Scarisbrick in *The Reformation and the English People* (1984) and Eamon Duffy in *The Stripping of the Altars* (1993), Alison Shell calls for the recognition of Southwell and Crashaw as important *English* poets, albeit writing in the Catholic baroque tradition. She points out that the practice in recent decades of calling metaphysical poetry seventeenth-century lyric or religious poetry has not helped the cause of Southwell either, as he was executed in 1595, five years before the century began. However, these formulations only reflect the fact that Southwell, the Jesuit priest martyr, was not taken very seriously as a poet. True, his significance as a precursor of Herbert and other contemporary religious poets is "a commonplace, and has inspired a number of critics to explore the relationship between devotional poetry and Ignatian meditation," especially as a result of Louis Martz's groundbreaking *The Poetry of Meditation* (1954).

But although Martz discusses Southwell at length, the tendency has been simply to treat Southwell as though he were important only as a harbinger of Herbert and Donne.

Southwell's poems—like Crashaw's and other Catholic poetry—could be read just as easily by Protestants as by Catholics, however differently Catholics might interpret them. His poems were not explicitly Catholic as opposed to Protestant, unlike the works of the writers who are the subject of this book: you could not tell, for example, from reading the most famous, "The Burning Babe," whether it was written by a Catholic or Protestant. Rather, it was the Catholic martyr, or traitor, who could not readily be acknowledged as an exemplar and influence. Because of their influence on seventeenth-century poets, Southwell's short lyrics have received the most attention, but Shell is anxious to emphasize how hugely popular and influential was his lengthy "Saint Peter's Complaint" among both Catholics and Protestants. It was this "long lachrymal elegy that had the greatest effect upon contemporary writers."

The most important successors of Southwell were two poets who were both converts to Catholicism—William Alabaster and Richard Crashaw. Because lachrymal or "tears literature" was intended as a call to repentance, which was a prelude to conversion, not least from Protestantism to Catholicism, the poetry of both Alabaster and Crashaw can reasonably be read as spiritual autobiography. True, unlike Alabaster's conversion which was sudden, Crashaw's took longer, and indeed most of his religious poetry was written while he was still at least outwardly conforming to the Church of England, although already a Catholic in his thinking. One of Crashaw's best known poems, "The Weeper," describes the penitence of Mary Magdalen, the prototype convert, about whom Southwell himself had written two poems. For Crashaw and Alabaster, tears signify devotion and love as against the Protestant emphasis on justification by faith. Shell suggests that the secularism of twentieth-century criticism has naturally favored the religious questioning and struggle that one finds in Donne and Herbert over the ecstatic faith of Crashaw. Thus both modern agnosticism and the English Protestant tradition have combined to deny Crashaw his proper place in English poetry. Nor has the neglect of Southwell helped in this marginalization of a poet whose baroque style and unquestioning religious devotion have of themselves been deemed sufficient to brand Crashaw as un-English and manifestly inferior to his Anglican contemporaries, Donne and Herbert.[6]

Less surprising than Newman's failure even to mention Crashaw is the omission of the name of Dryden, who converted to Catholicism some forty years later toward the end of his life, a conversion he announced in his long poem *The Hind and the Panther* (1687), although only five years before he had defended the Anglican position in *Religio Laici*. We do not know exactly when or why Dryden became a Catholic, only that it was at the end of a long process of religious searching. *The Hind and the Panther* is the longest and most complex of Dryden's original poems (as opposed to translations); it is, in the words of his modern biographer James Anderson Winn, "as a whole . . . a fascinating, risk-taking failure."[7] But if it does not succeed in being one of the major poems in the language, it has some great passages, including one dramatic tour de force where Dryden daringly compares the Catholic Church's acceptance of the heavy responsibility of infallibility with Christ's willingness to bear the sins of the world—in lines, moreover, that ironically echo the arch-Protestant poet Milton ("breathing hatred to the Catholic Church," as Newman puts it), for, as Winn points out, "The success of the analogy between a Church that lifts the burden of infallibility and a Saviour who lifts the burden of the world's sin thus depends upon a Catholic poet's ability to lift the 'glorious weight' of a great Protestant predecessor." And—especially in view of the conventional objection to Crashaw's style—it is a paradox that, while Dryden's "plays and much of his poetry display a baroque . . . exuberance of imagery," it is in his Catholic poetry that he is "most 'Calvinist'" in his style.[8]

Pope, born a Catholic in 1744 just over forty years after Dryden's death, is described by Newman as "personally an unsatisfactory one," while his "freedom . . . from Protestantism is but a poor compensation for a false theory of religion in one of his poems" (*An Essay on Man*).[9] On the other hand, as his modern biographer Maynard Mack puts it, Pope's poem "Eloisa" is notable for its "immersion in Catholic feeling," which "is more than skin-deep," frequently reflecting "the various structures of devotional meditation—exercises particularly recommended by the handbooks of the Counter-Reformation," in a "well-informed" if "sidelong" way. However, for all its "extreme Catholic cast . . . so much unlike anything else that Pope ever wrote," the poem is highly enigmatic, as "one cannot claim that the monastic vocation is treated here with much more respect than in the *Essay on Criticism*," which aroused criticism from his fellow Catholics. Indeed, Eloisa's harsh and melancholy surroundings and incarceration "might be felt to communicate his distaste for all confining practices and dogmas."

Still, it remains possible that "the turmoil of his co-religionists at this period" did "produce in him a special feeling of solidarity with the old faith and its practices, impelling him to write something substantial that, unlike the *Essay on Criticism* and *Rape of the Lock* . . . would be a work for his own people."[10]

Another critic, Thomas Woodman, has pointed out that although Pope is not so much a Catholic poet as a poet who happens to be a Catholic, nevertheless "Catholic influences and images are evident throughout." Even more significant "is the fascinating complex of identification and differentiation between papists and poets that is so built into Pope's conception of himself." No doubt poetry and Catholicism are inextricably linked in Pope's mind because his convert father guided his early literary exercises and studies. However, poets are seen as inherently irreligious because they are devotees of an alternative religion. Like Catholics, poets can expect to be persecuted—especially if they are also Catholics, in which case they are also exposed to criticism from their co-religionists. They can also expect poverty as their lot in life. Pope even sees poets, like Catholics, as martyrs for the truth. The Catholic motifs in Pope suggest a parallel with the apostate John Donne, a poet admired by Pope, whose childhood was spent in an atmosphere of martyrdom and persecution and whose early satires are notable for their Catholic ethos. In fact, circumstances led Pope to become the defender of orthodox Christianity against the skepticism of the Whigs and the theological liberalism of the Hanoverian court, which he saw as destructive of tradition and conducive to anarchy. His "'religion' of poetry," then, "is based not on the worship of art as such but on a commitment to the moral truth behind and in that art." The satirist has a valuable role in defending moral standards. Although Pope was not a practicing Catholic—certainly not after his mother's death, at any rate—and was skeptical about any church's claims to be the true form of Christianity, he resisted all attempts to make him give up the religion which brought so many disabilities and penalties. He also tried not to offend Catholics by his poetry and identified with their sufferings. But it seems it was essentially out of family loyalty rather than faith, since he appears not to have held any specific Catholic beliefs.[11]

Johnson is the last writer mentioned by Newman: "the special title of moralist in English literature is accorded by the public voice to Johnson, whose bias towards Catholicity is well known."[12] Newman is thinking of the conversations recorded by Boswell in which Johnson showed himself remarkably sympathetic to Catholicism, which he thought not very different in essentials from other forms of Christianity and certainly preferable to Presbyterianism, and whose specific tenets, such as mass, confession, purgatory, prayers for the dead, and invocation of the saints, he could see no great objection to, at least in theory if not in practice. And, in spite of what he saw as its corruptions, on one occasion Boswell reports him as saying that he would "be glad to be of a church where there are so many helps to get to heaven" and even that he "would be a papist" if he could, except for "an obstinate rationality," which he might be able to overcome "on the near approach of death," of which he had "a very great terrour."[13]

Finally, one other major figure that one might have thought Newman would include in his list is Walter Scott, who, Newman wrote in an 1839 article, "turned men's minds in the direction of the middle ages," not least through his romantic depiction of medieval Catholicism. In this article, which Newman quotes at length in his *Apologia pro Vita Sua,* the first literary influence on the Oxford Movement that he mentions is that of Scott, who "reacted on his readers, stimulating their mental thirst . . . setting before them visions, which, when once seen, are not easily forgotten."[14]

This book is not intended, like that of Alison Shell, to be a work of revisionism as much as one of *realization:* that is, in the very Newmanian sense, of making real the extent to which Catholicism informed and shaped a considerable and impressive corpus of literature in the nineteenth and twentieth centuries. Of the two dates in the subtitle, the first, 1845, the year of Newman's conversion, speaks for itself; it was the same year as the publication of his first work as a Catholic, *An Essay on the Development of Christian Doctrine,* written while he was still an Anglican to test his growing conviction of the truth of the Church of Rome's claims but not published till after his conversion; the first work he wrote as a Catholic appeared three years later in 1848, his first novel, *Loss and Gain.* The second date, 1961, is less obvious, but it is a significant date for three reasons: it is the beginning of the decade which saw the wholesale secularization of England and by the end of which one could no longer speak of the country as a Protestant country; it is also the year before the Second Vatican Council began, a council which effectively brought to an end the Counter-Reformation and Tridentine Catholicism; and finally, coincidentally, it is the year in which Evelyn Waugh, who was to be so horrified by the council, and not least the abolition of the Tridentine mass, published the last novel of his masterpiece, the trilogy *The Sword of Honour,* a book whose title, *Unconditional Surrender,* was intended to reflect Waugh's disillusion at the alliance of the Allies with the atheistic Soviet Union against Nazi Germany, but which could also be understood as presaging his despair at what was to happen to the Catholic Church in the next few years.

I should make it clear at the outset that this book is not meant in any sense to be a survey of the Catholic literary revival; the only chapter which resembles a survey is the present one. There is, in fact, already a recent, very thorough survey of the Catholic novel, which lists more novelists than Newman could have ever dreamed of in the 1850s.[15] I have already mentioned one curious coincidence; there are two others.

The first is that of all the many Catholic writers between 1845 and 1961, the six most important and significant figures were all writers whose work could not have been written without the formative Catholic influence. When I say "Catholic writers," I mean, of course, writers who really were Catholics, unlike, to take the most obvious case, Joseph Conrad, who seems to have abandoned his native Catholicism as thoroughly as he abandoned his Polish nationality. The other major figure who might be thought of as a Catholic writer was Conrad's friend and collaborator, Ford Madox Ford, a convert but a very intermittent Catholic. Unlike Conrad, Ford does include Catholicism in his fiction, especially in his most creative period when he wrote his masterpieces, *The Good Soldier* (1915) and the tetralogy *Parade's End* (1924–28). But, as Thomas Woodman remarks, these works "can hardly be considered 'Catholic' works in any full sense," although they do "explore in passing certain sociological and ethical dilemmas of English Catholicism with some evidence of inwardness on the subject." Woodman also points out that *The Good Soldier* uses the device of "the unreliable narrator," which is a helpful way for the Catholic novelist to present a Catholic point of view without appearing to do so by means of an impartial or even prejudiced observer, as Waugh does in *Brideshead Revisited* and Greene in *The End of the Affair.* The Catholicism of the wife of "the good soldier" determines her response to his adulteries.[16] The unsympathetic narrator who tells the story is forced to admit that Catholics have an extraordinary "sense of rectitude," as well as perhaps being "always right" when "dealing with the queer, shifty thing that is human nature."[17] Woodman notes how, in *Parade's End,* Ford's "nostalgic cultural Catholicism" plays its "special, if subordinate," part in his pessimism about the death of English civilization, and it is significant that the heir of Christopher

Tietjens, who represents the last of the Christian gentlemen, will be a Catholic and so inherit estates seized from Catholics at the Reformation.[18] Although only a more or less nominal, nonpracticing Catholic, whose faith was ambiguous, Ford found in Catholicism ceremony and tradition, which he linked with the feudal Toryism whose demise he lamented. Still, when all allowance has been made for the Catholic elements in Ford's work, the fact remains that he was not a Catholic writer in the sense in which the writers discussed in this book are *Catholic* writers, writing as they did *because* they were Catholics, and so producing exactly the kind of work that Newman desiderated but thought it vain to hope for.

A writer may happen to be a Catholic by birth, like Conrad, or by conviction, like Edith Sitwell, but neither necessarily makes the writer a Catholic writer in this sense. Like but unlike Conrad's works, Sitwell's poetry was unaffected by her conversion to Catholicism in 1955, nine years before her death, since her poetry was already written. Similarly, Siegfried Sassoon became a Catholic in 1957, but he had been a war poet, not a Catholic poet, and his poetry was also already written. Other writers may be Catholics and well known as Catholics, but their Catholicism may have even less effect on their writing than in the case of Ford.

From one point of view, there could not be a more Catholic poet than Francis Thompson, the protégé of the Meynells, and it is true that he made use of the liturgy and wrote poems on specifically Roman Catholic themes. In fact, however, not all that much of his poetry is specifically religious, and indeed his two best-known poems, which are religious poems ("The Hound of Heaven" and "The Kingdom of God"), could have been written by any religious poet and did not need a Catholic poet to write them. Coventry Patmore, who influenced Thompson, became a Catholic in 1862 when his best-known book of poetry, *The Angel in the House* (1854–63), a celebration of married love, was on the point of completion; but the erotic mysticism, for all its debt to Crashaw and St. John of the Cross, of his much less popular *The Unknown Eros* (1877) could just as easily have originated from an Anglo-Catholic poet. However, Anglo-Catholic writers fall outside the scope of this book, which is concerned only with specifically Roman Catholic writers—and moreover writers writing before the Second Vatican Council, as I have already indicated, within the Tridentine Church of the Counter-Reformation.

The convert poet David Jones has perhaps a better claim than Francis Thompson to be considered a specifically Roman Catholic writer. Like his fellow convert the historian Christopher Dawson, he saw Western culture and history as being determined and shaped by Catholicism. His *Anathemata* (1952), a long and complex work of both poetry and prose, uses the symbols of the mass to order and interpret history and nature; but Jones is closer to the Church fathers than to the Counter-Reformation, and among other scriptural references the antiphonal structure and parallelism reflect the antiphonal chanting of the psalms as well as the versicles and responses of the liturgy. His earlier more accessible *In Parenthesis* (1937), an epic work also of both prose and poetry, is often liturgical in its language, with references to the mass and liturgical year. Although the soldiers' physical life is sometimes set against a Christian, and on occasions explicitly Catholic, background, the work belongs more to the genre of war literature, specifically that of the trenches of World War I, than to the genre of religious or Catholic literature.

Turning to fiction, Robert Hugh Benson, the convert son of an archbishop of Canterbury, published his best-known Catholic novel, *Come Rack! Come Rope!*, in 1912, a story of persecution of Catholics under Elizabeth, which is a more gripping novel than the usual dismissal of it as melodramatic propaganda suggests. The first of his future fantasies, *Lord of the World* (1907), is another celebration of Catholic martyrdom, highly ultramontane in its view of the papacy, while *The Dawn of All* (1911) is unabashedly triumphalistic. Along with *The Average Man* (1913), which has a contemporary setting, these are Benson's best novels, all still very readable and intensely Roman Catholic.

Benson's sometime friend, the notorious Frederick Rolfe, or "Baron Corvo" as he liked to be called, wrote one book which is still read, *Hadrian the Seventh* (1904), a fictitious autobiography of wish fulfillment in which the protagonist, who has been dismissed from the seminary, is elected pope. Ronald Firbank, another homosexual convert who was received into the Church by Benson, resembles Rolfe in his decadence, exotic aestheticism, fantasies, and idiosyncratic style. It is doubtful whether he was a believing or practicing Catholic for long, but his elaborate parodies of Catholicism in novels like *Valmouth* (1919) and *Concerning the Eccentricities of Cardinal Pirelli* (1926) contain a curious note of sympathy, even devotion. Firbank was an influence on Evelyn Waugh—but the influence was literary, not religious. Another very similar convert homosexual was John Gray, whose future fantasy *Park* (1932) is also an idiosyncratic work of aestheticism, though, unlike Firbank's, it has the serious purpose of celebrating the Church's liturgy as the one true source of beauty in the world.[19]

The Scots nationalist novelist Compton Mackenzie became a Catholic in 1914, an event that he fictitiously predicted at the end of his best-known, and at the time very influential, novel, *Sinister Street* (1913–14), in the form of the semiautobiographical protagonist. But otherwise the book is not a Catholic novel, while his explicitly Catholic fictions, *The Altar Steps* (1924) and his most ambitious work, the six volumes of *The Four Winds of Love* (1937–45), are now hardly read. Another convert, Maurice Baring, wrote some successful social portraits of English upper-class society, especially *C.* (1924), *Cat's Cradle* (1925), and *Daphne Adeane* (1926), in which Catholicism is shown to offer the way of rendering personal suffering redemptive in a world where human love is ultimately doomed.[20]

In 1933 Antonia White published *Frost in May,* the story of her convent school days. It was the first of a quartet of autobiographical novels, the next of which was not published till nearly twenty years later: *The Lost Traveller* (1950), *The Sugar House* (1952), and *Beyond the Glass* (1954). A theme which she touches on several times is one that we shall see recurring in the course of this book, but it is not noticeable in the other, more important minor Catholic literature so briefly surveyed here: the paradox that Catholicism is so much more supernatural and otherworldly and yet at the same time more human and matter-of-fact than Protestantism.

Antonia White became a Catholic at the age of seven, when her father converted. Another woman novelist, Muriel Spark, was an adult convert from Judaism who was much influenced by Newman. She published her first novel three years later: *The Comforters* (1957). In this and *Memento Mori* (1959), *The Bachelors* (1960), *The Ballad of Peckham Rye* (1960), and *The Prime of Miss Jean Brodie* (1961), there is a strong awareness of the presence of the supernatural, especially evil and original sin. This last novel was published in the year where this study finishes. It is the same year in which Anthony Burgess, a lapsed Catholic with strong Manichaean tendencies, published *A Vision of Battlements.* His succeeding novels contain such Catholic motifs as the view of the Reformation as a disaster, the sense of being a foreigner in one's own country, a strong awareness of evil and original sin, and an antipuritanism.[21]

We shall find, interestingly enough, in the Catholic writers this book is concerned with—writers who are Catholic writers not just because they happen to be Catholics, or even because they happen to introduce Catholic ideas and themes into their work—that we are not dealing with such familiar and typical topics at all. The second coincidence I referred to earlier is that these six writers belong in pairs to three different periods of English literature. Not only did Newman receive Hopkins into the Catholic Church, but Hopkins's first job was at the Oratory School in Birmingham which Newman had founded, and his last job was at the university which Newman had also founded in Dublin. Belloc was a close friend and acknowledged influence on Chesterton. Greene and Waugh were contemporaries at Oxford who later became friends.

CHAPTER 1

John Henry Newman's Discovery of Catholicism

I

The story of John Henry Newman's conversion to Catholicism is not quite the same as the story of his discovery of Catholicism. The *Apologia pro Vita Sua*, which is subtitled *Being a History of His Religious Opinions*, is in effect his theological autobiography up to the year 1845, when he joined the Roman Catholic Church. In it we find a detailed account of the development of his ideas but barely anything of his inner spiritual life or of his wider religious experience. The aim of the book is to show how one man was led on logically and naturally from a belief in Christianity to belief in Catholicism. It was important for Newman to demonstrate not only the sincerity of his conversion but also its intellectual objectivity. As a result, other elements and factors are rigorously excluded, thus giving an impression of an austerely cerebral approach to religion, which was far from true of the man.

Nevertheless, it is the case that Newman's intellectual conversion did for the most part precede a more experiential and imaginative discovery of Catholicism. He became a Catholic, he always used to say afterwards, because he became convinced that "the modern Roman Communion was the heir and the image of the primitive Church."[1] Now while Newman knew a very great deal about the early Church, he knew extraordinarily little about contemporary Catholicism, apart from its formal doctrines and teaching. In 1835, two years after the beginning of the Oxford Movement, he had admitted to wanting "to fall across a Romanist to get into their system," but he was averse to "getting intimate" with any English Catholics because of their hostility to the Church of England and their readiness to enter into alliance with its political enemies.[2] However, what is interesting is that he saw quite clearly that one could not understand Catholicism merely by reading books about it, as there was no substitute for actually getting to know real Catholics so as to learn about the Catholic Church from within. In 1844, when he had all but decided to become a Roman Catholic, he could even say: "I have no existing sympathies with Roman Catholics. I hardly ever, even abroad, was at one of their services—I know nothing of them. I do not like what I hear of them."[3]

This is something of an exaggeration, since, as Newman gladly acknowledged in the *Apologia,* there was a Roman Catholic who *had* significantly influenced his conversion—a young Irish priest called Charles Russell, a professor at Maynooth, who had taken the initiative in writing to Newman and sending him a volume of St. Alfonso Liguori's sermons, in the hope that practical writings of this kind would do far more to make Catholicism better known and more attractive to English people than theology or apologetics. Russell could hardly have chosen more daringly, as the Neapolitan saint was a favorite target for anti-Catholic polemic because of his allegedly notorious Mariolatry. In reality, Newman found nothing of the kind, and the fact that certain passages had been admittedly omitted from one sermon on the Virgin Mary seemed to him to show that Catholic spirituality varied from country to country and was not as uniform as he had supposed. Russell had actually called on Newman a couple of times in Oxford, and Newman later commented, "He had, perhaps, more to do with my conversion than any one else."[4]

Still, it was true that Newman had avoided Catholics and Catholic churches—except, that is, when he was on his Mediterranean tour of 1832–33, and when he could hardly help being exposed to both. Even then, he had "religiously abstained from acts of worship, though it was a most soothing comfort" to go into churches, where, however, he claimed not to "know what was going on; I neither understood nor tried to understand the Mass service."[5] Like the relevant part of the *Apologia,* this passage from a postconversion letter hardly does justice to the effect on Newman of visiting Catholic countries and seeing Catholicism for the first time at firsthand.

Nevertheless, the *Apologia* does make some reference to the emotional and imaginative influence on his development of actually experiencing for himself a religion which, since his early Evangelically inspired conversion of 1816, he had regarded as the religion of the Antichrist predicted in the

Bible. In the first chapter, where he gives a summary account of these momentous months in his life, when for the first time he traveled abroad and witnessed both Catholicism in Italy and Malta and Orthodoxy in the Greek islands, he claims that "I saw nothing but what was external; of the hidden life of Catholics I knew nothing." But in the second chapter he effectively modifies this by admitting that he was certainly affected, indeed impressed, not to say moved, by what he saw:

> [W]hen I was abroad, the sight of so many great places, venerable shrines, and noble churches, much impressed my imagination. And my heart was touched also. Making an expedition on foot across some wild country in Sicily, at six in the morning, I came upon a small church; I heard voices, and I looked in. It was crowded, and the congregation was singing. Of course it was the mass, though I did not know it at the time. And, in my weary days at Palermo, I was not ungrateful for the comfort which I had received in frequenting the churches; nor did I ever forget it. . . . Thus I learned to have tender feelings towards her [the Catholic Church]; but still my reason was not affected at all.[6]

If one looks at the many letters Newman wrote home during the six months and more that he was away, one cannot help being struck by the contradictory attitude he finds himself adopting toward Catholicism. On the one hand, he retains all his theological objections to Tridentine Catholicism, objections which in some cases were only reinforced by the apparent scandals and superstitious practices he observed; on the other hand, not only is he clearly surprised by how much seemed quite unobjectionable and even admirable, but above all the effect of being in Rome itself was quite overwhelming. He thought it "a wonderful place," "of all cities the first," and all the cities he had seen were "but as dust, even dear Oxford inclusive, compared with its majesty and glory." But he was also affected by very different feelings. After all, Rome bore an "awful" aspect as "the great Enemy of God": its "immense . . . ruins, the thought of the purposes to which they were dedicated, the sight of the very arena where Ignatius suffered, the columns of heathen pride with the inscriptions still legible—brand it as the vile tool of God's wrath and again Satan's malice." Again and again in his letters to England, he spoke of his "mingled feelings" about the city:

You are in the place of martyrdom and burial of Apostles and Saints—
you have about you the buildings and sights they saw—and you are in
the city to which England owes the blessing of the gospel—But then
on the other hand the superstitions;—or rather, what is far worse, the
solemn reception of them as an essential part of Christianity—but
then again the extreme beauty and costliness of the Churches—and
then on the contrary the knowledge that the most famous was built (in
part) by the sale of indulgences—Really this is a cruel place.—There is
more and more to be seen and thought of, daily—it is a mine of all
sorts of excellences, but the very highest.[7]

Captivated as he obviously was by Rome, he felt obliged nevertheless
to continue to protest against its unreformed religion:

I cannot quite divest myself of the notion that Rome Christian is somehow under an especial shade as Rome Pagan certainly was—though I
have seen nothing here to confirm it. Not that one can tolerate for an
instant the wretched perversion of the truth which is sanctioned here,
but I do not see my way enough to say that there is anything peculiar
in the condition of Rome.[8]

True, it had to be admitted, there were "great appearances . . . of piety in
the Churches," but nonetheless as a "system" Catholicism was undoubtedly
"corrupt."[9] Thus, when he saw the Pope and his "court" at high mass, he
was scandalized by the "unedifying dumbshow":

[Y]et as I looked on, and saw . . . the Holy Sacrament offered up, and
the blessing given, and recollected I was in church, I could only say in
very perplexity my own words, "How shall I name thee, Light of the
wide west, or heinous error-seat?"—and felt the force of the parable of
the tares—who can separate the light from the darkness but the Creator Word who prophesied their union? And so I am forced to leave the
matter, not at all seeing my way out of it.—How shall I name thee?[10]

He was to ponder that question for a long time. In the meantime, he
contented himself with trying to distinguish between "the Roman C. system," which he had "ever detested," and "the *Catholic* system," to which he

confessed himself "more attached than ever." And while he feared that "there are very grave and farspreading scandals among the Italian priest-hood, and there is mummery in abundance," he could not help thinking that "there is a deep substratum of true Christianity, and I think they may be as near truth (at the least) as that Mr. B. whom I like less and less every day." Mr. Burgess was the Church of England chaplain in Rome, whom Newman described as "one of the most perfect watering place preachers I ever heard, most painfully so—pompous in manner and matter."[11] The "individual members of the cruel church," on the contrary, "who can but love and feel for them?" The baffling paradox was that in these very fol-lowers of the Antichrist who condemned Protestants as heretics, Newman found "so much amiableness and gentleness" and (the highest compli-ment) "so much Oxonianism."[12] At the time he did not realize the dis-turbing implications of the corruption he saw or thought he saw: "the lamentable mixture of truth with error which Romanism exhibits—the corruption of the highest and noblest views and principles, far higher than we Protestants have, with malignant poisons."[13] Much later, as a Catholic, he was to develop a veritable theology of corruption, but for the time being he did not appreciate the momentous corollary of the principle that the cor-ruption of the best is the worst.

The only explanation he could provide at the time was that there was an important distinction between Rome as a place (according to Protestant mythology one of the four beasts of the Apocalypse) and as a church: but "how a distinction is to be drawn between two powers, spiritual and dev-ilish, which are so strongly united, is . . . beyond our imagination." He could only attribute the corruption of Roman Catholicism to the fact that it was the "slave" of the evil spirit which must still be ruling Rome.[14]

As he waited for a ship to take him back to England from Palermo after his nearly fatal illness in Sicily, he felt "calmed" by visits to churches, al-though he still "knew nothing of the Presence of the Blessed Sacrament there" and did not attend any services.[15] But the "still retreats" which the cool churches offered from "the city's sultry streets" inspired the deeply ambivalent poem which begins:

> Oh that thy creed were sound!
> For thou dost soothe the heart, Thou Church of Rome,
> By thy unwearied watch and varied round
> Of service, in thy Saviour's holy home.[16]

Twelve years were to pass before Newman was to become convinced that it was the Roman Catholic Church's creed that was "sound" and that it was the Anglican position that was unsound. During those years he was never again to come into the same kind of close contact with Catholicism as he had experienced during those exciting, traumatic months away from England. The profound revolution in his theological views from Calvinist Evangelicalism to Roman Catholicism was the result of a gradual development that culminated in the recognition that the Church of the fathers was the same Church as that modern Church which alone dared call itself simply "the Catholic Church." In his own words, it was "the living picture" that "history presents" which finally opened his eyes to an identity that he admitted was not self-evident. And it was to that first "vision of the Fathers" which his boyhood reading of the Calvinist Joseph Milner's history of the Church had so vividly impressed on his mind that he ultimately traced his conversion: "The Fathers made me a Catholic."[17] However difficult it might be to show someone else the close resemblance that he saw between modern Catholicism and early Christianity, nevertheless it did seem obvious to him in later years that "the present Roman Catholic Church is *the only Church* which is like, and it is very like, the primitive Church": "It is almost like a photograph of the primitive Church; or at least it does not differ from the primitive Church near so much as the photograph of a man of 40 differs from his photograph when 20. *You know that it is the same man.*"[18]

Even so, Newman was still remarkably ignorant at the time of his conversion of the concrete system of Catholicism as it had developed through the Middle Ages and since the Council of Trent. In fact, the feature of his new religious life that most struck him came as a complete surprise to him.

> We went over not realizing those privileges which we have found *by* going. I never allowed my mind to dwell on what I might gain of blessedness—but certainly, if I had thought much upon it, I could not have fancied the extreme, ineffable comfort of being in the same house with Him who cured the sick and taught His disciples. . . . When I have been in Churches abroad, I have religiously abstained from acts of worship, though it was a most soothing comfort to go into them—nor did I know what was going on; I neither understood nor tried to understand the Mass service—and I did not know, or did not observe, the tabernacle Lamp—but now after tasting of the awful delight of wor-

shipping God in His Temple, how unspeakably cold is the idea of a Temple without that Divine Presence! One is tempted to say what is the meaning, what is the use of it?[19]

It is striking how it was the reservation of the Sacrament in the tabernacle in Catholic churches that more than anything else impressed and moved Newman. This is not what we might expect a convert as ignorant about Catholic devotional life as Newman claims he was, to emphasize above everything else, including the mass and the ritual. And it tells us, I suggest, something very important not only about Newman but also about a central aspect of the impact of Catholicism on the imagination of the English Protestant convert. Thus, when Newman informs a close Anglican friend, "I am writing next room to the Chapel—It is such an incomprehensible blessing to have Christ in bodily presence in one's house, within one's walls, as swallows up all other privileges.... To know that He is close by—to be able again and again through the day to go in to Him,"[20] he is not only making a devotional or spiritual point. He is also saying something very significant about objectivity and reality. For it was this concrete presence in a material tabernacle which above all, for Newman, at any rate, produced "the deep impression of religion as an objective fact" that so struck him about Catholicism—far more, for instance, than its discipline or its fervor. He admired in those early days "every where the signs of an awful and real system." Moreover, objectivity and reality also meant practicality: instead of being "a vague generality" or merely "an idea," Catholicism as compared with Anglicanism struck him as "a working religion." Had he not previously, he acknowledged, "kept aloof from Catholics from a sense of duty" but "known them and their religion from personal acquaintance," he would have been "exposed to a set of influences in their favour, from which in matter of fact" he "was debarred."[21] In Newman's case, in other words, the discovery of Catholicism was a consequence rather than a cause of conversion.

When Newman arrived in Italy nearly a year after his becoming a Catholic, he was immediately and vividly aware of a reality that powerfully impinged on his consciousness but of which he had been quite oblivious on his previous visit. Arriving in Milan, he immediately noticed that he had now an added reason for preferring classical to gothic architecture, since its simplicity meant that the high altar stood out as the focal point of the church. This meant that the reserved sacrament had particular prominence, for "[n]othing moves there but the distant glimmering Lamp which betokens the Presence of our Undying Life, hidden but ever working." His almost obsessive preoccupation with this "Real Presence" goes further than the devotional: "It is really most wonderful to see this Divine Presence looking out almost into the open streets from the various Churches. . . . I never knew what worship was, as an objective fact, till I entered the Catholic Church."[22] For what Newman had discovered was that the objectivity of the worship which so impressed him—and nothing else about the worship attracted his attention in the same way—only reflected the objectivity of Catholicism, which he came to believe was a quite different kind of religion from Anglicanism or Protestantism. Now he was delighted to find, as he thought, "a real religion—not a mere opinion such, that you have no confidence that your next door neighbour holds it too, but an external objective substantive creed and worship."[23]

Again, linked to this was the discovery of a highly practical kind of religion: instead of being something very special and removed from the ordinary mundane world, Catholicism, for all its supernatural claims—and, ever since that Mediterranean tour, it had always seemed to Newman a much more spiritual religion than that of the Church of England—seemed also, paradoxically, a far more matter-of-fact kind of "business":

> [A] Catholic Cathedral is a sort of world, every one going about his own business, but that business a religious one; groups of worshippers, and solitary ones—kneeling, standing—some at shrines, some at altars—hearing Mass and communicating—currents of worshippers intercepting and passing by each other—altar after altar lit up for worship, like stars in the firmament—or the bell giving notice of what is going on in parts you do not see—and all the while the canons in the choir going through matins and lauds, and at the end of it the incense rolling up from the high altar . . . lastly, all of this without any show or effort, but what everyone is used to—every one at his own work, and leaving every one else to his.[24]

Newman's fascination with the reservation of the Sacrament also reflects his celebrated philosophical distinction between the notional and the real: whereas notions are intellectual abstractions, reality is what we personally experience in the appropriate concrete form. Dogmatic as Catholicism is, it is not, Newman insisted, exactly a religion of dogmas, for what Catholics worship, he claimed, are not theological definitions but "Christ Himself, as He is represented in concrete in the Gospels." It is, then, to assist and enable this worship of the person of Christ that the consecrated bread is reserved in a prominent place in Catholic churches: "Do we not believe in a Presence in the sacred Tabernacle, not as a form of words, or as a notion, but as an Object as real as we are real?"[25]

An important part of Newman's apologetic for Catholicism lies in trying to show how different a religion in kind it is from Protestantism—that it is not as if Protestantism, seen from the Catholic perspective, is simply a truncated form of Catholicism, or as if Catholicism, from the Protestant point of view, is essentially Protestantism plus a great many more or less undesirable accretions or corruptions. To one inquirer he wrote, "I do not disguise that Catholicism is a *different religion* from Anglicanism." To the convert, he explained, Christianity is no longer something that you merely experience privately in your own heart or construct in your own mind from reading the Bible; it is now a reality that exists independently of the subjective self and that envelops one, so that "the Atonement of Christ is not a thing at a distance, or like the sun standing over against us and separated off from us, but . . . we are surrounded by an *atmosphere* and are in a medium, through which his warmth and light flow in upon us on every side."[26]

This reality of Christ, for Newman, is experienced not only through the reservation of the Sacrament but also through the whole Catholic system of sacraments and sacramentals, as well as the crucifixes and statues and pictures that surround the worshiper in a Catholic church. And the authority for one's religious beliefs is no longer oneself ultimately but the Church: "[C]onsider the vast difference between believing in a living authority, unerring because divine, in matters of doctrine, and believing none;—between believing what an external authority defines, and believing what we ourselves happen to define as contained in Scripture." This was why Newman was never in the least sanguine about reunion between the Church of England and the Church of Rome:

> [I]t is a mere deceit, I fully think, to suppose that the difference between Catholics and Anglicans is, that one believes a little more, and the other a little less; and therefore that they could unite. The religions never could unite . . . because they proceed on different *ideas;* and, if they look in certain external aspects alike, or have doctrines in

common, yet the way in which those doctrines are held, and the whole internal structure in the two religions is different; so that, even what a person has before he is a Catholic, being grafted on a new stock, becomes new, and he is like a Jew become Christian.[27]

Whatever the element of exaggeration in this stark analysis, Newman never substantially changed his mind in later years.

II

This whole postconversion process of discovering Catholicism was not only of theological significance, for, as we have already seen from his letters, it also powerfully engaged Newman's imagination. Certainly, it provided much of the creative stimulus that produced the most overtly literary period in his life, when he deliberately abstained from theology and instead turned to writing Catholic apologetics in the form of novels and satire. The book that he himself always considered his "best written book,"[28] although sadly it must be one of his least read works, was *Lectures on the Present Position of Catholics in England,* published in 1851. It contains some of the finest prose satire in the language, Swiftian in its savage imagery and grotesque in the vein of Dickens, whose satiric portrait of Mr. Podsnap in *Our Mutual Friend* (1865) is remarkably anticipated in one glorious passage on John Bull's chauvinism.[29] The delivery of these lectures was a significant moment in English cultural history, as for the first time since the Reformation a writer of genius confronted head-on the triumphalism of the "no Popery" tradition, which had captured the popular imagination.

There is a passage in *Present Position of Catholics* which is worth quoting at some length because, for Newman, it evokes the utterly alien atmosphere of a Catholic church as it may strike a Protestant observer.

One day he pays a visit to some Catholic chapel, or he casually finds the door open, and walks in. He enters and gazes about him, with a mixed feeling of wonder, expectation and disgust; and according to circumstances, this or that feeling predominates, and shows itself in his bearing and his countenance. In one man it is curiosity; in another, scorn; in another, conscious superiority; in another, abhorrence; over all their faces, however, there is a sort of uncomfortable feeling, as if they were in the cave of Trophonius or in a Mesmerist's lecture-room. One and all seem to believe that something strange and dreadful may happen any moment; and they crowd up together, as if some great ceremony is going on, tiptoeing and staring, and making strange faces, like the gargoyles or screen ornaments of the church itself. Every sound of the bell, every movement of the candles, every change in the grouping of the sacred ministers and the assistants, puts their hands and limbs in motion, to see what is coming next; our own poor alleviation, in thinking of them, lying in this,—that they are really ignorant of what is going on, and miss, even with their bodily eyes, the distinctive parts of the rite. What is our ground of comfort, however, will be their ground of accusation against us; for they are sure to go away and report that our worship consists of crossings, bowing, genuflections, incensings, locomotions, and revolvings, all about nothing.[30]

Part of Protestants' incomprehension lies simply in their ignorance of what is going on; but there is, Newman thought, a deeper reason for their bewilderment, which concerns the very nature of the worship rather than its exact meaning. For Newman's point is that there is a real sense in which comprehension is impossible, since Catholic worship, which is essentially dramatic as it consists in liturgical action, is incommensurate with Protestant worship, which is a religion of the word. In Protestant churches words are read and said and sung, accompanied by the minimum of action; in Catholic churches it is the words which accompany the liturgical and sacramental actions. Far from seeing Catholic worship as consisting of mere actions that signify nothing beyond themselves, Newman was now in effect struck by the force of the saying that actions speak louder than words.

As an Anglican, Newman had written, "Life is for action."[31] But "life," he had also insisted, was a note of the Church; and as a Tractarian he had been preoccupied with trying to show that the Church of England contained a "living principle," a note of the Church "equal to any,"[32] a view that seemed to be supported by the extraordinary "burst of hidden life" that the Oxford Movement had aroused and which seemed to him "the greatest note of the Catholicity of our Church."[33] A Church, therefore, that was living would be characterized by a life of action. On the eve of the Oxford Movement he had contrasted "that fresh vigorous Power of . . . the first centuries" and "the joyous swing of her advance" with the "do-nothing perplexity" of the Church of England.[34] Action meant life, and it was action that Newman found in Catholicism, not least in its worship. It was no longer a matter simply of saying words; things happened. The undergraduate hero of *Loss and Gain* wonders, "Why can only a clergyman read prayers in church?—Why cannot I?"[35] There is no answer to that question, he discovers, unless the clergyman is seen as a priest who alone can perform certain sacramental actions, as in "that Church which really breathes and lives."[36]

In *Difficulties of Anglicans,* the set of lectures which preceded *Present Position of Catholics* in 1850, and which were intended to persuade Anglo-Catholics to follow him into the Roman Catholic Church, Newman describes the difference between the faith of Protestants and that of Catholics by arguing that the former hold religious opinions, while for the latter the objects of belief are simply facts:

> Just as in England, the whole community, whatever the moral state of the individuals, *knows* about railroads and electric telegraphs; and about the Court, and men in power, and proceedings in Parliament; and about religious controversies, and about foreign affairs, and about all that is going on around and beyond them: so, in a Catholic country, the ideas of heaven and hell, Christ and the evil spirit, saints, angels, souls in purgatory, grace, the Blessed Sacrament, the sacrifice of the Mass, absolution, indulgences, the virtue of relics, of holy images, of holy water, and of other holy things, are of the nature of *facts,* which all men, good and bad, young and old, rich and poor, take for granted. They are facts brought home to them by faith.

To prove his point, Newman avers that if you were to "set up a large Crucifix at Charing Cross; the police would think you simply insane."[37]

But a faith which sees things or facts is also, according to Newman, a faith that may not be accompanied by the appropriate moral state, as he graphically illustrates with a vivid scene, again exemplifying the kind of activity and movement in Catholic churches that had made such a deep impression on him.

> You enter into one of the churches close upon the scene of festivity, and you turn your eyes towards a confessional. The penitents are crowding for admission, and they seem to have no shame, or solemnity, or reserve about the errand on which they are come; till at length, on a

penitent's turning from the grate, one tall woman, bolder than a score of men, darts forward from a distance into the place he has vacated, to the disappointment of the many who have waited longer than she. You almost groan under the weight of your imagination that such a soul, so selfish, so unrecollected, must surely be in very ill dispositions for so awful a sacrament. You look at the priest, and he has on his face a look almost of impatience, or of good-natured compassion, at the voluble and superfluous matter which is the staple of her confession. The priests, you think, are no better than the people. . . .

There is a feeble old woman, who first genuflects before the Blessed Sacrament, and then steals her neighbour's hankerchief, or prayer-book, who is intent on her devotions. . . . She worships and she sins; she kneels because she believes, she steals because she does not love.

Newman goes on to describe the fiesta scene outside the church, so calculated to shock Protestant susceptibilities. It is not only the popular superstition and corruption—"You come out again and mix in the idle and dissipated throng, and you fall in with a man in a palmer's dress, selling false relics, and a credulous circle of customers buying them as greedily as though they were the supposed French laces and India silks of a pedlar's basket"—but the extraordinary mingling of the religious and the secular. The town's guilds are laying on a play about the creation, but

the *chef d'oeuvre* of the exhibition is the display of fireworks to be let off as the *finale*. "How unutterably profane!" again you cry. Yes, profane to you . . . profane to a population which only half believes; not profane to those who, however coarse-minded, however sinful, believe wholly. . . . They gaze, and, in drinking in the exhibition with their eyes, they are making one continuous and intense act of faith.[38]

This intensity, however, in Newman's eyes, bore no relation to the seriousness of Protestantism, which, in "reforming" Catholicism, had fenced off religion from the rest of ordinary life and turned it into something special and removed from day-to-day living. The relief of finding religion integrated again into life more than compensated in his view for the kind of corruption that he thought was inseparable from a living religion: "Things that do not admit of abuse have very little life in them."[39]

As an Anglican, Newman had felt that Catholic priests did not have the "pompousness" of the clergy of the established Church.[40] It had not apparently occurred to him then that a popular religion which was notoriously characterized by superstition and vulgarity was hardly likely to possess the kind of pomposity that seemed to belong to Anglicanism, which, unlike Methodism, for instance, has never really been a "popular" religion, except in the ritualistic Anglo-Catholicism that, in a later phase of Tractarianism, established itself in the slums of the industrial cities. In a private memorandum he wrote as a Catholic, Newman observed that the Protestantism of the Church of England (he expressly excepted the embellishments of Anglo-Catholicism) could hardly be "*less* adapted to popularity. . . .[I]t goes as near to the wind, as a religion can." Apart from the unappealing sabbatarianism favored by Evangelicals, he had even as an Anglican himself "shivered" at the "dreary" liturgy of the Book of Common Prayer (he was, of course, speaking of its devotional rather than literary qualities).[41]

Dignity and good taste were not qualities one necessarily found in Catholicism, but what Newman did think he had found was *life*, whether it was the popular devotions in the churches or the hidden contemplation of the enclosed cloister. In both cases, the worshiper seemed to be actively directed to an external, objective reality, as Newman attempts to show in the passage that ends his account of this imaginary Catholic mise-en-scène:

> You turn to go home, and, on your way, you pass through a retired quarter of the city. Look up at those sacred windows. . . . Seclusion, silence, watching, meditation, is their life day and night. The immaculate Lamb of God is ever before the eyes of the worshippers; or at least the invisible mysteries of faith ever stand out, as if in bodily shape, before their mental gaze.[42]

There is a further point that Newman draws out in his concluding reflections. For if "faith impresses the mind with supernatural truths, as if it were sight," then "the faith of this man, and the faith of that, is one and the same, and creates one and the same impression." This meant that religion was not a private, subjective affair of an introverted nature, Newman claimed: "It is just the reverse among a Protestant people; private judgment does but create opinions, and nothing more; and these opinions are peculiar to each individual, and different from those of any one else. Hence it leads men to keep their feelings to themselves, because the avowal of them only causes in others irritation or ridicule."

We shall be returning to this idea of Catholicism as liberating one from the prison of self; but in the meantime it is worth noting the interesting link Newman makes between the inherently uncertain nature of a religion for which one is oneself the ultimate authority and the quality of pomposity:

> Since, too, they have no certainty of the doctrines they profess, they do but feel that they *ought* to believe them, and they try to believe them, and they nurse the offspring of their reason, as a sickly child, bringing it out of doors only on fine days. They feel quite clear and quite satisfied, while they are very still; but if they turn about their head, or change their posture ever so little, the vision of the Unseen, like a mirage, is gone from them. So they keep the exhibition of their faith for high days and great occasions, when it comes forth with sufficient pomp and gravity of language, and ceremonial of manner. Truths slowly totter out with Scripture texts at their elbow, as unable to walk alone. Moreover, Protestants know, if such and such things *be* true, what *ought* to be the voice, the tone, the gesture, and the carriage attendant upon them; thus reason, which is the substance of their faith, supplies also the rubrics, as I may call them, of their behaviour. This some . . . call reverence; though I am obliged to say it is . . . a mannerism, and an unpleasant mannerism. . . . They condemn Catholics, because, however religious they may be, they are natural, unaffected, easy, and cheerful, in their mention of sacred things; and they think themselves never so real as when they are especially solemn.[43]

Newman was thinking specifically of the "parsonic voice" Anglican clergy are famous for using in church, a voice which may seem not only to seal off religion in a special compartment from ordinary life but also to introduce the important element of class, since the "parsonic voice" carries distinct social overtones. Certainly, in the nineteenth century the Anglican clergyman was above all a "gentleman," distinguished by class and education from the majority of his congregation. In some of Hopkins's poems, by contrast, as we shall see, we find a kind of celebration of the classlessness of the Catholic priest.

In Newman's first novel, *Loss and Gain: The Story of a Convert,* published in 1848, the hero visits a Catholic church for the first time and exclaims to himself, "This *is* a popular religion." Having always been given to understand that Catholic worship was essentially "formal and external"—after all, Catholicism was notoriously priest-ridden with its clerical ritual and Latin liturgy—Charles Reding is astonished to discover that "it seems to possess all classes . . . indiscriminately." One might have thought that the vernacular language of the Prayer Book would make the liturgy of the Church of England much more accessible to the people, but although "the words were Latin . . . every one seemed to understand them thoroughly."

> Reding thought he never had been present at worship before, so absorbed was the attention, so intense was the devotion of the congregation. What particularly struck him was, that whereas in the Church of England the clergyman or the organ was everything and the people nothing, except so far as the clerk is their representative, here it was just reversed. The priest hardly spoke, or at least audibly; but the whole congregation was as though one vast instrument or Panharmonicum, moving all together, and what was most remarkable, as if self-moved. They did not seem to require any one to prompt or direct them, though in the Litany the choir took the alternate parts.[44]

After Newman became a Catholic, he commented not only on the "simple, natural, unaffected faith" of the Catholic clergy[45] but also on the fact that they were not required to be educated in the sense of receiving a liberal education at the university but rather had to undergo professional training in the seminary for the priesthood, which in a sense was a profession like any other.[46] Very different was the typical Church of England clergyman, who had received a classical education but usually only the most rudimentary theological formation, at least until the foundation of Anglican theological colleges in the latter half of the nineteenth century. Unlike the Catholic priest with his clearly defined sacramental function and the Dissenting minister with his preaching ministry, the Anglican clergyman seemed less of a professional and more of an amateur—and therefore a gentleman. His most characteristic clerical task was reading the services in the Prayer Book. But it was not at all clear why he and he only could do this. When Charles Reding raises the question, he is directed by another character in the novel to Jeremy Bentham's sarcastic proposal that "a parish-boy should be taught to read the Liturgy. . . . Why send a person to the University for three or four years at an enormous expense, why teach him Latin and Greek, on purpose to read what any boy could be taught to read at a dame's school? What is the *virtue* of a clergyman's reading?"[47]

Dickens makes exactly the same point in *Great Expectations* in his comic sketch of Mr. Wopsle, the parish church clerk, who

> had a deep voice which he was uncommonly proud of; indeed it was understood among his acquaintance that if you could only give him his head, he would read the clergyman into fits; he himself confessed that if the Church was "thrown open," meaning to competition, he would not despair of making his mark in it. The Church not being "thrown open," he was, as I have said, our clerk. But he punished the Amens tremendously; and when he gave out the psalm—always giving the whole verse—he looked all round the congregation first, as much as to say, "You have heard our friend overhead; oblige me with your opinion of this style!"[48]

So far as Mr. Wopsle is concerned, the professional expertise of the clergyman consists in his reading the service, which he, Mr. Wopsle, can do at least as well. What the clerk, of course, lacks is not professional training but the birth and education which would make him a gentleman. And the fact that he is not an educated gentleman means, of course, that he cannot read the sonorous cadences of the Prayer Book in the same way that his vicar can. The point is too obvious to Dickens and his readers to need comment or explanation.

Reading and appreciating the beautiful prose of the Prayer Book requires education and taste. But as Willis, the Catholic convert in *Loss and Gain*, remarks, "The idea of worship is different in the Catholic Church from the idea of it in your Church; for, in truth, the *religions* are different." Catholic worship does not essentially consist in reading out words: "I could attend Masses for ever and not be tired. It is not a mere form of words,— it is a great action, the greatest action that can be on earth. It is, not the invocation merely, but, if I dare use the word, the evocation of the Eternal.

He becomes present on the altar in flesh and blood, before whom angels bow and devils tremble." A verbal, cerebral religion requires education and intelligence; the Catholic mass, by contrast, is a drama centered on an event that is equally accessible to all the worshipers:

> Each in his place, with his own heart, with his own wants, with his own thoughts, with his own intention, with his own prayers, separate but concordant, watching what is going on, watching its progress, uniting in its consummation;—not painfully and hopelessly following a hard form of prayer from beginning to end, but, like a concert of musical instruments, each different, but concurring in a sweet harmony.[49]

Allowing for the element of convert enthusiasm on Newman's part, there is an important point being made here about the essentially egalitarian nature of a liturgy which depends on a sacramental action rather than "a hard form of prayer" requiring concentration "from beginning to end," a clear reference, of course, to the measured, solemn prose of the Prayer Book.

At the end of the novel it is not the mass that Reding witnesses but the service of benediction:

> A cloud of incense was rising on high; the people suddenly all bowed low; what could it mean? the truth flashed on him, fearfully yet sweetly; it was the Blessed Sacrament—it was the Lord Incarnate who was on the altar, who had come to visit and to bless His people. It was the Great Presence, which makes a Catholic Church different from every other place in the world.[50]

The next and final chapter again finds the newly converted Charles Reding praying in front of the reserved Sacrament after his reception into the Catholic Church. And so the novel ends on this strongly autobiographical theme of the objective reality of Catholicism.

Now, there is no doubt that Newman was reacting against more than what he would have seen as the inevitable subjectivism of Anglicanism or Protestantism. It was his adolescent Evangelicalism which followed his conversion experience in 1816 that had left a lasting horror in him of religious introspection. The Evangelical insistence on justification by faith alone as being at the heart of Christianity meant, Newman came passionately to feel, that religion was turned into a matter of feelings: "Instead of looking off to Jesus, and thinking little of ourselves, it is . . . thought necessary . . . to examine the heart with a view of ascertaining whether it is in a spiritual state or not." The "inherent mischief" of the doctrine, Newman explained, lay "in its necessarily involving a continual self-contemplation and reference to self":

> He who aims at attaining sound doctrine or right practice, more or less looks out of himself; whereas, in labouring after a certain frame of mind, there is an habitual reflex action of the mind upon itself . . . for, as if it were not enough for a man to look up simply to Christ for salvation, it is declared to be necessary that he should be able to recognise this in himself.

The consequence, then, of this theology of justification seemed to Newman to be psychological and spiritual introspection:

> [A] system of doctrine has risen up during the last three centuries, in which faith or spiritual-mindedness is contemplated and rested on as the end of religion instead of Christ. . . . And in this way religion is made to consist in contemplating ourselves instead of Christ; not simply in looking to Christ, but in ascertaining that we look to Christ, not in His Divinity and Atonement, but in our conversion and our faith in those truths.[51]

The extent to which this acute sense of self-imprisonment affected Newman can be gauged by his description of the heroine's conversion in his second novel, *Callista* (1856). The story is set in the third century, and so it is, Newman is well aware, a very different kind of Catholic Christianity from the Tridentinism of the nineteenth century. But while any portrayal of the tabernacle with the reserved Sacrament on the altar in the early Church would have been a complete anachronism, the external objective reality of Christianity is very much to the fore of the novel. This is shown nowhere more strikingly than in the most fundamental consideration that draws the pagan Callista to the Christian faith. Given that Newman is particularly associated with the argument from conscience as the best philosophical ground for theism, it is certainly remarkable how little part it plays in the only actual dramatization of the conversion process that he ever wrote.

It is in fact Callista's objection to the Christian doctrine of hell which the priest Caecilius turns on its head by explaining that hell is nothing other than the eternal prison of the self cut off from God. If there is any life after death, then "you will still live . . . you will still be *you*. You will still be the same being, but deprived of those outward stays and reliefs and solaces, which, such as they are, you now enjoy. You will be yourself, shut up in yourself. I have heard that people go mad at length when placed in solitary confinement." Similarly, when Juba finds himself possessed by an evil spirit, he hears it cry, "You cannot escape from yourself!" The happiness of the self depends on there being a reality outside itself, for "the soul always needs external objects to rest upon." If, then, ordinary human affectivity demands the existence of other people, so too human beings have religious "needs, desires, aims, aspirations, all of which demand an Object, and imply, by their very existence, that such an Object does exist also." And so, as Callista finds herself more and more drawn to Christianity as responding "to all her needs and aspirations," "the more it seemed . . . to have an external reality and substance."[52] In the end, the argument from conscience appears only toward the conclusion of the novel, just prior to Callista's conversion.

In one of the finest sermons he ever preached (as an Anglican), "The Thought of God, the Stay of the Soul" (1837), Newman maintains that one reason why "God alone is the happiness of our souls" is that "the contemplation of Him, and nothing but it, is able fully to open and relieve the mind, to unlock . . . our affections. . . . Created natures cannot open us. . . . None but the presence of our Maker . . . for to none besides can the whole heart in all its thoughts and feelings be unlocked." To the Augustinian thought that "He alone is sufficient for the heart who made it," it is highly characteristic of Newman to add the consideration that only God can liberate the human heart by freeing it from the prison of the self: "Withdraw the Object on which it rests, and it will relapse again into its state of confinement and constraint." Without God, "We are pent up within ourselves. . . . [W]e need a relief to our hearts . . . that they may not go on feeding upon themselves; we need to escape from ourselves to something beyond."[53]

It would be wrong to attribute all this preoccupation to Evangelicalism. Subjectivity is one of the most obvious characteristics of Romanticism, and Newman's own sensitivity to the personal and experiential elements in human reasoning can be seen to belong to a wider movement away from the objectivity and rationalism of the Enlightenment. But just as he felt that the way of logic by itself was a cul-de-sac, so also he was only too sensitive to the danger of turning the propositions of religion into mere expressions of attitude and emotion and imagination. While the significance of the individual judgment could not be too emphasized in any credible account of the human mind, on the other hand it was vitally important not to surrender, he believed, like Schleiermacher, all factual knowledge to science or to abandon the truth claims of religion.

The subjectivity, then, that was so pronounced an emphasis of Newman's thought had to be purified of the egocentric subjectivism that threatened both objectivity and reality. The fear that one might become the prisoner of one's own feelings and thoughts was never far from Newman's consciousness while he was still in the Church of England. To his delighted surprise, Catholicism provided the key that turned in the lock of this prison of the self. It is the attempt to give imaginative expression to this realization that is a prominent feature of his writings during those postconversion years when he was discovering Catholicism.

CHAPTER 2

From Oxford to Liverpool

The Conversion and Poetry of Gerard Manley Hopkins

I

Much has been written on the influences of the Ignatian method of meditation and the theology of Duns Scotus on the poetry of Gerard Manley Hopkins. Recently, however, two critics have suggested that the fact that his experimental prosody belongs more to the twentieth than the nineteenth century is bound up with Hopkins's conversion to the Church of Rome.

Geoffrey Hill has argued that, after losing the familiar "rhythm" of Anglican culture, Hopkins turned to sprung rhythm as the nearest to that of natural speech. Moreover, his predilection for the monosyllabic words of demotic speech as "the most elemental material" for his poems "could be reconciled" with "the mystic discipline of 'short prayer,' with the significance of the Corpus Christi procession, and with the sustained melody of Gregorian chant." Given Hopkins's devotion to his fellow Jesuit poets and martyrs, Edmund Campion and Robert Southwell, he "must also have known of the . . . death-cry of Prior Houghton," one of the Carthusians martyred at Tyburn in 1535. Referring to "the ambivalent power of the short words," Hill cites the last line of "Carrion Comfort," where "the expletive" and "the bare word of faith" can hardly be distinguished.[1]

More recently, Eric Griffiths has developed Hill's suggestion about the "abruption of familiar rhythm" which converts to Rome suffered, by arguing:

For writers such as Hopkins and Newman, the reciprocal adjustments of sociable locution and liturgical forms make up a central part of learning to live as English Catholics rather than as Anglo-Catholics. Known ways of speaking, linguistic habits, had to be faced, and turned in a new direction, had to be perfected, as a convert might have said, but, equally, the unfamiliar language of Catholicism had to be seen and heard as truly as English speech, not as something unutterably alien, if the convert's voice was to be persuasive to the as yet unconverted.

In Hopkins's own case, Griffiths claims that "the distinctiveness of his mature achievement does arise from such unformulable meshes of religious conviction and social experience. His move from Canterbury to Rome was also a move from Oxford to Liverpool, from the refined world he had known to a Church the majority of whose congregations consisted of Irish immigrant workers and their families." This achievement is seen as a kind of resurrection, for "he went through a death to arrive at his developed style, and the death he went through was his conversion to Catholicism."[2]

Newman's famous controversy with Charles Kingsley is cited by Griffiths as an indication of how, as "an English patriot and a Catholic priest, Hopkins found himself persistently vexed and troubled." Again, Newman's problems in founding the Catholic University of Ireland symbolize the cultural problem for both Newman and Hopkins in having to adjust to the relative inferiority of Catholics. This allegedly helps to explain Hopkins's fondness for an inverted order of words, which witnesses "to the bearing of this Catholic poet towards the world, and the character of the reaction of that bearing upon him." From another point of view, Griffiths maintains that the obscurities reflect "the silence and the severity of God" in regard to the language in which the poems are written. Thus, he suggests,

> Some features of Hopkins's style can be understood as attempts at a repair of and a reparation for the language which he felt had been wounded by the schism from Rome. . . . Hopkins's distinctive way of dwelling on a word, as if he were naming it rather than saying it, has a tenderness in it towards the language itself. . . . [I]t seems he feels the language needs to be cossetted back into harmony with itself.[3]

These interesting but more or less unsubstantiated speculations are hardly supported by the case of Newman, where it would be impossible to demonstrate any change in his postconversion prose—apart from his Catholic sermons, which are both more colloquial and more rhetorical than the Anglican sermons, a difference, however, which can easily be explained by the change from a preaching mode where the written text was read out to a much more extempore style (as well as to a certain Italianate influence in the case of *Discourses to Mixed Congregations* (1849), delivered in the years immediately following his ordination to the priesthood in Rome). Nevertheless, Geoffrey Hill's essential insight seems worth exploring in greater depth, not least by paying close attention to the actual religious forms and language in which Hopkins was immersed as a convert and as a Jesuit.

The monosyllabic rhythm of Hopkins's verse is linked by Hill, somewhat cryptically, to several different Catholic practices or phenomena. The significance of Corpus Christi processions is not made clear, but presumably a reference is intended to the chants in Latin that would have accompanied them. As for Gregorian chant, it is true that Hopkins, like any Catholic priest, would have been familiar with the official Gregorian chants that the priest was required to sing at a high mass, but the revival of plainsong came later, and in the larger Jesuit churches and communities where it was possible to have a sung mass and sung vespers on Sundays it is very unlikely that the choirs would have had much Gregorian music in their repertoires. It should also be remembered that Hopkins was not a monk or a friar, and the daily recitation or chanting in community of the liturgy of the Eucharist and the divine office was far from being a feature of Jesuit houses (indeed, it was an important part of the revolutionary nature of the Society of Jesus, when it was founded, that its members should have an independence and mobility that were denied to those in the cloister). Again, Hill's apparent reference to the repetition of the brief prayer formula (or "mantra") in contemplative prayer would hardly have played any part in Hopkins's spiritual life, not only because the systematic meditation of Loyola's *Spiritual Exercises* provided the fundamental, even exclusive, framework for the prayer life of a Jesuit, but because the revival in the twentieth century of contemplative prayer in the Catholic Church had not yet begun, and ever since the Quietist controversy in the seventeenth century it had tended to be regarded with extreme circumspection and even suspicion. It was certainly no part of Jesuit spirituality.

The particular devotional practice which *was* central to the life of a Jesuit, and indeed which was the common property of all ordinary Catholics up until the Second Vatican Council, was the very kind of prayer that, as we have seen, Newman portrays in *Loss and Gain* when he wants to depict the typical kind of popular Catholic service. When discussing that climactic scene, I pointed out the significance of the fact that Newman chose not to focus on the mass as he did in *Callista*. This is not meant to imply, of course, that the obligatory Sunday mass was not central to the religious life of a nineteenth-century Catholic, but merely to emphasize that the mass was not the liturgical service which encouraged the vocal participation of the people. The Tridentine mass was essentially the action or drama of the eucharistic sacrifice, to which the words of the liturgy were indeed a necessary accompaniment, but they were not in themselves the center of attention as in the Book of Common Prayer. It is interesting to find Newman commenting in 1837 on "the shortness of the prayers" in the Roman breviary, when he recalled how his friend Hurrell Froude "used to say that 'long prayers' . . . came in at the Reformation." And while there was more Scripture in the Prayer Book, Newman approved of the fact that in the breviary there were "not long passages of chapters—but short and broken portions." But even more to the point is Newman's later comment as a Catholic that the "repetition . . . of formularies simple and familiar to all, will be found, I think, by experience to be practically the best means of securing prayer, and the union of prayer, from masses of men. . . . Litanies answer the same purpose."[4]

Nowhere in Catholic worship was the quality of brevity more conspicuous than in the form of prayer called the litany. In its abrupt, rapid, heavily monosyllabic rhythm it was at the opposite extreme from the leisurely, lengthy, weighty periods of the prose of the Book of Common Prayer, on which converts like Newman and Hopkins had been nurtured. Unlike the latter, the litany, at least in English, had little or no aesthetic or literary quality to recommend it. As Chesterton was ruefully to remark:

> English Catholicism, having in the great calamity of our history gone into exile in the sixteenth and seventeenth centuries (at the very moment when our modern language was being finally made) naturally had to seek for its own finest enthusiasms in foreign languages . . . and it translated these things back into a language with which the exile had lost touch and in which his taste was not quite firm and sure.[5]

What the litany did have in its favor, as Newman implies, was that it was a vehicle of prayer that was totally accessible to the most uneducated, even illiterate person, and as such it could express the devotion of a community engaged in a common act of worship where all distinctions of class and education were irrelevant. Whereas there was no vocal participation in the mass by the people apart from the server and by the choir in a sung mass, at the very popular evening service of benediction the congregation would all have joined in the hymns and litanies. In *Loss and Gain*, the service of benediction is preceded by what is clearly the rosary. Newman's description of the impression made upon his hero by this first experience of Catholic worship is very significant: "It was rapid, alternate, and monotonous; and . . . it seemed interminable."[6] This comment on the apparently endless recitation of the same short vocal prayers, mostly the "Hail Mary" interspersed by the "Our Father" and a few other prayers, would also have fitted the Latin litany that follows at the benediction service, which in the novel is sung alternately by the choir and the people. Of course, a long, wordy prayer from the Book of Common Prayer might well also seem to have its own share of the interminable and monotonous, but the monotony would have been diametrically opposite to the monotony of rapid repetition that Newman is talking about. Since it is clear from Newman's description that the litany in the novel is a litany of the Virgin Mary or one of the saints, it is worth looking at one of the litanies that Newman himself composed on the basis of the standard litanies then to be found in ordinary Catholic prayer books (according to William Neville, his secretary and editor of the posthumously published *Meditations and Devotions,* these litanies represented "the finished portion of a Scheme of Litanies for the whole year").[7]

Take, for instance, Newman's "Litany of the Immaculate Heart of Mary." The format is quite typical, beginning with prayers to Christ and the Trinity, led by a priest, with the responses by the congregation following:

> Lord, have mercy./Lord, have mercy.
> Christ have mercy./Christ have mercy.
> Lord, have mercy./Lord, have mercy.
> Christ, hear us./Christ, graciously hear us.
>
> God the Father of Heaven,/Have mercy on us.
> God the Son, Redeemer of the world,/Have mercy on us.
> God the Holy Ghost,/Have mercy on us.
> Holy Trinity, one God,/Have mercy on us.

After these introductory prayers, we reach the heart of the litany, which here consists of seventeen invocations of Mary under different titles and descriptions. It is hard to convey the monosyllabic, monotonous rhythm of this form of prayer, so peculiar to anyone brought up on the more convoluted, long-winded prayers of the Anglican liturgy, without in fact quoting the whole. As we shall see, when we come to look at some of the quaint oddities in Hopkins's poetic diction, there is another reason, too, for giving the reader as generous a taste as possible of the kind of devotional language that was the common property of Catholics until the Second Vatican Council.

> Heart of Mary,/Pray for us.
> Heart, after God's own Heart,/Pray for us.
> Heart, in union with the Heart of Jesus,/Pray for us.
> Heart, the vessel of the Holy Ghost,/Pray for us.
> Heart of Mary, shrine of the Trinity,/Pray for us.
> Heart of Mary, home of the Word,/Pray for us.
> Heart of Mary, immaculate in thy creation,/Pray for us.
> Heart of Mary, flooded with grace,/Pray for us.
> Heart of Mary, blessed of all hearts,/Pray for us.
> Heart of Mary, throne of glory,/Pray for us.
> Heart of Mary, abyss of humbleness,/Pray for us.
> Heart of Mary, victim of love,/Pray for us.
> Heart of Mary, nailed to the Cross,/Pray for us.
> Heart of Mary, comfort of the sad,/Pray for us.
> Heart of Mary, refuge of the sinner,/Pray for us.
> Heart of Mary, hope of the dying,/Pray for us.
> Heart of Mary, seat of mercy,/Pray for us.

The litany continues with three invocations, "Lamb of God, who takest away the sins of the world," coupled with three different responses all asking for Christ's mercy, and concludes with a collect in form and length (though not content) similar to the collects of the Prayer Book.[8]

As a Jesuit, Hopkins was particularly steeped in this form of prayer, as the recitation of the various litanies was the one communal daily act of worship in a Jesuit community. Eighteen years after the death of Loyola in 1556, daily attendance at these litanies was made mandatory for all Jesuits, an edict which was reiterated even more strictly in 1594.[9] Particularly associated with the Society was the "Devotion of the Bona Mors," which consisted of prayers for a happy death and contained not only a litany of the saints but also a litany of the Passion. But such litanies, so strange for the most part to modern Catholics, were the common possession of all Catholics and to a large extent constituted such worship in the vernacular as there then was.

At this time, of course, the divine office or breviary was still in Latin and was considered the preserve of clerics and religious. Instead of the psalms, the laity had the "Jesus Psalter," dating probably from the fifteenth century, which consisted of fifteen "petitions," each containing several brief petitions, such as "Have mercy on me, dear Jesus, for I am weak; O Lord, help me, who am unable to help myself." Again, one notices the same kind of simple, brief, strikingly monosyllabic form of prayer. Indeed, there was an even terser form of prayer, which would have been completely unfamiliar to a convert, the so-called "ejaculatory" prayer. Nineteenth-century Catholic prayer books were full of these kind of prayers (to which indulgences were attached), such as, at their simplest, "My Jesus, mercy!", "Jesus, Mary!" At the most solemn moment of the mass, when the bread and wine were consecrated by the priest speaking barely audibly, a bell was rung as a signal for the faithful to adore the elevated Host and chalice, an act of adoration that was supposed to be accompanied by an ejaculatory prayer like "My Lord and my God!" or "O Sacrament most holy! O Sacrament divine!" Such prayers were to be found in a section of a typical Catholic prayer book (*The Catholic Manual of Instructions and Devotions*)[10] called "A Devout Method of Hearing Mass." The word *hearing* should be noted, as there was no vocal participation and not necessarily much hearing of the "blessed mutter" of the mass. It should also be remembered that only a handful of educated Catholics would have been able to follow the mass in their missals; the rest of the congregation could say their rosaries privately or follow the liturgy by means of their prayer books, where only a very few parts of the liturgy were reproduced, but instead prayers, many of them little more than ejaculations, were provided for silent recitation.

Geoffrey Hill's perfectly valid point about the death cries of the martyrs needs to be placed within this larger context, as these were no more after all than a particular form of ejaculatory prayer. The concluding words of the last line of "Carrion Comfort," "Of now done darkness I wretch lay wrestling with (my God!) my God," which he cites as an example of the powerfully ambivalent way in which Hopkins uses short words, does indeed hover between "the expletive" and "the bare word of faith." But then one need only listen to the ordinary speech of Irish Catholics today to see how a devotional ejaculation like "Sacred Heart!" can be used as an expletive to express various emotions. It is, of course, perfectly true that in the indigenous English tradition in which Hopkins was nurtured the name of God or Christ was commonly used as a swearword; but the language of Anglican devotion and worship gave no encouragement to that ejaculatory mode of prayer which is so close to demotic speech, and which therefore can give rise to the kind of dramatic ambivalence to which Hill refers.

This is not to say, however, that Catholic popular devotions in the vernacular were free of archaisms. In particular, as we saw in Newman's litany, it was still only acceptable to address God in the old second-person singular. To appreciate how traditional diction was blended with a devotional language capable of merging with demotic speech, one has only to look at the second stanza of "The Wreck of the *Deutschland*," where Hopkins marvellously exploits the possibilities, possibilities which he would not have found within his native Anglican culture:

> I did say yes
> O at lightning and lashed rod;
> Thou heardst me, truer than tongue, confess
> Thy terror, O Christ, O God...
> (lines 9–12)[11]

Are those final four words a prayer, or an oath, or a cry of pain? They are surely potentially all three at once.

The poet who explained that he employed sprung rhythm because it was "the nearest to the rhythm of prose, that is the native and natural rhythm of speech," also maintained that "the poetical language of an age shd. be the current language heightened, to any degree heightened . . . but not . . . an obsolete one."[12] To see how he developed his poetry in accordance with this ideal, and how this development was connected with his conversion to Roman Catholicism, it is instructive to compare two eucharistic poems, one written when he was still an Anglo-Catholic and the other when he was a Roman Catholic.

In the 1864 poem "Barnfloor and Winepress," we can detect distinct echoes of both the Authorized Version and the Book of Common Prayer. Thus lines 31–33,

> We scarcely call that banquet food,
> But even our Saviour's and our blood,
> We are so grafted on his wood,

can be traced back to this post-Communion prayer in the Book of Common Prayer, which is worth quoting in full for a reason that will soon be evident:

> Almighty and everliving God, we most heartily thank thee, for that thou dost vouchsafe to feed us, who have duly received these holy mysteries, with the spiritual food of the most precious Body and Blood of thy Son our Saviour Jesus Christ; and dost assure us thereby of thy favour and goodness towards us; and that we are very members incorporate in the mystical body of thy Son, which is the blessed company of all faithful people; and are also heirs through hope of thy everlasting kingdom, by the merits of the most precious death and passion of thy dear Son. And we most humbly beseech thee, O heavenly Father, so to assist us with thy grace, that we may continue in that holy fellowship, and do all such good works as thou hast prepared for us to walk in; through Jesus Christ our Lord, to whom, with thee and the Holy Ghost, be all honour and glory, world without end.

It is interesting to note that when Hopkins came to recast the poem in 1867, he ran into a difficulty: the "quotations or quasi-quotations" from the Authorized Version had to be revised in accordance with the Douay version which was the standard English Catholic translation, but unfortunately "the Douay is of course an inferior version."[13] Certainly, if we contrast this sonorous prayer, which, in spite of its length, consists of only two sentences, with, say, the "Anima Christi," a traditional post-Communion prayer used by Catholics, we notice immediately the lack of any literary pretension, even in Newman's elegant translation, as well as the simplicity of the single-line petitions, which have the ring of the speaking voice unlike the "obsolete" and literary diction of the Prayer Book.

> Soul of Christ, be my sanctification;
> Body of Christ, be my salvation;
> Blood of Christ, fill all my veins;
> Water of Christ's side, wash out my stains;

Passion of Christ, my comfort be;
O good Jesu, listen to me;
In thy wounds I fain would hide,
Ne'er to be parted from thy side;
Guard me, should the foe assail me;
Call me when my life shall fail me;
Bid me come to thee above,
With thy saints to sing Thy love,
World without end. Amen.[14]

If we turn to a poem on the same subject, written fifteen years later, "The Bugler's First Communion," we can detect the influence of a wholly different religious culture on the language and rhythm of the poetry:

Forth Christ from cupboard fetched, how fain I of feet
        To his youngster take his treat!
Low-latched in leaf-light housel his too huge godhead.
                                                            (lines 10–12)

These three abrupt, pointed lines well illustrate Newman's point about the businesslike, practical nature of Catholicism. They also bring out another striking and controversial feature of Hopkins's mature poetry, namely, his capacity to embarrass with a word like *treat*. But then the devotional language of English Catholicism, which Chesterton found so tasteless, has exactly the same capacity to embarrass. Take, for instance, this extract from a typical contemporary litany of the Blessed Sacrament, with the people responding "Have mercy on us" to each invocation:

Living Bread, that camest down from heaven,
Hidden God and Saviour,
Corn of the elect,
Wine whose fruit are virgins,
Bread of fatness, and royal Dainties,
Perpetual Sacrifice,
Clean oblation,
Lamb without spot,
Most pure Feast,
Food of Angels . . .

Anyone coming for the first time to this kind of insistent determination to squeeze the last devotional juice out of the doctrine of transubstantiation is bound to feel somewhat confused, not to say amused or embarrassed, by sentiments like "Wine whose fruit are virgins" or "Bread of fatness, and royal Dainties"! But what does surely strike one is how easily an archly incongruous word like *treat* can slip into a poem about the Eucharist, when a commonly used litany can so readily and unembarrassedly use the term *dainties* for the consecrated bread and wine.

There is, in fact, a poem of Hopkins, "Duns Scotus's Oxford," which appears not only to contain an unmistakable echo of the best known of all the litanies, but even itself to be based on the form of a litany:

> Towery city and branchy between towers;
> Cuckoo-echoing, bell-swarmed, lark-charmed, rook-racked,
>   river-rounded;
> The dapple-eared lily below thee; that country and town did
> Once encounter in, here coped and poised powers ...
>
> (lines 1–4)

As commentators have noticed, the image of "towery" anticipates the reference to the Virgin Mary in the last line, since in the litany of Loretto (on which Newman composed a lengthy set of meditations[15]) she is called "Tower of David" and "Tower of Ivory."[16] What is in effect a quasi-litany moves from titular invocations to a relative descriptive clause in the last line: "Who fired France for Mary without spot." This again is very characteristic of the litany form, as can be seen, for instance, in Newman's "Litany of Penance," where, the titular invocations,

> God the Father of Heaven,
> God the Son, Redeemer of the world,
> God the Holy Ghost,
> Holy Trinity, one God,
> Incarnate Lord,
> Lover of souls,
> Saviour of sinners,

are followed by a series of descriptive clauses, beginning with

> Who didst come to seek those that were lost,
> Who didst fast for them forty days and nights ...[17]

Hopkins's most ambitious, longest, and perhaps greatest poem, "The Wreck of the *Deutschland*," begins with lines which, with their accumulation of titular invocations, immediately recall the form and rhythm of the litany. The difference from the earlier Anglican religious poems is that, instead of the poet having the rich literary resources of Anglican culture to hand, he now has only the demotic sound of Catholic vernacular piety ringing in his ear. But the gain far exceeds the loss, as Hopkins uses ("heightens") the effect of the repetitive monotony of such staple Catholic devotions as the rosary and the litany to produce a completely new sound in English poetry, a sound which evinces strong religious feeling without losing touch with spoken speech:

> Thou mastering me
> God! giver of breath and bread;
> World's strand, sway of the sea;
> Lord of living and dead . . .
>
> (lines 1–4)

The poem ends in the same way as it began, although it is the dead martyr nun and Christ, the "martyr-master" (line 167), who are now invoked in a final stanza which is again reminiscent of the litany:

> Dame, at our door
> Drowned, and among our shoals,
> Remember us in the roads, the heaven-haven of the
> reward:
> Our king back, Oh, upon English souls!
> Let him easter in us, be a dayspring to the dimness of us,
> be a crimson-cresseted east,
> More brightening her, rare-dear Britain, as his reign rolls,
> Pride, rose, prince, hero of us, high-priest,
> Our hearts' charity's hearth's fire, our thoughts' chivalry's
> throng's Lord.
>
> (lines 273–80)

To hear the same rhythm, particularly the accumulative effect of the last two monosyllabic lines, we should turn, not to the polysyllabic cadences of the Authorized Version or the Book of Common Prayer, but to the simple incantation of, say, Newman's "Litany of the Resurrection":

Jesus, Redeemer of mankind,/Have mercy on us.
Jesus, conqueror of sin and Satan,/Have mercy on us.
Jesus, triumphant over Death,/Have mercy on us.
Jesus, the Holy and the Just,/Have mercy on us.
Jesus, the Resurrection and the Life,/Have mercy on us.
Jesus, the Giver of grace,/Have mercy on us.
Jesus, the Judge of the world,/Have mercy on us.[18]

If this development and refinement of Geoffrey Hill's essential insight has truth in it, then there emerges the somewhat strange conclusion that the unliterary language of a now largely discarded (and, since the biblical and liturgical revival, discredited) Catholic piety played an important part in helping Hopkins to escape from derivative poetic conventions and become "the first modern English poet," as he is often called. And if so, then a significant part of "the most elemental material" that Hopkins employed to connect poetry again with the spoken language turns out to be the diction and rhythm of a minority religion that appeared foreign and un-English, had no literary claims or pretensions, at least in the vernacular language, and existed outside the mainstream of English culture and religion.

II

Evelyn Waugh, at the end of his life, appalled by the liturgical revolution that followed the Second Vatican Council, wrote in his diary that he had been drawn to the Catholic Church "not by splendid ceremonies but by the spectacle of the priest as a craftsman" who "had an important job to do."[19] This fascinating comment tallies with what has already been said in the first chapter about the Catholic priest as a doer of things (i.e., sacraments) rather than as a reader or preacher of words. It seems to me that this point is of special interest in understanding a wholly new dimension that Hopkins brought to English religious poetry.

The point can be made in a more general way by noting that, although Hopkins was not the first English religious poet to be in holy orders, he is the first such poet actually to write about what a clergyman in fact does, in the sense in which Conrad wrote about the work of a merchant seaman or Wilfred Owen about being a soldier. A poet like T. S. Eliot has written about war, memorably indeed in "Little Gidding," but that does not make him a "war poet" in the way in which Owen is. Similarly, Hopkins is more than a religious poet—he is quite literally a priest-poet.

Commentators have noted how even in an early poem, "Easter Communion," written while Hopkins was still an Anglican, the poet seems already to be a priest addressing the communicants from the altar.[20] Another Anglican poem, "Habit of Perfection," written a year later in 1866, was certainly influenced by George Herbert's "The Priesthood":

> But th' holy men of God such vessels are,
> As serve him up, who all the world commands:
> When God vouchsafeth to become our fare,
> Their hands convey him, who conveys their hands.
> O what pure things, most pure must those things be,
>   Who bring my God to me!
>
> (lines 25–30)

One can easily see how the homeliness of Herbert's diction appealed to Hopkins; but there is already a difference perhaps in the highly practical detail of Hopkins's

> But you shall walk the golden street
> And you unhouse and house the Lord.
>
> (lines 23–24)

By now a change has taken place in the Anglican Church, thanks to the Tractarian Movement: the Sacrament is now reserved in many of its churches, which may even look indistinguishable from Roman Catholic churches, and Anglo-Catholic clergy, like their Roman counterparts, also bring out and take back the consecrated wafers kept in the tabernacle at the back of the altar. And so one detects a sign of that practicality of Catholicism, that "working" religion which so impressed Newman after his conversion, as opposed to the "vague generality" of Anglicanism.

It is, I suggest, this very paradoxical practicality, this very mundane aspect of a religion which laid claims to "mysteries" rejected by Anglicanism and Protestantism, that found poetic expression in Hopkins, just as it helped shape the novels and satires of Newman in the decade or so after his conversion. A poem like "Felix Randal," for example, introduces a wholly new element into English religious poetry. Far from rural Bemerton in Wiltshire, where Herbert was rector, we are now in the slums of Liverpool, where Hopkins worked in a parish for nearly two years. Instead of the genteel family conversation of an Anglican vicarage, we overhear the professional conversation of priests in a presbytery: "Felix Randal the farrier, O is he dead then?"(line 1). Like professionals such as nurses and undertakers, for whom death is a daily occurrence and part of the business of the day, so too the priest, who also has to attend deathbeds, not only, or even primarily, in order to utter spiritual sentiments, but essentially to do a job, also with his hands, inevitably speaks in the same matter-of-fact, even casual, way of the dead. Because this is so unlike what is assumed to be "religious" behavior, it is not surprising that some critics have professed themselves to be shocked by Hopkins's dispassionate attitude. But if Hopkins is to be criticized for "emotional inadequacy,"[21] then, as another critic realizes, the same must be said about his "strange indifference . . . towards the sacraments themselves," as "can be heard in the very colloquial 'Being anointed and all.'"[22] Since, however, it is inconceivable that Hopkins had ever the slightest lack of reverence for the sacraments of the Church, this suggests that such critics are to be counted among the children of a Protestant (or post-Protestant) culture, who, in those words of Newman already quoted, "condemn Catholics, because, however religious they may be, they are natural, unaffected, easy, and cheerful, in their mention of sacred things; and they think themselves never so real as when they are especially solemn."[23]

There is, I think, too, another unusual element in the poem which deserves mention, and that is the sense of the priest as himself, like the farrier, a kind of craftsman, a man who does things as opposed to saying things. There is no hint at all in the poem that Hopkins ever said anything to the sick man at all. Instead, he "anointed" him and—again with his hands—"tendered" him Communion ("our sweet reprieve and ransom"). It was not a sermon or words of spiritual exhortation that Hopkins offered him, but two concrete sacraments, the first of which "mended" him and the second of which induced "a heavenlier heart" (lines 6–8). Of course, these details emphasize the power of Catholic sacramentalism as opposed to Protestant reliance on the preaching of the Word. But there is also a hint of the priest's solidarity with the working man, as what he has to offer him does not come from his (inevitably superior) knowledge of the Bible and spiritual books but consists of simple things such as (blessed) oil and (consecrated) bread which he brings and ministers with his own bare hands. In other words, the priest too is a kind of workman, whose importance lies not in the knowledge or influence he derives from education or class but in the power he possesses to perform certain actions with his hands and the ordinary things of this world.

What makes many of Hopkins's religious poems different from any other modern English religious poetry is the fact that they are "pastoral": that is, they are about the work of a working pastoral priest, whose occupation provides him as a poet with much of his subject matter. Thus "Felix Randal" describes how the priest did his "duty" to a sick man and "watched" over him (lines 1–2). Hopkins himself wrote to Robert Bridges in 1879, while he was working in the Jesuit parish in Oxford, "I find within my professional experience now a good deal of matter to write on."[24] He made the comment at the end of a discussion of the sonnet called "The Handsome Heart," where he describes how he asked an altar boy what gift he would like in recompense for services rendered during Holy Week and ends by praying for

> None but this, all your road your race
> To match and more than match its sweet forestalling strain.
> (lines 13–14)

In a number of poems the same note of priestly concern is heard. In "The Wreck of the *Deutschland*," the contrast Hopkins draws between his own tranquil security and the shipwrecked nuns' agony—

> Away in the loveable west,
> On a pastoral forehead of Wales,
> I was under a roof here, I was at rest,
> And they the prey of the gales
> (lines 185–88)

—is surely not only the kind of comparison anyone may mentally make on learning of some accident or disaster; but there is also the sense of the priest's failure to be there at the side of his sisters in religion at their hour of need. The lament over the "unconfessed" (line 244) among the crew and passengers, who lack not only a priest but also the Catholic faith, is repeated in the other shipwreck poem, "The Loss of the *Eurydice*," where the priest poet bewails

> These daredeaths, ay this crew, in
> Unchrist, all rolled in ruin—
> (lines 94–95)

and prays that his "prayer" for them may be "heard" (lines 113, 115). Similarly, in "Henry Purcell," Hopkins offers a retroactive prayer of intercession for his beloved composer who died in heresy:

> Have fair fallen, O fair, fair have fallen, so dear
> To me, so arch-especial a spirit as heaves in Henry Purcell,
> An age is now since passed, since parted; with the reversal
> Of the outward sentence low lists him, listed to a heresy, here.
> (lines 1–4)

"At the Wedding March" is a very different "prayer poem," a kind of verse equivalent of the blessing the priest gives to the couple celebrating the sacrament of marriage. Again, the Catholic priest has to preach sermons, as well as administer sacraments, and "Morning, Midday, and Evening Sacrifice" is in effect a poetic homily on the importance of giving oneself in one's youth to God, as can be seen from a parallel passage in an actual sermon Hopkins preached contemporaneously in August 1879.[25] But even when no specific pastoral or sacramental task is the subject of the poem, there is the sense of the poet as the concerned priest. In "The Lantern out of Doors," for example, Hopkins begins with the common enough experience of speculating about the identity of a passerby or stranger one will never see again:

> Sometimes a lantern moves along the night.
>   That interests our eyes. And who goes there?
>   I think; where from and bound, I wonder, where,
> With, all down darkness wide, his wading light?
> (lines 1–4)

But as the poem progresses, culminating in the reassurance that "Christ minds" (line 12), we realize that more than curiosity is involved: the poet is actively engaged as a priest anxious to save souls, who nevertheless feels his own helplessness:

> Death or distance soon consumes them: wind:
>   What most I may eye after, be in at the end
> I cannot, and out of sight is out of mind.
>   (lines 9–11)

"The Candle Indoors" is a very similar poem, again set at night, but this time it is the poet who is passing by in the street:

> Some candle clear burns somewhere I come by. . . .
> By that window what task what fingers ply,
> I plod wondering, a-wanting, just for lack
> Of answer the eagerer a-wanting Jessy or Jack
> There / God to aggrandise, God to glorify.—
>   (lines 1, 5–8)

The poem ends with the poet reproaching himself for worrying about his neighbor instead of examining his own conscience; but to say simply that it is a religious poem seems to me to miss the specifically priestly note which sounds through so much of Hopkins's poetry.

III

The third effect of Hopkins's conversion that I want to look at is his attitude to death. In his detailed study of *Death and the Future Life in Victorian Literature and Thought,* Michael Wheeler examines at length four literary texts: Tennyson's *In Memoriam,* Dickens's *Our Mutual Friend,* Newman's *The Dream of Gerontius,* and Hopkins's "The Wreck of the Deutschland." For Wheeler, the main factor that distinguishes the former two from the latter two writers is that, while Tennyson and Dickens "both sympathized with Anglican Broad Church opinion on most of the major doctrinal issues of the day, and grounded their writing on the subject of death and the future life . . . on the authority of the heart and a liberal interpretation of scripture," Newman and Hopkins, "both Roman Catholic priests[,] . . . based their treatments of purgatory and martyrdom . . . on the authority and theology of the church to which they had converted."[26]

What is strikingly absent from Wheeler's discussion is any appreciation of the enormous difference in these Protestant and Catholic writers' attitude to death, a difference which is explained by the fact that the Reformation had abolished both the doctrine of purgatory and the invocation of the saints. This meant that for both Tennyson and Dickens the dead person was no longer in any contact or relationship with the living, apart from a continuing existence in the memory. If the only two destinations for the dead were heaven and hell, there was no point in praying for them. And if, as the Protestant Reformers maintained, there was only one mediator between God and man, Jesus Christ, and the saints in heaven remained again only in the memory of the living as models to admire and be inspired by, but certainly not as members of the Church triumphant of whose intercession the members of the Church militant could avail themselves, then there could no longer be any real or practical relationship between the dead and the living. To quote the memorable words of Eamon Duffy in *The Stripping of the Altars* on the English Reformation's effect on the position of the dead:

> The dead, whose names were recited week by week . . . at the parish Mass, remained part of the communities they had once lived in. . . . But in the world of the 1552 [prayer] book the dead were no longer with us. They could neither be spoken to nor even about, in any way that affected their well-being. The dead had gone beyond the reach of human contact, even of human prayer. . . . [T]he dead person is spoken not to, but about, as one no longer here, but precisely as departed: the boundaries of human community have been redrawn.[27]

The important point, then, to emphasize is not that Tennyson and Dickens were liberal theologically while the conservative Newman and Hopkins rested their poems on dogma—but rather that, while Tennyson cannot pray for Arthur Hallam, Hopkins can and does pray for Henry Purcell. This is not to imply that this crucial difference affects the quality of the poetry one way or the other; but it is to affirm that we are dealing with an essentially different kind of literature of death. Not only does the *Dream of Gerontius* contain a litany of the saints, which is recited by the Assistants for the dying Gerontius, but after death the soul of Gerontius is aware of the prayers that are being offered for it:

> . . . I surely heard a priestly voice
> Cry "Subvenite;" and they knelt in prayer.
> I seem to hear him still; but thin and low . . .
>
>   (sec. 2)

And at the end of the poem, when Gerontius is in purgatory, the Angel assures Gerontius's soul that "masses on the earth, and prayers in heaven, / Shall aid thee." (sec. 7).

Hopkins's poetry contains not only priestly prayers for the dead but also the prayers of the saints for the living. As an English Catholic, and especially as an English Jesuit, Hopkins was keenly aware of the English martyrs, among whom the Jesuits were prominent, who had given their lives for the Catholic faith during penal times. In his untitled poem on Margaret Clitheroe, the York woman crushed to death in 1586 for harboring priests, Hopkins makes it clear that, although she had not yet been beatified or canonized, nevertheless she was a true martyr in her death: for, after three ejaculatory prayers calling on the holy name of Jesus ("She told His name times-over three"), she uttered as her last words: "*I suffer this* she said *for thee*" (lines 56–57).

This poem is significant for understanding Hopkins's purpose in "The Wreck of the *Deutschland*," where the tall nun is hardly a candidate for formal beatification or canonization, yet is seen by Hopkins as a genuine martyr, as she cries to the "martyr-master," "O Christ, Christ, come quickly." As a good nun, she has often prayed for "a happy death" or "Bona Mors"— and her prayer is now answered: "The cross to her she calls Christ to her, christens her wild-worst Best" (st. 24). Far from there being any need to postulate any miraculous apparition in stanza 28, as some commentators have done,[28] it would seem that to do so would diminish the faith of the nun which wins a martyr's crown. The point surely is that in embracing willingly her cross, the tall nun also embraces the cross of Christ: in the acceptance of death she encounters her crucified Savior, or, in other words, she sees with the eye of faith Christ in the waves that engulf her. For the subject of religious persecution to be a martyr rather than just a victim, it is essential that the suffering be freely embraced as a sharing in the passion of Christ. The poem, therefore, ends on not a tragic but a triumphant note, as the nun has accomplished more by her death, seen as a self-oblation, than she could ever have done as a nursing sister in America. Persecuted by Bismarck's Protestant Prussia, she has now been shipwrecked on the shores of another Protestant country. But far from it being a mere waste of life, Hopkins sees her drowning as of immense benefit to his heretical countrymen:

Dame, at our door
Drowned, and among our shoals,
Remember us in the roads, the heaven-haven of the
reward:
Our king back, Oh, upon English souls!

(stanza 35)

Convinced that her cry indicates she died the death of a martyr, Hopkins is free to believe she is in heaven, from where, according to the doctrine of the communion of saints, she can now be expected to be praying for the people whose coast brought death to her.

In Tennyson and Dickens the dead may continue to live in the memory of the living and to be a source of inspiration, but in themselves the deaths of Arthur Hallam and of little Johnny are nothing but tragic: the only consolation lies in "the hope of a future life in Christ."[29] But in Newman and Hopkins the dead and the living are linked by more than memory, since if the dead are in purgatory, they depend on the prayers of the living, and, if they are in heaven, the living depend on their intercession. This does not mean that *The Dream of Gerontius* is a better poem than *In Memoriam*—it is manifestly not. What, however, it does mean is that death may, in the hands of the Catholic writer, be actually celebrated joyfully in a way in which it cannot be in a culture where the dead are excluded (except in memory) from the community of the living. The triumphant conclusion of "The Wreck of the *Deutschland*" strikes an altogether fresh note in the nineteenth-century literature of death, as well as enabling a poem that may not be a wholly great poem in all its parts to finish on a superbly confident burst of enthusiasm.

CHAPTER 3

Hilaire Belloc and the Catholic "Thing"

Hilaire Belloc stands apart from the other central writers of the Catholic revival. Unlike the others he was neither a convert nor wholly English, being French on his father's side. Again, he is neither a major writer nor a figure of the intellectual stature of Newman or even Chesterton. There are two reasons for giving him a chapter to himself in this book. First, he is an integral part of the tradition, if only because he was educated at the Oratory School, which was founded by Newman and where Hopkins briefly taught, and because he was an important influence on Chesterton. Second, he did write one book which certainly belongs as a minor classic to the revived Catholic tradition and which continues to be read and reprinted.

Apart from his comic verse, and particularly the incomparable verses he wrote for children, which are almost certainly the best things he ever wrote, there is only one other among his prolific writings which will always draw readers, and that is his book *The Path to Rome,* published in 1901, which is substantially more than a mere book of travel. It is his most important prose work, which established him as a writer, as well as the book where the ideas of his controversial writings on culture, history, religion, and society achieve their fullest imaginative expression. For once, Belloc found the perfect outlet for the particular conversational style in which he excelled, so that he was able to realize creatively the polemical views he had expounded through a host of books now largely relegated to secondhand bookshops.

The first and most important thing to be said about them is that they all flow from the fundamental premise that all questions are ultimately theological. This determining principle Belloc learned not from Cardinal Newman at the Oratory School but from conversations with Cardinal Manning, the convert Ultramontane Archbishop of Westminster, after he left school: "The profound thing which Cardinal Manning said to me was this: *all human conflict is ultimately theological.*"[1] (It was also Manning, not

Newman, who influenced Belloc's mother, Bessie Parkes, into becoming a Roman Catholic before her marriage.)[2] This saying became for Belloc "a searchlight," he explained in *The Cruise of the "Nona"* (1925). Obvious as the point had been to people in past ages, now it was not generally realized that political conflict turned on what were "really points of theology." Doctrine was not merely "a private, individual affair"; rather, "it is doctrine that drives the State." Belloc was passionately convinced that events were determined by what people believed, "for men live by religion."[3]

It was this deep-seated conviction that shaped Belloc's views on economics, history, and politics. As he emphasized in *Survivals and New Arrivals* (1929): "[R]*eligion* is at the root of every culture, and . . . on the rise and fall of *religions* the great changes of society have depended." This is because "[t]he form of any society ultimately depends upon its philosophy, upon its way of looking at the universe, upon its judgment of moral values: that is, in the concrete, upon its religion." It did not matter for him whether a given society "calls its philosophy by the name of 'religion' or no," since "into what *is,* in practice, a religion of some kind, the philosophy of any society ultimately falls." He was using the word in the large sense of one's attitude to life: "The ultimate source of social form is the attitude of the mind; and at the heart of every culture is a creed and code of morals: expressed or taken for granted."[4]

This was why anyone interested in understanding the history of Europe could not afford to underestimate the importance of the Christian heresies. Thus Arianism was not just a terminological dispute, if only because "an Arian world would have been much more like a Mohammedan world than what the European world actually became." Doctrinal error had distinct "social effects," just as "[c]ultures spring from religions," so that cultural differences reflected religious differences. By rejecting the full divinity of Christ, Arianism undermined human dignity and produced "a gradual social degradation following on that loss of the direct link between human nature and God which is provided by the Incarnation." Belloc had no doubt that the growing secularization of Europe would have a devastating influence on its culture; as he grimly predicted:

> [T]here is . . . a certain indissoluble Trinity of Truth, Beauty and Goodness. You cannot deny or attack one of these three without at the same time denying or attacking both the others. Therefore with the advance of this new and terrible enemy against the Faith and all that civiliza-

tion which the Faith produces, there is coming not only a contempt for beauty but a hatred of it; and immediately upon the heels of this there appears a contempt and hatred for virtue.[5]

So far as Belloc was concerned, the most important event in modern European history was the Reformation. Before that historical phenomenon all else paled into insignificance. He was convinced that this was the single ultimate cause of all the cultural, economic, moral, political, and social problems that beset Western society. To understand the Reformation was to understand

> how the united body of European civilization has been cut asunder and by what a wound. The abomination of industrialism; the loss of land and capital by the people . . . the failure of modern discovery to serve the end of man; the series of larger and still larger wars following in a rapidly rising scale of severity and destruction—till the dead are now counted in tens of millions; the increasing chaos and misfortune of society—all these attach one to the other, each falls into its place, and a hundred smaller phenomena as well, when we appreciate . . . the nature and the magnitude of that fundamental catastrophe.[6]

This characteristically uncompromising passage from Belloc's most triumphalist of books, *Europe and the Faith* (1920), sums up the various, but related, themes of his polemical writings.

To understand Belloc's point of view, one must first ask the question, What after all had created Europe? To quote Belloc's own famous—notorious—words, "The Faith is Europe, and Europe is the Faith." Out of the pagan Roman Empire emerged Christian or European civilization, "which the Catholic Church has made and makes"; so far as it was still Catholic, it "was by that influence still one," even though its unity had since the sixteenth century been "suffering from the grievous and ugly wound of the Reformation."[7] It is not surprising that Belloc saw "the denial of unity" as the essential principle of Protestantism. It was this denial of the necessity of the Church as "a visible, definable and united personality," as "a united spiritual authority," which he thought had destroyed European civilization. Europe was intended to be "by nature one; but it has forgotten its nature in forgetting its religion."[8] Belloc saw it as his mission to proclaim this message in season and out of season, not only because he was a

Catholic and half-French but because, as an English writer writing for English-speaking people, he considered that the success of the Reformation in Europe would not have been possible but for the fact that popular resistance to the Reformation had tragically failed in Britain. The importance of Britain for Belloc, with his deep sense of continuity and tradition, was that unlike northern Germany and Scandinavia it had been once part of the old Roman civilization; now it was the only part of that world "in which a conscious antagonism to the ancient and permanent civilization of Europe exists." If the Reformation was the greatest tragedy to befall Western culture, it was the country of Belloc's adoption that was responsible: "The breakdown of Britain and her failure to resist disruption . . . made the Reformation permanent. It confirmed a final division in Europe." This was why in Belloc's eyes "the defection of Britain from the Faith of Europe" was the most crucial historical event since the conversion of Constantine.[9]

What, specifically, did Belloc think were the consequences of the Reformation? In the first place, obviously, the loss of European unity had led to and had encouraged the virulent growth of nationalism and wars which Belloc insisted were civil, not foreign, conflicts. These had culminated in the First World War, although in this the most terrible of the wars Protestantism bore a special responsibility because, according to Belloc, Prussian militarism owed its rise to the Reformation, which was "essentially the reaction of the barbaric, the ill-tutored and the isolated places external to the old and deep-rooted Roman civilization."[10] German Protestantism he saw too as being responsible for the new paganism of Hitler and Nazism.[11] European disunity was not simply a negative but also a positive cause of war, as nationalism, "this making of the nation an end in itself," became a "a novel religion" resulting in "the splitting up of our common cultural tradition, our general quality as Europeans, into a number of isolated fragments." As Belloc laments the casual way a British politician "thinks of Japan as he would of Italy—one rigid unit in an uncoordinated mechanical jumble of separate isolated peoples," one is struck by how a notoriously reactionary writer, most of whose books now gather dust on the shelves, can actually sound far ahead of his time in a way he could hardly have dreamed or hoped.[12]

The theme of isolation takes one to the heart of Belloc's creative imagination, but it also informs his economic and social thinking, again in connection with his vision of the destruction wrought by the Protestant Reformation. One of the Reformation's results was to persuade people that religion was "an individual thing . . . its object being . . . the salvation of the individual soul," whereas the "corporate quality" is of the very essence of Catholicism, which therefore is necessarily concerned with politics. Not only that, but since, as we have seen, for Belloc social habits and institutions are always underpinned by some doctrine or other, the wrong religious doctrine inevitably produces bad social arrangements.[13]

Now it was Calvin, not any of the other great Reformers, who was the real heresiarch; he had "set up a counter-Church" and was responsible for all that was "lively and effective in the Protestant temper."[14] Given the Calvinist discrimination between those predestined for salvation and those for damnation, Protestantism was unlikely to be enthusiastic about what Belloc called "the mystic Catholic doctrine of human equality."[15] Moreover, the Calvinist "devotion to material success" and its "antagonism to poverty" were consonant with a "vision of a Moloch God" who arbitrarily condemned so many of his creatures to damnation.[16] Capitalism Belloc blamed on "false religion," particularly the malign influence of Calvin.[17] By permitting usury and free competition, first in Calvinist Holland, Protestantism had destroyed "the old safeguards of the small man's property."[18] Finally, the absolutism of the modern state began "with the affirmation of the Protestant princes that their power was not responsible to Christendom or its officers, but independent of them."[19]

In *The Servile State* (1912), Belloc's trenchant analysis of capitalism and socialism, he lauded what he termed the "*distributive* system" of the Catholic Middle Ages, which "was guaranteed by the existence of co-operative bodies, binding men of the same craft or of the same village together; guaranteeing the small proprietor against loss of his economic independence, while at the same time it guaranteed society against the growth of a proletariat." This "co-operative tradition" had died at the English Reformation, when the "lands and the accumulated wealth of the old monasteries were taken out of the hands of their old possessors with the intention of vesting them in the Crown—but they passed . . . not into the hands of the Crown, but into the hands of an already wealthy section of the community who . . . became . . . the governing power of England."[20] The logical conclusion of this process would be a return to the pre-Christian servile society: the more society fell back into paganism, the more "the institution of slavery" would begin to reappear in new laws regulating labor.[21] By total contrast, in the Middle Ages, "poor men might go where they willed,"[22] with monasteries "nourishing hundreds . . . based upon the populace, drawn from the populace."²³ It was "Popular Monarchy" which had kept the people free, before the Reformation "made wealth supreme."²⁴ For it was the English Reformation "which killed popular monarchy by enriching the squires with the loot of the Church and making them and their great working committee, Parliament, the master and supplanter of the Crown."²⁵

Again, unlike Protestantism, which saw the Church "to be an institution merely human, and therefore naturally subjected, as an inferior," to the political powers, Catholicism made the Church free and self-governing, and thus made it "the guarantee of the plain man's healthy and moral existence against the threat of the wealthy, and the power of the State." Indeed, so far as Belloc was concerned, the English Reformation had succeeded only because of "the small wealthy class which used the religious excitement of an active minority as an engine to obtain material advantage for themselves." It was not until the last part of the twentieth century that revisionist historians like Eamon Duffy and J. J. Scarisbrick have come to support the truth of Belloc's more or less intuitive insight that at the Reformation the rich "who worked the movement to their enrichment took advantage of genuine religious excitement in a few brave, sincere, and often unbalanced, men; but it was not these last who made England Protestant— it was a pack of robbers," who "licked their lips" at the opportunity they were given. Supported by Protestant theologians—who could be simply dismissed as dons in Belloc's demonology—they robbed the ordinary people of their protector, the Church: "The Iconoclasts of greed joined hands with the Iconoclasts of blindness and rage and with the Iconoclasts of academic pride." A free, independent peasant society, in which "agriculture is, in the main, conducted by men possessed . . . of their instruments of production and of the soil, either through ownership or customary tenure," was from now on to survive only in Catholic countries.²⁶

There is a passing comment in *The Cruise of the "Nona,"* the nearest thing to an autobiography that Belloc ever wrote, which illuminates the fundamental reason for his aversion to Protestantism. Speaking of Protestant culture, he refers to its replacement of the Church with the Bible as its ultimate authority but then adds: "It had, of course, its profound spiritual origin, an excessive and enthusiastic passion for lonely communion with God."²⁷ Belloc does not stop to elaborate for the reader the significance of this comment; but for that we can turn to the concluding chapter of *Europe and the Faith,* which begins with this single-sentence paragraph: "The

grand effect of the Reformation was the isolation of the soul." This preg-
nant statement is followed by another one-sentence paragraph, indicating
that from this one cause came all the effects so abominated by Belloc: "This
was its fruit: from this all its consequences proceed: not only those clearly
noxious, which have put in jeopardy the whole of our traditions and all our
happiness, but those apparently advantageous, especially in material things."
In the succeeding pages he explains that "the isolation of the soul" is a question not simply of the unhappiness of the individual but of social dissolu-
tion: "In the first place and underlying all, the isolation of the soul releases
in a society a furious new accession of *force*." Then, as a result of "the corporate sense" and "corporate religion" being abandoned, "a reaction"
sets in "towards corporate life in the shape of a worship of nationality—
patriotism." Next comes the idolatry of scientific discovery: "Men acting in
a fashion highly corporate will not so readily question, nor therefore so
readily examine, as will men acting alone" when "an accepted philosophy"
has been abandoned as a "guide." It is not scientific progress that Belloc
objects to, but its misuse, which aided the rise of capitalism in Protestant
countries. According to Belloc, capitalism "arose directly in all its branches
from the isolation of the soul," which "permitted an unrestricted competition," "gave to superior cunning and even to superior talent an unchecked
career," and "gave every license to greed," while at the same time "it broke
down the corporate bonds whereby men maintain themselves in an economic stability."[28] As we read of the "fearful emptiness" of "the unsupported soul," we may begin to wonder if a particular personal element is
present in Belloc's horror at the economic and social consequences of the
Reformation: "Calvinism produced the Puritan movement and from there
proceeded as a necessary consequence the isolation of the soul, the breakup
of corporate social action, unbridled competition and greed, and at last the
full establishment of what we call 'Industrial Capitalism' today."[29]

In an introduction to a reprint of Belloc's verse, his biographer A. N.
Wilson notes that he once assumed that the mood of desolate solitude
which inspired the best of Belloc's poetry (apart from his comic and satirical poems) was the result of the various tragedies which blighted his life;
but he now believes that in fact Belloc was born with an elegiac sense.[30] It
would seem, however, from the way in which Belloc harped so much in his
prose writings on the theme of "the isolation of the soul" as the fundamental evil of the culture he lived in, that he himself saw it as a general
social problem of the culture he lived in. At any rate, it is this sense of

isolation, according to Wilson, which informs not only "all his best poems" but also "possibly the best lines he ever wrote":[31]

> The only part about it I enjoy
> Is what was called in English the Foyay.
> There will I stand apart awhile and toy
> With thought, and set my cigarette alight;
> And then—without returning to the play—
> On with my coat and out into the night.[32]

If there is no antidote to this loneliness in the poetry, Wilson points out that in the prose works Belloc did find an "acceptable collective . . . the Catholic Church, which he believed to provide hearth and home for the human spirit."[33] True as that is, I think there is an even more basic point to be made about the Catholic Church in relation to the "isolation of the soul."

It is a point which relates not so much to the influence of Manning's social Catholicism as to Newman's psychological and spiritual preoccupation with the self-imprisonment of the self and the possibility of liberation through the external and objective reality of the Catholic Church. Consider, to begin with, another of Belloc's frequent sayings in his prose writings, to the effect that there is no such thing as Christianity, only the Church. He will have no truck with the "mere Christianity" of Richard Baxter and C. S. Lewis:

> There is and always has been the Church, and various heresies proceeding from a rejection of some of the Church's doctrines by men who still desire to retain the rest of her teaching and morals. But there never has been and never can be or will be a general Christian religion professed by men who all accept some central important doctrines, while agreeing to differ about others. There has always been, from the beginning, and will always be, the Church, and sundry heresies either doomed to decay, or, like Mohammedanism, to grow into a separate religion. Of a common Christianity there never has been and never can be a definition, for it has never existed.

"Christianity," Belloc even declares, is an entirely "imaginary" religion.[34]

Far from this being an example just of Belloc's provocatively militant Catholicism, the fact is Belloc did not exactly believe in a concept called

"Catholicism" either. He points out that, far from the early Christians using the word *Christianity,* which is a post-Reformation term connoting "an opinion or a theory; a point of view; an idea," "[u]pon the contrary, they were attached to its very antithesis. They were attached to the conception of a *thing:* of an organized body instituted for a definite end, disciplined in a definite way, and remarkable for the possession of definite and concrete doctrine." This "thing," as opposed to a "theory," existed in the form of "an organism, and that organism was the Catholic Church."[35] For Belloc the Church came first, not its doctrine or even the individuals composing it: "The Catholic Church was from Her origin a thing, not a theory. She was a society informing the individual, and not a mass of individuals forming a society."[36] Like Newman, Belloc loves to emphasize the sheer concreteness of Catholicism—it is decidedly a thing, not a theory: "Here is the corporate tradition which made Europe: the Thing which is the core and soul of all our history for fifteen hundred years, and on into the present time: the continuator of all our Pagan origins, transformed, baptised, illumined; the matrix of such culture as we still retain."[37] God revealed himself to the world "through a corporation—a thing not a theory . . . an organism by which He may continue to be known to mankind for the fulfilment of the great drama of the Incarnation."[38]

Linked to this, and again recalling a favorite theme of Newman, is Belloc's recurring allusion to "reality." Thus, at their zenith, the Catholic Middle Ages were distinguished for all kinds of things, not least a just social order, but, says Belloc, "[a]bove all" for "a perception of reality. . . . They saw what was before them, they called things by their names."[39] This "desire for reality" Belloc calls "a kind of humility," and it is even the chief benefit of religion in this life: "Nor does religion exercise in our common life any function more temporarily valuable than this, that it makes us be sure at least of realities, and look very much askance at philosophies and imaginaries and academic whimsies." One cannot imagine Belloc having any sympathy at all with Newman's theory of the *Via Media,* if only because he would have said it was just the kind of thing that only a don could believe in! In one of his conversational essays in *Hills and the Sea* (1906), he offers a casual but quite deliberate definition of faith: "[W]hen I had thought out carefully where the nearest Don might be at that moment, I decided that he was at least twenty-three miles away, and I was very glad: for it permitted me to contemplate . . . with common sense and with Faith, which is Common Sense transfigured."[40] It is not surprising that Belloc had far more sympathy with materialists than with anyone else outside the Catholic Church. For at least they were "full of common sense" in noticing "all around . . . manifest innumerable examples—visible, tangible, real—of material cause apparently preceding every effect": in other words, they were "at least in touch with reality, as we are also of the Faith in a grander fashion."[41] At least atheistic materialists are concerned with external reality even if they fail to see the whole of it: "The specific difference between the Catholic and the non-Catholic . . . lies in what is roughly called . . . the 'acceptation of the supernatural.'" Nevertheless, the "Faith," too, says Belloc, is nothing else but "an attitude of acceptance towards an external reality." He wonders at the end of *The Cruise of the "Nona"* if his love of sailing is not due to the fact that at sea he experiences the "salt of reality": "The sea puts ever before us those twin faces of reality: greatness and certitude." So powerfully does he feel this sense of reality at sea that he even concludes the book by calling it "the common sacrament of this world."[42]

When A. N. Wilson commented that Belloc found in the Catholic Church "hearth and home for the human spirit," he was in fact echoing or misquoting what Belloc himself declares, vehemently but movingly, in his terse statement of faith toward the end of *Essays of a Catholic* (1931): "One thing in this world is different from all other. It has a personality and a force. It is recognised, and (when recognised) most violently loved or hated. It is the Catholic Church. Within that household the human spirit has roof and hearth." Nowhere else does Belloc express his fundamental faith more succinctly than when he says that this "thing," the Catholic Church, "is a grasp upon reality." And among the proofs for its claims, none is more convincing in Belloc's eyes than "its consonance with reality." In approaching the skeptic, he recommends first instructing him as to the mystery of the Incarnation—not, however, he hastens to add, in the sense of "didactic . . . exercises" but in the sense of "getting a man in touch with some real thing," as "a man is instructed in seafaring by going to sea." The skeptic has to experience "by taste" the Faith's "consonance with external and historical reality upon every side." The Catholic Church is the place "wherein alone the human spirit can repose," because it alone is "in full touch with reality." On the other hand, it is "the very mark of false doctrine" that it is "remote from reality . . . that it has not roots in the soil: it cannot come down to earth."[43] This is why Catholic Europe would have been saved from the Reformation by the "inherent force attaching to reality," had it not been that the rich saw their opportunity.[44]

Being in touch with reality has certain important consequences. First, in contrast to "the unhealthy gloom of the spirit originating with Calvin," a Catholic culture is characterized by "moral health and joy." This is because the Catholic faith, which is "the most reasonably human of things," not only "demonstrably enlarges" human life but also "explains" it; and by giving "life its rationale" it "morally and aesthetically rectifies—that is, sanely guides and maintains in health—the same." Again, Belloc, consciously or unconsciously, echoes Newman in insisting that everyone in fact goes by some "authority," the difference between Catholics and non-Catholics being that the latter "accept their authority without enquiry." The influence of what would now be called the media is so pervasive that people have their minds made up for them without realizing it, and so "outside the Faith, men are abandoning reason."[45] The "virile" intellect of the greatest of Catholic philosophers, St. Thomas Aquinas, and the healthy rationality of the Middle Ages are contrasted with the "tottering . . . insecurity" of the modern European mind, itself the result of the "isolation" of "the unsupported soul" which is condemned as "the prime product of the Reformation."[46] Having "begun by exaggerating the power of human reason" against the Church, Protestant culture is now "ending by abandoning human reason." The soul is left not only isolated but paralyzed: "When reason is dethroned, not only is Faith dethroned (the two subversions go together), but every moral and legitimate activity of the human soul is dethroned at the same time."[47]

The second consequence of being in contact with reality is a kind of carefree matter-of-factness. As in Newman and Hopkins, religion is treated as a perfectly natural part of life—or at least of a healthy life. For Belloc, as we have seen, it is a mark of the true faith that it should be earthy and rooted in the soil of ordinary life. Famously, Belloc likes to associate it particularly with eating and drinking, especially wine. Speaking of the pagans of his beloved Sussex to whom St. Wilfrid brought the Christian gospel in the eighth century, he says they lacked "the jolly energy which all decent Western religion gives a man," which also meant that they were "by the wrath of God deprived of the use of wine." A pilgrimage is a particularly Catholic kind of thing because it combines religion with the most mundane things of life: "It is better occasionally to travel . . . to some beloved place (or to some place wonderful and desired for its associations), haunted by our mission, yet falling into every ordinary levity, than to go about a common voyage in a chastened and devout spirit." The curse of the Reformation was that it sealed off religion into a separate compartment from the rest of life: "It is a very great error, and one unknown before our most recent corruptions, that the religious spirit should be so superficial and so self-conscious as to dominate our method of action at special times and to be absent at others." But it is the refusal to separate the sacred from the secular which, for example, enables Belloc without embarrassment to call "the memory of a complete repose" after eating "strongly" and drinking "largely" "a sort of sacrament."[48] He enjoys shocking his puritanical fellow-countrymen by writing a poem for Easter Sunday called "Upon God the Wine-Giver," which begins, "Though Man made wine, I think God made it too," and which contains an almost flippant allusion to the Eucharist: "And now by God are we not only bakers / But vintners also, sacraments to yield." Nor did ecumenical considerations trouble Belloc, least of all when he was in a Catholic celebratory mood:

> Heretics all, whoever you be,
> In Tarbes or Nimes, or over the sea,
> You never shall have good words from me.
> *Caritas non conturbat me.*
>
> But Catholic men that live upon wine
> Are deep in the water, and frank, and fine;
> Wherever I travel I find it so,
> *Benedicamus Domino.*

One can be familiar with a faith that is in the air one breathes, and Belloc's irreverence is meant to convey a message to solemn Protestants who keep their religion for special occasions:

> Noël! Noël! Noël! Noël!
> A Catholic tale have I to tell!
> And a Christian song have I to sing
> While all the bells in Arundel ring.
>
> I pray good beef and I pray good beer
> This holy night of all the year,
> But I pray detestable drink for them
> That give no honour to Bethlehem.

May all good fellows that here agree
Drink Audit Ale in heaven with me,
And may all my enemies go to hell!
Noël! Noël! Noël! Noël!
May all my enemies go to hell!
Noël! Noël![49]

Belloc likes to make his point by deliberately setting out to shock the English Protestant mind. He is delighted, for instance, to confirm the worst suspicions of Protestants about the paganism of the Catholic cult of the saints by telling how once in a storm "in despair" he "prayed to the boat itself (since nothing else could hear me), 'Oh, Boat,' for so I was taught the vocative, 'bear me safe round this corner, and I will scatter wine over your decks'"—a promise he duly carried out.[50] Believers, too, in the doctrine of justification by faith are unlikely to have their fears about Catholic sacramentalism allayed when Belloc recounts in *The Four Men* (1912) how one character "very quickly and suddenly, hurled over" another character "all that was in the pint pot of beer, saying hurriedly as he did so, 'I baptize you in the name of the five senses.'"[51] As for prayer, Belloc is more than happy to commend what Protestants traditionally accuse Catholics of doing, that is, gabbling their prayers: "[M]owing should be like one's prayers—all of a sort and always the same, and so made that you can establish a monotony and work them, as it were, with half your mind: that happier half, the half that does not bother."[52] In other words, praying should be as much a natural part of life as mowing the grass and should be done as mechanically, because nothing is worse than the earnest self-consciousness that the Reformation brought into religion.

Apart from the verse, there is no more readable book of Belloc than *The Path to Rome,* where he succeeded in bringing together the various ideas and themes we have been examining in an imaginative form. Not since the *Canterbury Tales* of Chaucer had any English writer attempted to write a book about a pilgrimage, so the work is in a very obvious way an attempt to revive a very Catholic form of literature. A. N. Wilson has commented that Belloc "is always best, whether in poetry, or in his essays, or in his historical writings, when he is *observing*."[53] Probably the most memorable parts of *The Path to Rome* are the vividly depicted encounters with strangers, people the traveler will never meet again, about whom he knows next to nothing, but who are often of more or less critical significance at a particular juncture or crisis; such strangers, as anybody who has traveled will know, retain an extraordinarily prominent place in the memory, out of all proportion to their importance in one's life as a whole. Even when these meetings are barely sketched, they provide Belloc with a dramatic channel for expressing his pet preoccupations. Thus, for example, of the French anarchist he bumps into on the road in Switzerland we learn next to nothing, but his anarchism gives Belloc the chance to expound his own distributist philosophy: "I also told him . . . that as for property, a man on his own land was the nearest to God." However, there was no time to "preach" his "full doctrine," namely, that the economic problems of Europe would be solved "if we once again had a united doctrine in Europe."[54] A common Catholicism had once united Europe; it still does to some extent, as Belloc reflects when on the feast of Corpus Christi he comes upon the landlady of an inn in German-speaking Alsace:

> She was of a very different sort from that good tribe of the Moselle valley beyond the hill; yet she also was Catholic—(she had a little tree set up before her door for the Corpus Christi: see what religion is, that makes people of utterly different races understand each other; for when I saw that tree I knew precisely where I stood. So once we Europeans understood each other, but now we are divided by the worst malignancies of nations and classes. . . .[55]

The tragedy of the English Reformation, on the other hand, had produced the invincibly ignorant Protestantism of a "Mr. Benjamin Franklin Hard, a kindly merchant of Cincinnati, O., who had no particular religion, but who had accumulated a fortune of six hundred thousand dollars, and who had a horror of breaking the Sabbath." This well-meaning American capitalist decided, on taking early retirement, to visit Europe: "He had not been in Europe five weeks before he ran bang up against the Catholic Church. He was never more surprised in his life." Salvation comes to him when he gets "to know, among others, a certain good priest that loved a good bottle of wine, a fine deep dish of *poulet à la casserole,* and a kind of egg done with cream in a little platter."[56] There is no other prose work of Belloc where he succeeds to the same extent in achieving the outrageously funny, and yet deadly serious, comedy of his verse satires.

The sacred and secular intermingle quite naturally, even though incongruously for the Protestant readers, to whom Belloc wants to show off his

Catholic Europe. Religion comes into map reading, for instance, when the author tries to take a short cut in the Moselle country: "This error came from following private judgment and not heeding tradition, here represented by the highroad which closely follows the river."[57] But he is sufficiently observant of the Faith to stick to the letter of his vow not to take a lift on any "wheeled thing," while practicing the casuistry of clinging on to a wagon that happens to arrive at an opportune moment "in such a manner that it did all my work for me, and yet could not be said to be actually carrying me." The danger, on the contrary, of the preference ("not far removed from Heresy") for "the Spirit and Intention" in moral matters, as opposed to a careful Catholic blend of juridicalism and casuistry, is illustrated by the story of the drinking man whom Belloc advised never to drink anything but the "feeding, fortifying, and confirming beverages that our fathers drank in old time" (in other words before the Reformation). All

> went well. He became a merry companion, and began to write odes. His prose clarified and set, that had before been very mixed and cloudy. He slept well; he comprehended divine things; he was already half a republican, when one fatal day . . . I went with him to the Society for the Prevention of Annoyances to the Rich, where a certain usurer's son was to read a paper on the cruelty of Spaniards to their mules. As we were all seated . . . the host of that evening offered him whisky and water, and, my back being turned, he took it. Then when I would have taken it from him he used these words—"After all, it is the intention of a pledge that matters"; and I saw that all was over, for he had abandoned definition, and was plunged back into the horrible mazes of Conscience and Natural Religion.
>
> What do you think, then, was the consequence? Why, he had to take some nasty pledge or other to drink nothing whatever, and became a spectacle and a judgment, whereas if he had kept his exact word he might by this time have been a happy man.[58]

In this kind of comic passage in *The Path to Rome* Belloc admirably succeeds in transmuting his convictions about the religious underpinning of culture into his particular kind of offhand conversational literary art.

The sheer matter-of-factness of Catholicism is another recurring theme in *The Path to Rome*. This is the point, for example, of Belloc's terse comment about the mass he attended on the feast of Corpus Christi—it "was low and short—they are a Christian people"![59] Although the Catholic claim is that something infinitely more important takes place at a Catholic mass than at a Protestant service of the word, nevertheless—or therefore—there is no need to make a fuss about it, since there is nothing of appreciable significance that man can add to what God has done. On a pilgrimage, says Belloc, one should "hear Mass every morning"; however, not only for strictly religious reasons—after all, religion is meant to be part of, not separate from, life—but also because of "the pleasing sensation of order and accomplishment which attaches to a day one has opened by Mass; a purely temporal, and, for all I know . . . a carnal feeling, but a source of continual comfort to me." Significantly, for Belloc the mass delivers one from oneself and from one's own self-consciousness: as a "rapid ritual," it has "the function of all ritual . . . to relieve the mind by so much of responsibility and initiative and to catch you up (as it were) into itself, leading your life for you during the time it lasts. In this way you experience a singular repose." The ritual of the mass conveys another secular (for those who separate religion from life) benefit, for it offers a kind of historical consolation: "[y]ou are doing what the human race has done for thousands upon thousands upon thousands of years." And if we want to be happy, then we must do what "is buried right into our blood from immemorial habit." Consequently, "in the morning Mass you do all that the race needs to do and has done for all these ages where religion was concerned; there you have the sacred and separate Enclosure, the Altar, the Priest in his Vestments, the set ritual, the ancient and hierarchic tongue, and all that your nature cries out for."[60] In fact, human nature cries out for the mass just as it cries out for a good meal and a good wine, as at Lucca, when Belloc "ordered such a meal as men give to beloved friends returned from wars. I ordered a wine I had known long ago in the valley of the Saone. . . . While they cooked it I went to their cool and splendid cathedral to follow a late Mass. Then I came home and ate their admirable food and drank the wine."[61]

As Michael Novak has said, *The Path to Rome* is an attempt to introduce Protestant England to "the Catholic sensibility," to show that Catholicism "is not only a set of abstract doctrines . . . but also . . . habits, sights, sounds, smells, imaginings, and feelings: a sensibility."[62] Again, Belloc makes no concessions to Protestant susceptibilities. Thus bargaining and paying money are portrayed as part and parcel, as it were, of Catholic devotions, so that at one particularly perilous moment on the journey Belloc "vowed one candle to Our Lady of Perpetual Succour if she would see that all went well, and this candle I later paid in Rome."[63] Less seriously, the pilgrim Belloc "vowed a franc to the Black Virgin of La Délivrande (next time I should be passing there) because I was delivered from being a tourist, and because all this horrible noise was not being dinned at me (who was a poor and dirty pilgrim, and no kind of prey for these cabmen, and busmen, and guides and couriers), but at a crowd of drawn, sad, jaded tourists."[64]

Michael Novak agrees with A. N. Wilson that *The Path to Rome* records a particularly decisive moment in Belloc's life, when he witnessed the entire population (as it seemed) of the Alpine village of Undervelier attending vespers.[65]

> At this I was very much surprised, not having been used at any time of my life to the unanimous devotion of an entire population, but having always thought of the Faith as something fighting odds, and having seen unanimity only in places where some sham religion or other glozed over our tragedies and excused our sins. Certainly to see all the men, women, and children of a place taking Catholicism for granted was a new sight, and so I put my cigar carefully down under a stone on the top of the wall and went in with them.[66]

The fact that the author thinks it worth mentioning the care taken over a thing like a cigar—which will be carefully retrieved and relit—is symbolic of this quasi-conversion experience in which the full force of the concreteness of Catholicism as a "thing" strikes Belloc with a new power. As he put it in his private correspondence, Catholicism is "a living thing . . . not a document nor a mere record," for "the Faith" is a *Thing.*" Without the external reality of the Church, Belloc admitted that he would be a skeptic— "my whole nature is sceptical." But it was "the Faith, Reality," which kept him from "the extreme of harm, final harm, despair." It was "like pure air, or sufficient sleep, a food and necessity for men."[67]

In Undervelier that evening at the parish vespers, this reality of the Church was experienced by Belloc in a manner that resembles a conversion:

> My whole mind was taken up and transfigured by this collective act, and I saw for a moment the Catholic Church quite plain, and I remembered Europe and the centuries. Then there left me altogether that attitude of difficulty and combat which, for us others, is always associated with the Faith. . . . I took less heed of the modern noise. I went out with

them into the clear evening and the cool. I found my cigar and lit it again, and musing much more deeply than before, not without tears, I considered the nature of Belief.[68]

But this decisive episode does not end with reflections on how the "Thing" which is the Catholic Church liberates one from "the isolation of the soul." For there is no place for the solemn separation of religion from ordinary life in Belloc's scheme of things. And so he ends with the casual comment, "They cook worse in Undervelier than any place I was ever in, with the possible exception of Omaha, Neb."[69]

CHAPTER 4

The Dickensian Catholicism
of G. K. Chesterton

Is G. K. Chesterton a major English writer? Today he is generally regarded as a minor novelist and short story writer—and an even more minor poet—who happened also to be a significant literary biographer and critic, particularly of Dickens. His works of political and religious controversy would not normally be regarded as of any special literary interest. However, there is another way of looking at Chesterton's literary achievement which has gone by default, and that is to admit that the author of the Father Brown stories and even of *The Man Who Was Thursday* (1907), his best novel, is indeed a fairly slight figure, but on the other hand to see the nonfiction prose writer, the Chesterton who wrote such studies as *Charles Dickens* (1906), *The Victorian Age in Literature* (1913), and *St. Thomas Aquinas* (1933), as well as the apologetic classics *Orthodoxy* (1908) and *The Everlasting Man* (1925), as a successor to the great Victorian "sages" or "prophets," who was indeed often compared to Dr. Johnson in his own lifetime, and who can be mentioned without exaggeration in the same breath as Carlyle, Ruskin, Arnold, and especially, of course, Newman.

Newman himself wrote two (underrated) novels—the first of which, *Loss and Gain,* which introduces a new element of satirical comedy as well as introspection into the religious novel, is at least as interesting a work of fiction as *The Man Who Was Thursday,* with its fantastic, Kafkaesque quality of nightmare—and a good deal of verse, which, like Chesterton's, includes a handful of well-known poems; but his literary claims too must rest principally on his nonfictional prose: that is, precisely, on those works, to a large extent also of controversy, where he is expounding his religious and theological views. Similarly, Chesterton's classic study of Dickens not only should have established him as a creative literary critic, comparable to the very greatest English critics—perhaps because he was writing about the novel rather than poetry this has not been sufficiently recognized—but also should be seen as revealing his literary genius and originality in a way that none of his novels do. As he frankly admits in his *Autobiography* (1936): "I could not be a novelist; because I really like to see ideas or notions wrestling naked, as it were, and not dressed up in a masquerade as men and women." He adds, however: "But I could be a journalist because I could not help being a controversialist."[1] One recalls that Newman himself was the editor of two periodicals and that one of his most brilliant books, *The Tamworth Reading Room* (1841), consisted of letters to the *Times*. Newman's brother, F. W. Newman, commenting on his powers as a controversialist, remarked that he could have been an "eminent" barrister; one might add that he could have been an eminent journalist, like G. K. Chesterton.[2]

Charles Dickens not only constitutes a literary achievement that Chesterton never surpassed, or even equaled, in any of his other books but also is the book which reveals most luminously both the sense in which Chesterton is a Catholic writer and why conversion to Catholicism was the natural and inevitable outcome of his progression from the vague Unitarianism in which he had been brought up. It is a typical Chestertonian paradox that while Dickens was nothing if not ignorant of and prejudiced against Catholicism as well as the Middle Ages, it is his unconsciously Catholic and medieval ethos and imagination that are at the heart of Chesterton's critical study. It is often said that Chesterton's conversion to Roman Catholicism was not very significant, as it was only the logical conclusion of the Catholic Christianity which he had long come to believe in, not least because of the influence of his Anglo-Catholic wife. One of his biographers has even suggested that it was only the death of his beloved brother Cecil, who was a convert to Roman Catholicism, that impelled Chesterton to embrace his dead brother's religion. After all, it is alleged, the differences between Anglo- and Roman Catholicism were relatively insignificant, lying "primarily in matters of daily discipline and habits as well as in a certain lack of social 'acceptability,' an un-Englishness."[3] But this is to ignore what Chesterton himself says in his *Autobiography*, where he explains quite clearly, if reluctantly, why he could not remain an Anglo-Catholic:

> I do not want to be in a religion in which I am *allowed* to have a crucifix. I feel the same about the much more controversial question of the honour paid to the Blessed Virgin. If people do not like that cult, they

are quite right not to be Catholics. But in people who are Catholics, or call themselves Catholics, I want the idea not only liked but loved and loved ardently, and above all loudly proclaimed. I want it to be what the Protestants are perfectly right in calling it; the badge and sign of a Papist. I want to be allowed to be enthusiastic about the existence of the enthusiasm; not to have my chief enthusiasm coldly tolerated as an eccentricity of myself.[4]

Chesterton's exuberant wonder at life itself precluded half-measures: enthusiasm about Catholicism meant going the whole hog and embracing the fullest, most unapologetic kind of Catholicism. A halfway house like Anglo-Catholicism could never ultimately have satisfied Chesterton, not because it was illogical or inconsistent, as it came to seem to Newman, but simply because it was less than the whole of Catholicism: if there was a papacy, then that too had to be part of Chesterton's Catholicism. The more that there was to believe the merrier, as Chesterton himself explains:

As an apologist, I am the reverse of apologetic. . . . I am very proud of my religion; I am especially proud of those parts of it that are most commonly called superstition. I am proud of being fettered by antiquated dogmas and enslaved by dead creeds . . . for I know very well that it is the heretical creeds that are dead, and that it is only the reasonable dogma that lives long enough to be called antiquated. I am very proud of what people call priestcraft; since even that accidental term of abuse preserves the medieval truth that a priest like every other man, ought to be a craftsman. I am very proud of what people call Mariolatry; because it introduced into religion in the darkest ages that element of chivalry. . . . I am very proud of being orthodox about the mysteries of the Trinity or the Mass; I am proud of believing in the Confessional; I am proud of believing in the Papacy.[5]

It is as if Catholicism must be true because it has a largeness and vitality that no other form of Christianity has: its very priests—to pick up again a theme we noted in connection with Hopkins and Waugh—are not just clergymen but craftsmen, too, who can do something with their hands as well as their minds. Catholicism was the only "creed that could not be satisfied with a truth, but only with the Truth, which is made of a million such truths and yet is one." It was "the only theology that has not only thought, but thought of everything." Instead of liberty enabling individual ideas best to flourish, it was—and this is a key Chestertonian theme to which we shall return—the ordered Catholic garden with its well-defined boundaries in which "such flowers grow best . . . and even grow biggest," for "in the wilderness they wither and die."[6]

There were two ideas or facts about the world that were crucial for Chesterton's conversion first to Christianity and then to Catholicism as the form of Christianity that best realized them. They corresponded to the two attitudes to life that Chesterton called optimism and pessimism, each of which is a recognition of one of the undeniable aspects of reality but each of which without the other is a serious distortion of reality. On the one hand there is the sheer goodness of human life and the world, which calls for gratitude and wonder, and on the other hand the no less striking evil that vitiates them and creates despair. These two contradictory truths, Chesterton came to believe, could be explained only by the two basic, complementary doctrines of Christianity, namely, that creation is good because created by God but also bad because spoilt by fallen human beings. As he puts it in *Orthodoxy*, "God had written, not so much a poem, but rather a play; a play he had planned as perfect, but which had necessarily been left to human actors and stage-managers, who had since made a great mess of it." This accounted for his own experience of finding "this hole in the world: the fact that one must somehow find a way of loving the world without trusting it; somehow one must love the world without being worldly."[7] It explained both our attachment to and simultaneously our alienation from the world, our optimism and our pessimism.

These two truths were for Chesterton most fully embodied in Catholicism, which on the one hand emphasized the goodness of creation through the sacramental principle and refused (unlike Calvinism) to reject human nature as wholly corrupt, and on the other hand, unlike liberal Protestantism, was unflinching in its acknowledgment of the awful reality of sin, for which it provided an antidote in the form of confession. This was indeed the explanation that Chesterton always gave when asked why he had converted to Roman Catholicism: "'To get rid of my sins.' For there is no other religious system that *does* really profess to get rid of people's sins." However, this sacrament not only relieved Chesterton of his own guilt but also affected what he called "the chief idea of my life," namely, "the idea of taking things with gratitude, and not taking things for granted." For it was not until he "happened to open the Penny Catechism and read the words, 'The two sins against Hope are presumption and despair,'" that he "saw the two sides of this single truth stated together anywhere." In other words, the sacrament of confession restores a person to his or her childhood innocence—which Chesterton saw as the time when one simply gazes at the world with gratified wonder—by giving "a new life" that enables a person to "step out again into that dawn of his own beginning." It is not the cheap comfort offered by optimists, since this "gift is given at a price, and is conditioned by a confession," which is to say that "the name of the price is Truth, which may also be called Reality; but it is facing the reality about oneself." Catholicism, then, provided Chesterton with the means of escape from the "two dangers" of which he had had "from the first an almost violently vivid sense"—"the sense that the experience must not be spoilt by presumption or despair." Meanwhile the modern philosophies of both optimism and pessimism had "missed and muddled this matter; through leaving out the ancient conception of humility and the thanks of the unworthy"—which allows, for example, "the yellow star of the dandelion" to be "startling, being something unexpected and undeserved."[8]

I

I said that *Charles Dickens* is probably Chesterton's greatest work—the work in which more than in any other he expressed his own self and his philosophy of life—and the book that explains most clearly and fully his Catholicism—his Roman Catholicism—and the sense in which he is a Catholic writer in his most creative works. As I also pointed out, the book is built on the paradox that outwardly Dickens was as far from Catholicism as any Englishman can be. Chesterton emphasizes this fact. When in Italy, Dickens never really left England, or rather, "Dickensland": "the great foreign things which lie in wait for us in the south of Europe," such as the Catholic Church, he never "really felt." Paradoxically again, Chesterton could not really regret it, as Dickens "could only have understood them by ceasing to be the inspired cockney that he was"![9] In one of his *Appreciations and Criticisms of the Works of Charles Dickens* (1911), Chesterton remarks that "[w]hen he found a thing in Europe which he did not understand, such as the Roman Catholic Church, he simply called it an old-world superstition, and sat looking at it like a moonlit ruin." Because Dickens had, in spite of this, what Chesterton conceived of as a naturally Catholic spirit, he could not bring himself to condemn that innocent ignorance which enabled Dickens, for example, to criticize "the backwardness and idleness of Catholics who would not build a Birmingham in Italy," while seemingly "quite unconscious of the obvious truth, that the backwardness of Catholics was simply the refusal of Bob Cratchit to enter the house of Gradgrind."[10]

Chesterton's own primary—religious—experience, that wonder at the unexpectedness of the ordinary world, is for him the outstanding feature of Dickens's novels. But whereas the scene of the childhood experiences was also London, it was a very different city from the comfortable middle-class world of Chesterton's happy childhood. One might have thought that the environment of Dickens's miserable childhood could hardly have evoked wonder, let alone gratitude. Nevertheless it was during the nightmare of "drudging" at the blacking factory that the young Dickens "drifted over half London" and discovered those streets that "[f]or him ever afterwards . . . were mortally romantic; they were dipped in the purple dyes of youth and its tragedy," and yet "rich with irrevocable sunsets." As Chesterton explains in one of the great passages in *Charles Dickens:*

> He did not go in for "observation," a priggish habit; he did not look at Charing Cross to improve his mind or count the lamp-posts in Holborn to practise his arithmetic. But unconsciously he made all these places the scenes of the monstrous drama in his miserable little soul. He walked in darkness under the lamps of Holborn, and was crucified at Charing Cross. So for him ever afterwards these places had the beauty that only belongs to battlefields. For our memory never fixes the facts which we have merely observed. The only way to remember a place for ever is to live in the place for an hour; and the only way to live in the place for an hour is to forget the place for an hour. The undying scenes we can all see if we shut our eyes are not the scenes that we have stared at under the direction of guide-books; the scenes we see are the scenes at which we did not look at all—the scenes in which we walked when we were thinking about something else—about a sin, or a love-affair, or some childish sorrow. We can see the background now because we did not see it then. So Dickens did not stamp these places on his mind; he stamped his mind on these places.

The dramatic quality of this kind of writing does not support the common supposition that Chesterton's paradoxes are merely clever rhetorical devices to highlight his admittedly acute powers of insight and observation. Here, rather, the inescapable truth of the apparently contradictory only adds to the sense of a perfectly lucid nightmare which one knows to be only a dream but from which one cannot wake.

> Herein is the whole secret of that eerie realism with which Dickens could always visualize some dark or dull corner of London. There are details in the Dickens descriptions—a window, or a railing, or the keyhole of a door—which he endows with demoniac life. The things seem more actual than things really are. Indeed, that degree of realism does not exist in reality: it is the unbearable realism of a dream. And this kind of realism can only be gained by walking dreamily in a place; it cannot be gained by walking observantly. Dickens himself has given a perfect instance of how these nightmare minutiae grew upon him in his trance of abstraction. He mentions among the coffee-shops into which he crept in those wretched days one in St. Martin's Lane, "of which I only recollect that it stood near the church, and that in the door there was an oval glass plate with 'COFFEE ROOM' painted on it, addressed towards the street. If I ever find myself in a very different kind of coffee-room now, but where there is such an inscription on glass, and read it backwards on the wrong side, MOOR EEFFOC (as I often used to do then in a dismal reverie), a shock goes through my blood." That wild word, "Moor Eeffoc," is the motto of all effective realism; it is the masterpiece of the good realistic principle—the principle that the most fantastic thing of all is the precise fact. And that elvish kind of realism Dickens adopted everywhere. His world was alive with inanimate objects. The date on the door danced over Mr. Grewgious's, the knocker grinned at Mr. Scrooge, the Roman on the ceiling pointed down at Mr. Tulkinghorn, the elderly armchair leered at Tom Smart—these are all moor eeffocish things. A man sees them because he does not look at them.[11]

Unlike Chesterton, who had good reason for delighting in the fact of life in his boyhood, Dickens could be said to belong to those "higher optimists" whose joy is in inverse proportion to their grounds for so rejoicing; for these "do not approve of the universe; they do not even admire the universe; they fall in love with it. They embrace life too close to criticize or even to see it. Existence to such men has the wild beauty of a woman, and those love her with most intensity who love her with least cause."[12]

Unlike Chesterton, then, the evil and pain of life did not come later but formed part of Dickens's boyish experience. For those early years of misery "gave him many moral and mental wounds, from which he never recovered." Nevertheless "the practical depression of his life at this time did nothing to prevent him from laying up those hilarious memories of which all his books are made." And so it was the coexistence of these two funda- mental aspects of life, which for Chesterton were the inevitable basis of a Christian conception of the world, that was also at the heart of Dickens's genius as a novelist: "He was delighted at the same moment that he was desperate. The two opposite things existed in him simultaneously, and each in its full strength. His soul was not a mixed colour like grey and purple, caused by no component colour being quite itself. His soul was like a shot silk of black and crimson, a shot silk of misery and joy."[13]

From one of these two points of view, the exaggeration of Dickens's caricatures only reflects the fact that their creator knew "what it is to feel a joy so vital and violent that only impossible characters can express that." No other novelist "*encouraged* his characters so much as Dickens." Just as Catholic Christianity—unlike Calvinism—says that "any man could be a saint if he chose," so Dickens believed in the "encouraging of any body to be anything"—so much so that, although he "tried to make some of his people appear dull people . . . he could not keep them dull."[14] Even in Scrooge Chesterton finds "a heartiness in his inhospitable sentiments that is akin to humour and therefore to humanity," for there "glows" through him "the great furnace of real happiness . . . that great furnace, the heart of Dickens."[15]

That this allusion to the heart of Dickens has a quasi-religious resonance—in Catholic terminology an echo of the "Sacred Heart" of Jesus—should not surprise us, for Chesterton attributes divinity to the creativity of Dickens: "One of the godlike things about Dickens is his quan- tity, his quantity as such, the enormous output, the incredible fecundity of his invention." But like the divine Creator, Dickens does not create card- board characters; they have the same sort of relation to him as human crea- tures to God; they are dependent on him, but they are not puppets: "He is not come, as a writer, that his creatures may copy life and copy its nar- rowness; he is come that they may have life, and that they may have it more abundantly." And like God, he loves and values even his most unattractive creations, like Mr. Toots: "He makes us not only like, but love, not only love, but reverence this little dunce and cad. The power to do this is a power truly and literally to be called divine."[16] Because Dickens "conceives an endless joy" in conceiving his immortal creations, he is "close to popular religion, which is the ultimate and reliable religion." That this popular religion is Catholicism is made plain a few pages later, when Chesterton speaks of how the "fragments" and "the wrecks of that enormous religion," the huge popularity of Dickens, have entered into the ordinary English language spoken by people who may never have opened a novel by Dickens—"just as Catholics can live in a tradition of Christianity without having looked at the New Testament."[17]

The Catholicism, if one may call it that, of the world of Dickens is not confined to the goodness of creation. There is also the sheer holiness of creation, which Chesterton finds most strikingly in a type of character quite unknown to the Protestant culture of Victorian England, but familiar to the Catholic (and even more the Orthodox) tradition: the so-called "holy fool." Chesterton himself uses the word of Miss Podsnap in *Our Mutual Friend,* who "is, like Toots, a holy fool." These holy fools, like the Misses Pecksniff in *Martin Chuzzlewit,* are certainly not treated with solemn reverence, otherwise they would be cardboard characters, as the characters Dickens "tried to treat unsmilingly and grandly" are the very characters who are not human: "Dickens had to make a character humorous before he could make it human . . . when once he has laughed at a thing it is sacred for ever." The secret, Chesterton even claims, of the "humble characters," of "the great characters of Dickens is that they are all great fools," a "great fool" being someone "who is above wisdom rather than below it." And the fool is defined not just in Christian but in Catholic terms: "The present that each man brings in hand is his own incredible personality. In the most sacred sense and in the most literal sense of the phrase, he 'gives himself away.' Now, the man who gives himself away does the last act of generosity; he is like a martyr, a lover, or a monk. But he is almost certainly what we commonly call a fool."[18]

A character like Toots is "turned from a small fool into a great Fool" not by being altered "in any vital point" but by Dickens's "enthusiasm," which "fills us, as does the love of God, with a glorious shame; after all he has only found in Toots what we might have found for ourselves." It is Dickens again who has properly understood the gospel "injunction to suffer fools gladly": "We always lay the stress on the word 'suffer,' and interpret the passage as one urging resignation. It might be better, perhaps, to lay the stress upon the word 'gladly,' and make our familiarity with fools a delight, and almost a dissipation."[19]

In his introduction to *Dombey and Son*, Chesterton goes so far as to say that the study of Toots is "in some ways the masterpiece of Dickens." This remarkable estimate of one of Dickens's lesser known characters provides the key to understanding why Chesterton was never so much himself as when writing about Dickens, and also the profound sense in which Chesterton saw Dickens as a deeply Christian and Catholic spirit.

> Nowhere else does Dickens express with such astonishing insight and truth his main contention, which is that to be good and idiotic is not a poor fate, but, on the contrary, an experience of primeval innocence, which wonders at all things. Dickens did not know, any more than any great man ever knows, what was the particular thing that he had to preach. He did not know it; he only preached it. But the particular thing that he had to preach was this: That humility is the only possible basis of enjoyment; that if one has no other way of being humble except being poor, then it is better to be poor, and to enjoy; that if one has no other way of being humble except being imbecile, then it is better to be imbecile, and to enjoy.[20]

If one may speak of the greatness of Chesterton, then Chesterton himself falsifies his own assertion that the great man never knows what he has to preach; but it is easy to agree that Dickens himself could not have celebrated his own genius as Chesterton does, any more than the painters Ruskin writes about could have evoked their art as he does.

It is, of course, the affinity that Chesterton feels for Dickens that provides him with the perfect medium that enables him to express his own sense of wonder at the world, as he was never able to do so exuberantly in his other prose writings, or even in his novels or verse. Recognizing that Dickens, like himself, belonged to the "brotherhood" of journalism, he notes how "some of the best work that Dickens ever did, better than the work in his best novels, can be found in these slight and composite scraps of journalism." And this overflowing creative power is likened to "the virtue of a saint," which "is said to be shown in fragments of his property or rags from his robe."[21] The "vision of a monstrous magazine, entirely written by

Himself," which "floated before him," was conceived, Chesterton imagined, "as a kind of vast multiplication of himself, with Dickens as editor opening letters, Dickens as leader-writer writing leaders, Dickens as reporter reporting meetings, Dickens as reviewer reviewing books, Dickens, for all I know, as office-boy opening and shutting doors."[22] Now in this comic evocation of Dickens's unremitting energy Chesterton is himself expressing not only his own characteristic comic genius but also his own "incomparable hunger and pleasure for the vitality and the variety, for the infinite eccentricity of existence."[23] He attributes this craving to Dickens, but in so doing he actually enacts his own extraordinary sense of the wonder of existence. We recognize Dickens, perhaps as never before, but the words are not, could not be, Dickens's; they are pure Chesterton.

Dickens's delight at the extraordinary unexpectedness of life, at the "wild and utterly unexplained" character of the world ("It is the best of all impossible worlds"), contains what was for Chesterton the fundamental religious perspective: "It is, perhaps, the strongest mark of the divinity of man that he talks of this world as 'a strange world,' though he has seen no other." Dickens transforms the commonplace because it is not commonplace to him; for him life is not normal or ordinary but "eccentric": "This sentiment of the grotesqueness of the universe ran through Dickens's brain and body like the mad blood of the elves. He saw all his streets in fantastic perspectives, he saw all his cockney villas as top heavy and wild, he saw every man's nose twice as big as it was, and every man's eyes like saucers."[24]

This explains how Dickens could express "with an energy and brilliance quite uncommon the things close to the common mind," that mind which is "common to the saint and the sinner, to the philosopher and the fool." This quality of "commonness" was what Dickens "grasped and developed"—in both his humor and his horror, which were deeply human because "they belong to the basic part of us, below the lowest roots of our variety." This ability both "to make the flesh creep and to make the sides ache"[25] reflected the Christian view of creation as inherently good but terribly damaged by evil. Thus, on the one hand, Dickens's humor sprang from the hope and joy that constitute an "exhilaration" that is simply "mystical" or "infinite": "[A] joke can be so big that it breaks the roof of the stars. By simply going on being absurd, a thing can become godlike; there is but one step from the ridiculous to the sublime."[26] But, on the other hand, as well as Dickens's "beatific Buffoonery,"[27] there was another kind of "exhilaration" which Dickens shared with the Catholicism of the Middle Ages,

"that amazingly healthy period when even the lost spirits were hilarious"—
in the creation of such evil characters as Quilp, whose "atrocious hilarity"
makes him want to "hurt people in the same hearty way that a good-natured
man desires to help them." And just as Dickens's Victorian limitations prevented him from appreciating or understanding Roman Catholicism and
the Middle Ages, so too Chesterton doubts if, "in the kindly rationalism
of his epoch, he kept any belief in a personal devil in his theology, but he
certainly created a personal devil in every one of his books."[28]

Not only is Dickens's celebration of the commonplace and ordinary at
the heart of Chesterton's view of him as a writer, but the theme is also integral to Chesterton's own conception of Catholic Christianity. The novelist
of the streets of London, whose "tales always started from some splendid
hint in the streets" and for whom "shops, perhaps the most poetical of
all things, often set off his fancy galloping," opening to him "the door of
romance,"[29] confounded the usual distinction between "the dull man who
likes ordinary things mildly, and the extraordinary man who likes extraordinary things wildly." For not only did Dickens like "quite ordinary things,"
but he "made an extraordinary fuss about them," sharing the same interests as the ordinary person but feeling "all of them more excitedly."[30] Dickens's desire to bring out the romance in real life, to show that realism is
romantic, to create "real people romantically felt," led him to write "in a
kind of ecstasy of the ordinary," in the knowledge that "the things that are
common are the things that are not commonplace" but rather "terrible and
startling, death, for instance, and first love."[31] And so "the real gospel of
Dickens," who taught that "[i]t is in our own daily life that we are to look
for the portents and the prodigies," is "the inexhaustible opportunities
offered by the liberty and variety of man." So far as Chesterton is concerned, the caricatures of Dickens, in all their grotesqueness, are terribly
real, not absurdly unreal, for "[i]t is in our private life that we find people
intolerably individual, that we find them swelling into the enormous con-
tours, and taking on the colours of caricature."[32]

The reason why Dickens "was always most accurate when he was most
fantastic" is simply that he "exaggerated when he had found a real truth
to exaggerate." The person who discovers a truth "breaks into extravagances, as the Christian churches broke into gargoyles." And Chesterton
brilliantly perceives that Dickens "could only get to the most solemn emotions adequately if he got to them through the grotesque." It was essential
for Dickens "to be ridiculous in order to be true": "His characters that

begin solemn end futile; his characters that begin frivolous end solemn in the best sense. His foolish figures are not only more entertaining than his serious figures, they are also much more serious."

This realism of the absurd has an explicitly religious connotation for Chesterton. For Chesterton's explanation of why "Dickens had to make a character humorous before he could make it human" is that "once he had laughed at a thing it is sacred for ever."[33] Humor, says Chesterton, was Dickens's "medium; his only way of approaching emotion." This is why, as Dickens develops a character, the character "grows more and more into a gargoyle or grotesque."[34] Again, there is a Christian allusion as Chesterton explains that this is why Dickens's "great, grotesque characters are almost entirely to be found where Dickens found them—among the poorer classes," who "are too great to get into the public world" but who can "enter into the kingdoms of the earth."[35]

The symbol of the grotesque gargoyle is a deliberate reference to the Catholic Middle Ages, as Chesterton saw Dickens as—unconsciously—totally medieval in his attitude to life, a view he expounds in one of the most amusingly penetrating passages in *Charles Dickens:*

> Upon him descended the real tradition of "Merry England," and not upon the pallid mediaevalists who thought they were reviving it. The Pre-Raphaelites, the Gothicists, the admirers of the Middle Ages, had in their subtlety and sadness the spirit of the present day. Dickens had in his buffoonery and bravery the spirit of the Middle Ages. He was much more mediaeval in his attacks on mediaevalism than they were in their defences of it. It was he who had the things of Chaucer, the love of large jokes and long stories and brown ale and all the white roads of England. Like Chaucer he loved story within story, every man telling a tale. Like Chaucer he saw something openly comic in men's motley trades. Sam Weller would have been a great gain to the Canterbury Pilgrimage and told an admirable story. . . .
>
> In fighting for Christmas he was fighting for the old European festival, Pagan and Christian, for that trinity of eating, drinking and praying which to moderns appears irreverent, for the holy day which is really a holiday. He had himself the most babyish ideas about the past. He supposed the Middle Ages to have consisted of tournaments and torture-chambers, he supposed himself to be a brisk man of the manufacturing age, almost a Utilitarian. But for all that he defended the

mediaeval feast which was going out against the Utilitarianism which was coming in. He could only see all that was bad in Mediaevalism. But he fought for all that was good in it. . . . He cared as little for mediae-valism as the mediaevals did. He cared as much as they did for lusti-ness and virile laughter. . . . He would have been very much bored by Ruskin and Walter Pater if they had explained to him the strange sun-set tints of Lippi and Botticelli. He had no pleasure in looking on the dying Middle Ages. But he looked on the living Middle Ages, on a piece of the old uproarious superstition still unbroken; and he hailed it like a new religion. The Dickens characters ate pudding to an extent at which the modern mediaevalists turned pale. They would do every kind of honour to an old observance, except observing it. They would pay to a Church feast every sort of compliment except feasting.[36]

That medieval Catholic spirit that Chesterton paradoxically found in Dickens not only was sustained by dogmas unknown to or rejected by Dickens but was actually built on the very principle of dogma that was in itself inimical to the latitudinarian Christianity of Dickens. But this prin-ciple was for Chesterton simply the religious version of the principle of limitation that lay at the heart of his philosophy of life. It appears through-out his writings, not least as a defense of middle-class values, as in this pas-sage from *Charles Dickens,* which brings together several characteristic Chestertonian themes, again illustrating why Roman Catholicism was only the natural fulfillment of what Newman would have called his "first principles":

Molière and his marquises are very much amused when M. Jourdain, the fat old middle-class fellow, discovers with delight that he has been talking prose all his life. I have often wondered whether Molière saw how in this fact M. Jourdain towers above them all and touches the stars. . . . It would be better for us all if we were as conscious that sup-per is supper or that life is life, as this true romantic was that prose is actually prose. M. Jourdain is here the type, Mr. Pickwick is elsewhere the type, of this true and neglected thing, the romance of the middle classes. . . . Decadents talk contemptuously of its conventions and its set tasks; it never occurs to them that conventions and set tasks are the very way to keep that greenness in the grass and that redness in the roses. . . . Stevenson, in his incomparable "Lantern Bearers," describes the ecstasy of a schoolboy in the mere fact of buttoning a dark lantern under a dark great-coat. If you wish for that ecstasy of the schoolboy, you must have the boy; but you must also have the school. Strict opportunities and defined hours are the very outline of that enjoyment.[37]

The word *defined* recalls the definitions of doctrine that are the dogmas of Roman Catholicism which Chesterton came to feel were essential to account for and reconcile those extremes of "gloom and gaiety" that brought Dickens "close to religion" and that for Chesterton flowed inexorably from the two essential facts about life and the world, creation and the Fall. In Dickens, who could create both "the humane hospitalities of Pickwick" and "the inhuman laughter of Fagin's den," the "strands of festivity and fear" were "tied up together in a strange knot."[38]

The festive note on which *Charles Dickens* ends picks up what Chesterton had observed earlier about the "abnormal amount of drinking" to be found "in a page of Dickens":

> If you reckon up the beers and brandies of Mr. Bob Sawyer, with the care of an arithmetician and the deductions of a pathologist, they rise alarmingly like a rising tide at sea. Dickens did defend drink clamorously, praised it with passion, and described whole orgies of it with enormous gusto. . . . But it was a part of his humane philosophy, of his religion, that he did drink wine. To healthy European philosophy wine is a symbol; to European religion it is a sacrament.[39]

In Chesterton's eyes Dickens belongs to Merry, not Puritan, England because, albeit unconsciously, he believed in the same "trinity of eating, drinking and praying" and "the holy day which is really a holiday," just like the authors of the *Canterbury Tales* and *The Path to Rome,* for whom religion was a part of ordinary daily life as it had not been in England since the Reformation. And the vision with which Chesterton ends his great critical work, which tells us at least as much about Chesterton as it does about Dickens, is of an eternal inn where we shall enjoy the heavenly banquet of which the Sacrament of the Eucharist is the pledge: "And all roads point at last to an ultimate inn, where we shall meet Dickens and all his characters: and when we drink again it shall be from the great flagons in the tavern at the end of the world."[40]

II

If we turn now to Chesterton's two major woi ks of Christian apologetics, we can see how closely many of the themes of Charles Dickens reflect the principal arguments of both *Orthodoxy,* which Chesterton wrote as a Catholic-minded Christian, and *The Everlasting Man,* which he wrote as a Roman Catholic. *Orthodoxy* indeed begins with the idea of the romance of the commonplace that was so central to his appreciation of Dickens: "I wish to set forth my faith as particularly answering this double spiritual need, the need for that mixture of the familiar and the unfamiliar which Christendom has rightly named romance." The need, says Chesterton, "so to view the world as to combine an idea of wonder and an idea of welcome" is the "achievement of my creed that I shall chiefly pursue in these pages."[41] Similarly, in *The Everlasting Man* Chesterton claims that Catholicism safeguards "life considered as a romance," while Catholic Christianity itself, having grown too familiar, needs to be made "vivid" again by being seen to be "new and strange," if needs be in a "deliberately grotesque" manner.[42] But although this life should evoke gratified wonder, there is another unmistakable fact about it, apart from its innate goodness, and that is that "there is something the matter" with it, which explains why pagans always "were conscious of the Fall, if they were conscious of nothing else."[43] Or, as he puts it in *Orthodoxy,* original sin "is the only part of Christian theology which can really be proved." And so for Chesterton, "The primary paradox of Christianity is that the ordinary condition of man is not his sane or sensible condition; that the normal itself is an abnormality."[44]

This innate sense of the flawed goodness of the world was what enabled Dickens to have that "religious conception of life" which made him, unlike other writers, a successful social reformer, conscious always of the "degradation" yet the "dignity" of people. It was through "a kind of mystical contradiction" that he was able to "have two apparently antagonistic emotions . . . at the same time": to feel that "the oppressed man" was "intensely miserable, and at the same time intensely attractive and important."[45] Simple optimism or pessimism about the world discourages reform, whereas Christianity makes us "fond of this world, even in order to change it," and moreover "fond of another world . . . in order to have something to change it to." We have to "hate it enough to change it, and yet love it enough to think it worth changing." Or, to use a characteristically paradoxical metaphor, "We have to feel the universe at once as an ogre's castle, to be stormed, and yet as our own cottage, to which we can return at evening." Only Christianity explained "this need for a first loyalty to things, and then for a ruinous reform of things"—which accounted for the fact that it "was accused, at one and the same time, of being too optimistic about the universe and of being too pessimistic about the world." To believe that "one must somehow find a way of loving the world without trusting it; somehow one must love the world without being worldly," is to have a Christian optimism which "is based on the fact that we do *not* fit in to the world" and which views "the unnaturalness of everything in the light of the supernatural." Paradoxically, and indeed prophetically, Chesterton argues in *Orthodoxy,* an age of unbelief will be an age of conservation: "Let beliefs fade fast and frequently, if you wish institutions," like the established Church of England, "to remain the same." Whereas for evolutionary progressives the "vision of heaven is always changing," and therefore the "vision of earth will be exactly the same[,] . . . for the orthodox there must always be a case for revolution; for in the hearts of men God has been put under the feet of Satan, so that there can always be a revolution; for a revolution is a restoration." Again, there is the Chestertonian idea of definition or limitation: "A strict rule is not only necessary for ruling; it is also necessary for rebelling" for a "fixed and familiar ideal is necessary to any sort of revolution," and "a permanent ideal is as necessary to the innovator as to the conservative."[46] Not that Chesterton is arguing in favor of conservatism, which "is based upon the idea that if you leave things alone you leave them as they are": "But you do not. If you leave a thing alone you leave it to a torrent of change. If you leave a white post alone it will soon be a black post. If you particularly want it to be white you must be always be painting it again; that is, you must be always having a revolution. Briefly, if you want the old white post you must have a new white post."[47] Here Chesterton reminds one of the Newman of development, who wrote that Christianity "changes . . . in order to remain the same."[48]

There is a paradox, not commented upon by Chesterton himself, in his stress on the importance of defined limits. For the peculiar note of modern secular philosophies, according to Chesterton, is their combination of "logical completeness" with "spiritual contraction," a "narrow universality" offering only "a small and cramped eternity," "an expansive and exhaustive reason with a contracted common sense," a "thin explanation" carried "very far," an "insane simplicity" of "covering everything and . . . leaving everything out," a "cosmos" which has "shrunk." Thus deterministic materialism is "much more limiting than any religion" and far from being "a liberating force" only uses "free thought to destroy free will." Or again, skepticism "is equally complete in theory and equally crippling in practice."[49] These heresies are contrasted with orthodox Christianity, which evinces just those very qualities of liberality and vitality which drew Chesterton to the genius of Dickens.

The word *orthodox* needs emphasis, for it is a favorite paradox of Chesterton that the liberal Protestant is the most illiberal of Christians: it "always means a man who wishes at least to diminish the number of miracles; it never means a man who wishes to increase that number. It always means a man who is free to disbelieve that Christ came out of His grave; it never means a man who is free to believe that his own aunt came out of her grave." A miracle, after all, Chesterton points out, "only means the liberty of God"; but the descendant of Calvinist Protestantism, the liberal Protestant, far from being a freethinker, is really only somebody who has reached certain conclusions, such as "the material origin of phenomena, the impossibility of miracles, the improbability of personal immortality," none of which ideas are "particularly liberal." Indeed, this kind of so-called liberal theology which seeks "to bring freedom into the church is simply a proposal to bring tyranny into the world" by "freeing that peculiar set of dogmas loosely called scientific, dogmas of monism, of pantheism, or of Arianism, or of necessity," every one of which "can be shown to be the natural ally of oppression." And Chesterton's deep insight into the Victorian mind is nowhere better seen in this paradoxical comment on its religious doubts:

> The man of the nineteenth century did not disbelieve in the Resurrection because his liberal Christianity allowed him to doubt it. Tennyson, a very typical nineteenth-century man, uttered one of the instinctive truisms of his contemporaries when he said that there was faith in their honest doubt. There was indeed. Those words have a profound and even a horrible truth. In their doubt of miracles there was a faith in a fixed and godless fate; a deep and sincere faith in the incurable routine of the cosmos. The doubts of the agnostic were only the dogmas of the monist.

Far from Protestantism having brought freedom to human beings enslaved by Catholic dogmas and priests, for Chesterton its actual development or history showed the opposite was true:

> The Catholic Church believed that man and God both had a sort of spiritual freedom. Calvinism took away the freedom from man, but left it to God. Scientific materialism binds the Creator Himself; it chains up God as the Apocalypse chained the devil. It leaves nothing free in the universe. And those who assist this process are called the "liberal theologians."[50]

In fact, Chesterton claims, it is Catholic or orthodox Christianity which frees people, unlike the "modern philosophies . . . which . . . fetter," by, for example, abolishing the "heroic and monumental manner in ethics" that "has entirely vanished with supernatural religion." For it is "by insisting that God transcends man" that "man has transcended himself." Nor is there anything "in the least liberal . . . in the substitution of pure monotheism for the Trinity," which affords "the conception of a sort of liberty" within the Godhead. By believing in free will rather than predestination, Christianity enables life to be a "*story,* which may end up in any way," a "narrative romance," "full of danger, like a boy's book."[51] It is the very liberality of Catholic Christianity which makes it a target for contradictory accusations: one moment it is being "reproached with its naked and hungry habits; with its sackcloth and dried peas"; the next moment with "its pomp and its ritualism; its shrines of porphyry and its robes of gold." This combination of "bodily austerity" and "artistic pomp" is typical of that "exact and perilous balance; like that of a desperate romance," which Christianity maintains between "passions apparently opposite," although "not really inconsistent," only "hard to hold simultaneously," and therefore presenting an apparent "paradox" but in reality a "picture composed" of various "elements in their best proportion and relation." It is just such a "careful . . . balance" which ensures "[m]ental and emotional liberty." Catholic ethics was "the discovery of the new balance," parallel to the intricacies of Gothic architecture, so different from paganism, which "had been like a pillar of marble, upright because proportioned with symmetry," whereas "Christianity was like a huge and ragged and romantic rock." Theologically, this accounted for the Church's dread of heresy, being unable "to swerve a hair's breadth on some things if she was to continue her great and daring experiment of the irregular equilibrium." This "is the thrilling romance of Orthodoxy . . . the equilibrium of a man behind madly rushing horses, seeming to stoop this way and to sway that, yet in every attitude having the grace of statuary and the accuracy of arithmetic." The Church swerved "to left and right, so exactly as to avoid enormous obstacles"—"the heavenly chariot" flying "thundering through the ages, the dull heresies sprawling and prostrate, the wild truth reeling but erect."[52]

The munificent largeness of Christianity opposes itself to so-called liberal theological attempts to "diminish or to explain away the divinity of Christ," if only because its unique "boast" is that God "could have His back to the wall," as Chesterton explains in one of those dramatically paradoxical passages of his, the excitement of which even those who are most averse to the Chestertonian paradox must surely feel:

> Christianity is the only religion on earth that has felt that omnipotence made God incomplete. Christianity alone has felt that God, to be wholly God, must have been a rebel as well as a king. . . . In a garden Satan tempted man: and in a garden God tempted God. He passed in some superhuman manner through our human horror of pessimism. When the world shook and the sun was wiped out of heaven, it was not at the crucifixion, but at the cry from the cross: the cry which confessed that God was forsaken by God. . . . [There is] only one religion in which God seemed for an instant to be an atheist.[53]

This orthodox Christianity not only enlarges the human idea of God but also enhances the things of this world as "the mother of all worldly energies," as opposed to the beliefs of the secularists who "have not wrecked divine things; but . . . secular things, if that is any comfort to them."[54] Far from the priesthood suppressing and devitalizing the people in Catholic countries, Chesterton claims: "Those countries in Europe which are still influenced by priests, are exactly the countries where there is still singing and dancing and coloured dresses and art in the open-air. Catholic doctrine and discipline may be walls; but they are the walls of a playground. Christianity is the only frame which has preserved the pleasures of Paganism."[55] (Again we notice the reference to the paradoxical importance of bounds and limits for freedom.) Such societies are also more truly democratic, for their culture depends upon a religion of tradition, and "tradition is only democracy extended through time," for "[t]radition means giving votes to the most obscure of all classes, our ancestors. It is the democracy of the dead." It means trusting the testimony of ordinary people in matters of religion, since the "democratic thing is to believe an old apple-woman when she bears testimony to a miracle."[56]

The religion of the God who experienced human pessimism is also the religion of an optimism beyond the reach of the pagan or the secularist, who "have both been miserable about existence, about everything, while mediaevals were happy about that at least," for "joy is the fundamental thing . . . and grief the superficial," and joy should be "expansive," whereas "grief" should be "contracted."[57] Laughter indeed is a recurring topic in *Orthodoxy,* as it was in *Charles Dickens.* Thus, for example, the "essence" of the evolutionary and pantheistic view of the world is that "Nature is our mother"; whereas to a Christian like Francis of Assisi, instead of being "a solemn Mother," as she is to Wordsworth, for instance, she is rather "a little, dancing sister, to be laughed at as well as loved."[58] The reference to solemnity reminds one of Newman's discovery that Catholicism lacked the solemnity of Anglicanism. For Chesterton solemnity is explicitly a sign of pride:

> Pride is the downward drag of all things into an easy solemnity. . . . It is really a natural trend or lapse into taking one's self gravely, because it is the easiest thing to do. It is much easier to write a good Times leading article than a good joke in Punch. For solemnity flows out of men naturally; but laughter is a leap. It is easy to be heavy: hard to be light. Satan fell by the force of gravity.

The "one thing," Chesterton thought, the Pre-Raphaelites could not imitate or recover was "the deep levity of the Middle Ages," which characterized even "the most earnest mediaeval art," simply because they lacked the humility that came from a supernatural faith.[59] It was this same faith that produced the gargoyles of Gothic architecture: "Greek heroes do not grin: but gargoyles do—because they are Christian." When the solemn people of Christ's day, "respectable people (such people as now object to barrel organs) objected to the shouting of the guttersnipes of Jerusalem," he "prophesied the whole of Gothic architecture in that hour" by saying, "If these were silent, the very stones would cry out."[60] Chesterton even speculates in the last sentences of *Orthodoxy* that "[t]here was something that He covered constantly by abrupt silence or impetuous isolation. There was some one thing that was too great for God to show us when He walked upon our earth; and I have sometimes fancied that it was His mirth."[61]

There remain two other themes to be discussed that connect Chesterton's apologetics with his celebration of the genius of Dickens. They come together in his attack on the then fashionable so-called philosophy of anarchism, which removes "the liberty to bind myself":

> Complete anarchy would not merely make it impossible to have any discipline or fidelity; it would also make it impossible to have any fun. . . . For the purpose even of the wildest romance results must be real; results must be irrevocable. Christian marriage is the great example of a real and irrevocable result; and that is why it is the chief subject and centre of all our romantic writing.[62]

The sheer insanity of a philosophy which denies all laws and rules introduces the theme of sanity which runs so persistently through Chesterton's writings. Paradoxically, even Dickens, with all his wild exaggerations and extravagances, was, Chesterton emphasizes, thoroughly sane and sensible: "Even when he raved like a maniac he did not rave like a monomaniac. . . . [H]e was merely a normal man minus a normal self-control." He never lost his common sense, Chesterton insists, and "perhaps the best evidence of this steadiness and sanity is the fact that, dogmatic as he was, he never tied himself to any passing dogma." He was not fond of "extraordinary things"; rather, "he liked quite ordinary things; he merely made an extraordinary fuss about them." Always "sanity was his ideal, even when he seemed almost insane." Indeed, so able was he "to see things sanely" that he was able "to satirize even his own faults."[63] Now in *Orthodoxy* Chesterton claims that the same healthy sanity came into the world with the Christian revelation, which supplies "the proper first principles" without which one "goes mad": "Mysticism keeps men sane. As long as you have mystery you have health; when you destroy mystery you create morbidity." It is the only religion which provides a "balance of apparent Contradictions" that is the "buoyancy of the healthy man."[64]

The other theme that emerges from the comment on anarchism is, of course, that the absolutely imperative principle that protects mirth, romance, and sanity is the principle diametrically opposed to anarchism: namely, the need for limits. I mentioned earlier the paradox that Chesterton, for all his expansiveness and exuberance, should have insisted so vehemently on the principle of limitation, which in religion becomes the principle of dogma. But the resolution of the paradox is simple enough: namely, that it is edges which create a space as opposed to a void. In fact, limitation, Chesterton points out, is the inevitable accompaniment of any act of will, of any action: "When you choose anything, you reject everything else." Free art, for example, is a contradiction in terms: "Art is limitation; the essence of every picture is the frame.... The artist loves his limitations: they constitute the *thing* he is doing." Life itself is limitation: "The moment you step into the world of facts, you step into a world of limits." That there should be limits in religion—that is, dogmatic definitions—is no more illiberal than is the requirement that "[i]f you draw a giraffe, you must draw him with a long neck." Chesterton's logic is as funny as it is compelling:

> If, in your bold creative way, you hold yourself free to draw a giraffe with a short neck, you will really find that you are not free to draw a giraffe.... You may, if you like, free a tiger from its bars; but do not free him from his stripes. Do not free a camel of the burden of his hump: you may be freeing him from being a camel. Do not go about as a demagogue, encouraging triangles to break out of the prison of their three sides. If a triangle breaks out of its three sides, its life comes to a lamentable end.

The revolutionary anarchist "is always engaged in undermining his own mines," for "[b]y rebelling against everything he has lost his right to rebel against anything." Those who oppose "expansion and largeness" to "strict limits and conditions" are the very people who turn their vast materialist universe into one "very large" "prison," knowing nothing of "the poetry of limits," which is what makes Chesterton "frightfully fond of the universe" and able to experience a "feeling of cosmic cosiness."[65]

Now this infinite, varied universe for which Chesterton has such an insatiable craving owes its very fascination and richness to the fact that it is so extremely complex and so unlike the universe of materialistic determinism, so complete in its simplicity. If, therefore, there is any key to understanding this world in all its largeness and spaciousness, one would expect this key to be as intricate, with as hard and defined edges, as the lock which it has to fit: "And if a key fits a lock, you know it is the right key." Accordingly, there is nothing to be embarrassed about in the elaborate doctrines of Christianity—one should be "proud of its complexity, as scientists are proud of the complexity of science." But to try and explain "this accumulation of truth," this "belief . . . so big," induces "a kind of huge helplessness," if only to know where to begin: "All roads lead to Rome; which is one reason why many people never get there."[66]

When Chesterton wrote those words in *Orthodoxy,* he had himself not yet reached Rome. But by the time he came to write *The Everlasting Man,* he had been a Roman Catholic for three years, and by then the rather vague "Church" or "Christian" or "Catholic" "Church" was quite explicitly the Roman Catholic Church. This professed key to life was notoriously complicated by dogmas and laws. But it was this very intricacy that seemed to Chesterton to correspond to the complexities of life: it was "a complete and complex truth with something to say about everything" which was provided by a Church able to "provide . . . for all sides of life," which "is newer in spirit than the newest schools of thought; and . . . almost certainly on the eve of new triumphs," which "grows younger as the world grows old."[67] No religion makes such great claims as Christianity, and no form of it appears more incredible than Catholicism; but while it "seems at first so outrageous," nevertheless it "remains solid and sane in substance . . . the moderator of all . . . manias; rescuing reason from the Pragmatists exactly as it rescued laughter from the Puritans." The emphasis on balance and sanity— "the soul" of Catholicism, he claims, is "common sense"—is very Chestertonian; but we are reminded of a recurring theme in this book when he adds that "[t]he mystery is how anything so startling should have remained defiant and dogmatic and yet become perfectly normal and natural," how "something so supernatural should have become so natural." This indeed is the note on which *The Everlasting Man* ends: "It has endured for nearly two thousand years; and the world within it has been more lucid, more level-headed, more reasonable in its hopes, more healthy in its instincts, more humorous and cheerful in the face of fate and death, than all the world outside."[68] All this health, humor, naturalness, sanity are ultimately based for Chesterton upon the "single paradox" of the Incarnation—"we might almost say upon this jest"—"that the hands that had made the sun and stars were too small to reach the huge heads of the cattle."[69]

The Everlasting Man also celebrates that complexity and richness of Catholicism which make it "the key that could unlock the prison of the whole world." The symbol of the key is important for Chesterton's version of Catholicism in three respects. First, the fact that it may seem "narrow" is of no significance, for the importance of a key lies not in its size but in its "shape"—and it "depends entirely upon keeping its shape." Similarly, Catholicism "is above all things the philosophy of shapes and the enemy of shapelessness," for otherwise it cannot be the key to the meaning of this life: "A man told that his solitary latchkey had been melted down with a million others into a Budhist [sic] unity would be annoyed. But a man told that his key was gradually growing and sprouting in his pocket, and branching into new wards or complications, would not be more gratified." Second, to those who find Catholicism fantastic, Chesterton has an easy answer: "[T]he shape of a key is in itself a rather fantastic shape. A savage who did not know it was a key would have the greatest difficulty in guessing what it could possibly be. And it is fantastic because it is in a sense arbitrary. A key is not a matter of abstractions; in that sense a key is not a matter of argument. It either fits the lock or it does not." Third, the complexities of Catholicism are exactly what we should expect if it is the key it claims to be:

> [A]s the key is necessarily a thing with a pattern, so this was one having in some ways a rather elaborate pattern. When people complain of the religion being so early complicated with theology and things of the kind, they forget that the world had not only got into a hole, but had got into a whole maze of holes and corners. . . . If the faith had faced the world only with the platitudes about peace and simplicity some moralists would confine it to, it would not have had the faintest effect on that luxurious and labyrinthine lunatic asylum. . . . [T]here was undoubtedly much about the key that seemed complex; indeed there was only one thing about it that was simple. It opened the door.[70]

At the most fundamental level, for Chesterton Catholic Christianity was complex because it was "a vision . . . not a pattern but a picture" of the mixture of good and evil that is the most basic fact about the world, unlike "those simplifications which resolve everything into an abstract explanation" of either good or evil.[71] Rejecting the "insane simplifications" of philosophers, it is also "at one with common sense" in declaring that "things are really there; or in other words that things are really things."[72] Again, it is complex because it is the "answer" to the "riddle" of the Gospels, which told a story that was "anything but . . . a simple Gospel."[73] It had defended the "balance of . . . interdependence" of a Trinitarian God against "the cold compromise" of Arianism, as well as the "sanity" of that "humane complexity" against Islam.[74] It is impossible "to make something larger than the Creed," which is "a very complex thing," its "unique note" being "the simultaneous striking of many notes."[75] Its dogmas are "incredible" because they are "incredibly liberal," "too liberal to be likely." For example, the Christian God is like "a liberal and popular prince, receiving petitions, listening to parliaments and considering the cases of a whole people"; and it is "the Catholic, who has the feeling that his prayers do make a difference, when offered for the living and the dead, who also has the feeling of living like a free citizen in something almost like a constitutional commonwealth."[76]

III

These themes that we have been tracing in Chesterton's greatest critical study and his most brilliant apologetic writings are to be found in the early *Heretics* (1905), the book to which *Orthodoxy* was the sequel, as well as in the more explicit defenses of Roman Catholicism, if less powerful than *The Everlasting Man,* that follow his conversion to Rome (1922): *Where All Roads Lead* (1922), *The Catholic Church and Conversion* (1927), *The Thing: Why I Am a Catholic* (1929), *The Well and the Shallows* (1935).

Similarly, the same ideas, but in nothing like the same profusion and richness as in *Charles Dickens,* appear in his other critical biographical studies, such as *Robert Browning* (1903) and *Robert Louis Stevenson* (1927). In *Chaucer* (1932), the medieval subject matter allows the themes to be developed in an overtly Catholic way. The "hearty and expansive" largeness of Chaucer's spirit is contrasted with the illiberal, simplistic, joyless world in which Robert Burns grew up: "Poor Burns never got out of the Puritan fog for one breath of that fresh air and daylight, of . . . spontaneous spiritual joy and gratitude." Chaucer's soul, by contrast, "had not been poisoned and blackened and blasted by the monomaniac horrors of a Simple Christianity":

> He had not seen all theology shrivel to a single thought; its very thunders of indignation all on one note; or the whole great Christian philosophy hardened into one harsh doctrine. . . . He did not suffer the particular kind of suffocation that comes in the *cul-de-sac* of a single idea, which is called a simple creed. He had the breadth and the blessings of a complicated creed.[77]

Again, the dogmas of Catholicism are paradoxically seen as enlarging rather than narrowing. For what unites Chaucer's very different Canterbury pilgrims is the fact that there is a "definite goal" to the pilgrimage; what keeps them together, in spite of their differences, is that they are bound by the same supernatural "facts"—Chesterton uses the same word as Newman employed in describing what distinguishes a Catholic from a Protestant culture:

> The truth is that the broad religion creates the narrow clique. It is what is called the religion of dogmas, that is of facts . . . that creates a broader brotherhood and brings men of all kinds together. This is called a paradox; but it will be obvious to anyone who considers the nature of a fact. All men share in a fact, if they believe it to be fact. Only a few men commonly share a feeling. . . . [I]f religion is an intuition, it must be an individual intuition and not a social institution. . . . [I]t is much easier to build a social institution on something that is regarded as a solid fact. . . . A religion of miracles turned all this crowd of incongruous people into one company. A religion of moods would never have brought them together at the tavern, far less sent them trotting laboriously to the tomb.

Like Newman, too, Chesterton rejoices in the way in which the sacred and the secular mingle in a Catholic culture: "One of the quarrels in *The Canterbury Tales* sounds exactly like a quarrel in a public-house to-day, between a boisterous bookie and a surly north-country groom." Such encounters may still be possible in public houses, but not the kind of intimate intercourse that a pilgrimage involves: "That is the measure of the difference between an objective religion, worshipped as an object by the whole people, and a subjective religion, studied as a subject only by the religious." Such a common journey would be impossible in a Protestant or secular society, where there is no such common purpose: the Miller will want to go to Ramsgate, while the Merchant will refuse

> to ride beyond Chatham, because all his interests are limited to the progressive industry of that wealthy and dirty town. . . . [T]he Prioress, not content with pitying mice, will withdraw to a Vegetarian Hostel on the hills of Westerham, inhabited by cranks; while the now aged

Knight, swearing that the Service is going to the dogs, and that these damned pacifists haven't a damned patriotic instinct left, shall devote himself furiously to the fortifications of Dover. As their counterparts stand to-day, it is easier to imagine the Wife of Bath wanting to go sun-bathing at Margate, or the Clerk instantly returning, with refined disgust, to Oxford, than to imagine either of them wanting to toil together to a particular tomb in Canterbury.[78]

Chesterton sees Chaucer as anticipating Dickens in his "fantastic," "irrational" humor, "that new and powerful use of the comic, which seems sometimes almost more tremendous than the tragic," that "pure folly" of humor for the sake of humor. But the frivolity of Chaucer came from having the "equilibrium" of the Catholic faith, a frivolity excluded by "pure" Protestantism in the form of the "simple system" of Puritanism. It was a "cheerfulness or sanity" that Dickens also possessed, but without the "theology" that "broadened" the mind of Chaucer by providing "a centre of gravity" which was for him "always a centre of gaiety." For Chaucer's "balance" and "common sense" existed against the background of a common Christian philosophy, in particular "the colossal common sense of St. Thomas Aquinas," while his "normality" was to be understood in the light of the medieval insistence on the "equilibrium" and "just balance" of all the doctrines of Christianity, as opposed to heresy, which only seeks "to develop a solitary doctrine."[79] As for Chaucer's "gratitude" and "wonder at the very existence of the World," those too arose out of a Catholic "glimpse" of the goodness of creation.[80]

If the reader of Chaucer is constantly reminded (sometimes by the author) of Chesterton on Dickens, the same is true of his two other explicitly Catholic biographical studies. The subject of *St. Francis of Assisi* (1923), however "wild and romantic" he might seem, "always hung on to reason by one invisible and indestructible hair," just as the "sense of humour which salts all the stories of his escapades alone prevented him from ever hardening into the solemnity of sectarian self-righteousness."[81] Apart from his essential sanity, Francis for Chesterton was above all the saint of praise of nature, "which no one will ever understand while he identifies it with nature-worship or pantheistic optimism." But praise of nature was fundamentally that gratitude for existence itself which lay at the heart of Chesterton's whole philosophy of life and of all his best writing.

This sense of the great gratitude and the sublime dependence was not a phrase or even a sentiment; it is the whole point that this was the very rock of reality. It was not a fancy but a fact; rather it is true that beside it all facts are fancies. That we all depend in every detail, at every instant, as a Christian would say upon God, as even an agnostic would say upon existence and the nature of things . . . is the fundamental fact which we cover up with curtains. . . . He who has seen the whole world hanging on a hair of the mercy of God has seen the truth.

Francis was like a man "transported with joy to discover that he is in debt," that is, the "infinite debt" for life itself, which he can never pay back—but "[i]t is the highest and holiest of the paradoxes that the man who really knows he cannot pay his debt will be for ever paying it back." His passionate enjoyment of poverty was like Dickens's passionate enjoyment of the simple pleasures of life: "It was not self-denial merely in the sense of self-control. It was as positive as a passion; it had all the air of being as positive as a pleasure. He devoured fasting as a man devours food."[82] Again, like Dickens, he delighted in the individual person: he was a "very genuine democrat" because "[h]e only saw the image of God multiplied but never monotonous. To him a man was always a man and did not disappear in a dense crowd any more than in a desert. He honoured all men; that is, he not only loved but respected them all." Like Dickens and his "holy fools," Francis "treated the whole mob of men as a mob of kings" as he moved "swiftly through the world with a sort of impetuous politeness."[83] But as with Francis's praise of nature, this deep interest in every human being he met was only one aspect of a profound "thanksgiving" for life itself: "He knew that the praise of God stands on its strongest ground when it stands on nothing. He knew that we can best measure the towering miracle of the mere fact of existence if we realise that but for some strange mercy we should not even exist."[84]

Just as, for all its factual errors and one or two idiosyncratic critical judgments, Chesterton's *Charles Dickens* has been hailed by many Dickens scholars as the one great study ever written of the novelist, so his *St. Thomas Aquinas* (1933) was considered by the leading Thomist scholar of the time, Etienne Gilson, to be a work of genius in that Chesterton had expressed the essence of Aquinas's thought as no scholar had ever been able to do.[85] As in his study of St. Francis, Chesterton fastens on what he calls "the primary and fundamental Part" of Thomism "or indeed the Catholic philosophy," namely, "the praise of Life, the praise of Being, the praise of God as the Creator of the World." For Chesterton, "Everything else follows a long way after" the essential point, namely, the goodness of creation, which is never in doubt, although things have been complicated by the Fall. Thomas "did, with a most solid and colossal conviction, believe in Life," so much so that his mind was "filled and soaked as with sunshine with the warmth of the wonder of created things."[86] If Francis was Dickensian in his asceticism, Thomas was Dickensian "in his hunger and thirst for Things." These were not "things to eat or drink or wear, though he never denied to these their place in the noble hierarchy of Being; but rather things to think about, and especially things to prove, to experience and to know." Philosophically, "he was avid in his acceptance of Things," holding that "there really are things; and not only the Thing; that the Many existed as well as the One." It was this realism of Aquinas that led him to God: the fact that there really were things, but things that were not "complete" in themselves, meant not that there were no things but that "their reality can only be explained as part of something that is complete," namely, God. Thomas "saw a thing that was thicker than a thing; that was even more solid than the solid but secondary facts"; since the secondary facts were "real, any elusive or bewildering element in their reality cannot really be unreality; and must be merely their relation to the real reality." Thomas had too much Christian humility to deny that he had seen a real stick or stone: whatever philosophical doubts there might be about their reality, he was "faithful to his first love; and it is love at first sight"; in the face of all sophistries, he remained "stubborn in the same objective fidelity. He has seen grass and gravel; and he is not disobedient to the heavenly vision." The sense of the sheer strangeness of existence that struck Chesterton so deeply was also, he claims, what inspired Aquinas: "There is no thinker who is so unmistakably thinking about things." What Chesterton sees as "the elemental and primitive poetry that shines through all his thoughts; and especially through the thought with which all his thinking begins," was "the intense rightness of his sense of the relation between the mind and the real thing outside the mind." Chesterton generalizes the point: "That *strangeness* of things, which is the light in all poetry, and indeed in all art, is really connected with their otherness; or what is called their objectivity." Similarly, in Thomas's philosophy, "the energy of the mind forces the imagination outwards . . . because the images it seeks are real things. All their romance and glamour, so to speak, lies in the fact that they are real things; things *not* to be found by staring inwards at the mind." Thomism avoids both materialism and subjectivism: "The mind is not merely receptive, in the sense that it absorbs sensations like so much blotting-paper.... On the other hand, the mind is not purely creative, in the sense that it paints pictures on the windows and then mistakes them for a landscape outside." It sees the relation between mind and reality quite differently:

> If the mind is sufficient to itself, it is insufficient for itself. For this feeding upon fact *is* itself; as an organ it has an object which is objective; this eating of the strange strong meat of reality.... In other words, the essence of the Thomist common sense is that two agencies are at work; reality and the recognition of reality; and their meeting is a sort of marriage.[87]

The common sense and sanity of St. Thomas indeed form another key theme in the book. Thus Thomas's emphasis on the Incarnation as against an excessively spiritual Christianity is seen by Chesterton as being simply the "common sense" of "the holy familiarity of the word made flesh." Blessed with "any amount of Common Sense," he fought against the Platonizing Augustinians, whose "Logos was the Word; but not the Word made flesh," for "a religion of common sense" that would once again be a "popular" religion. That Thomism is "the philosophy of common sense is itself," Chesterton insists, "a matter of common sense," as Aquinas "is almost always on the side of simplicity, and supports the ordinary man's acceptance of ordinary truisms," his whole system hanging on "one huge yet simple idea," the fact of being or existence. Whereas the practicality of pragmatism paradoxically "turns out to be entirely theoretical," the "Thomist begins by being theoretical, but his theory turns out to be entirely practical." Thus the fact of being is followed by its "shadow the first fundamental creed or commandment; that a thing cannot be and not be."[88] Again, in his orthodoxy Aquinas can be said to have "saved the sanity of the world" by insisting on the importance of the body against those Platonizing tendencies that led to the Albigensian denial of marriage. Asceticism, Chesterton argues, "or the war with the appetites, is itself an appetite," which "is indulged in much saner proportion under Catholic Authority than in Pagan or Puritan anarchy." The book ends with what is for Chesterton the highly suggestive story that Martin Luther publicly burned the works of St. Thomas.

> All the close-packed definitions that excluded so many errors and extremes; all the broad and balanced judgments upon the clash of loyalties or the choice of evils; all the liberal speculations upon the limits of government or the proper conditions of justice; all the distinctions between the use and abuse of private property; all the rules and exceptions about the great evil of war; all the allowances for human weakness and all the provisions for human health; all this mass of medieval humanism shrivelled and curled up in smoke before the eyes of its enemy; and that great passionate peasant rejoiced darkly, because the day of the Intellect was over.[89]

It is not only the common sense and sanity of Aquinas that Chesterton sees as being destroyed by the Reformation, but also his liberalism in the sense of liberality. As Dickens had sought to liberate his fellow human beings from the inhumanities of the Victorian age, so Aquinas in Chesterton's eyes "was one of the great liberators of the human intellect" by reconciling religion with reason and by insisting that "the senses were the windows of the soul and that the reason had a divine right to feed upon facts, and that it was the business of the Faith to digest the strong meat of the toughest and most practical of pagan philosophies." Unlike the Protestant reformers who deprived faith of reason, Aquinas fought for "all that is liberal and enlightened." It was because of the "liberality" of his "liberal theology" that "he insisted that God and the image of God had come in contact through matter with a material world," for his "humanising of divinity" meant that he was "insisting on the immense importance of the human being in the theological scheme of things." In short, like the Franciscan movement, Thomism, distinguished for its "humanistic liberality," "was an enlargement and a liberation."[90]

I cannot say I am sorry to have quoted Chesterton so liberally in this chapter. For I believe that the writer who has emerged from these pages will be scarcely recognizable to those who know only the author of the Father Brown stories and *The Man Who Was Thursday* and *The Ballad of the White Horse* (1911). If I am right in seeing Chesterton's literary achievement as primarily akin to that of the great Victorian prose writers, then I should want to add that Chesterton's literary studies, particularly of Dickens, are books that may be placed—incongruously, perhaps, but not impertinently—on the shelf alongside Arnold's *Essays in Criticism,* and his biographies of Francis of Assisi and Thomas Aquinas alongside Carlyle's biographical portraits in *On Heroes, Hero-Worship and the Heroic in History* and *Past and Present.* As for *Orthodoxy* and *The Everlasting Man,* these are works that Newman would not have been ashamed to have written. But whether or not I am also right in thinking that Chesterton's greatest book is *Charles Dickens,* it is, I am convinced, the book that is the key to understanding Chesterton's Catholicism and the way in which this is reflected in his thought and writings.

CHAPTER 5

The Catholicism of Greeneland

In Marie-Françoise Allain's *The Other Man: Conversations with Graham Greene* (1979), the novelist several times denied that he believed in hell, as opposed to "a sort of purgatory." On one of these occasions, according to the record, he even said, "I have never believed in hell," while admitting that "the evil which surrounded" him at boarding school "prepared" him "for the paradoxes of Christianity."[1] But what he described in his essay "The Lost Childhood" (1947) as the "perfect evil" which he had experienced at school suggests something more hellish than purgatorial.[2] And this is confirmed in the prologue to *The Lawless Roads* (1939), where Greene stated explicitly: "I began to believe in heaven because I believed in hell, but for a long while it was only hell I could picture with a certain intimacy—the pitch-pine partitions of dormitories where everybody was never quiet at the same time; lavatories without locks." In contrast to the hell of school life, the Church of England "could not supply the same intimate symbols for heaven; only a big brass eagle, an organ voluntary, 'Lord, Dismiss Us with Thy Blessing.'" These symbols changed when Greene became a Roman Catholic in 1926: "The Mother of God took the place of the brass eagle: I began to have a dim conception of the appalling mysteries of love moving through a ravaged world—the Curé d'Ars admitting to his mind all the impurity of a province, Péguy challenging God in the cause of the damned."[3]

If the conventional Anglicanism in which Greene had been brought up could not convey any real sense of heaven and God's love, neither did it believe in hell in the way the Roman Catholic Church did. One could only appreciate "the appalling Mysteries" of divine love if one also had a lively faith in the possibility of damnation. For not only did the Catholicism to which Greene was introduced preach about the possibility of damnation, it also left the believer in no doubt about the kinds of action that sent one to hell—"mortal sins" or those sins which merited eternal damnation. A later kind of Catholicism, less anxious to apply the ultimate sanction to lapses such as missing mass on Sunday, may have a more nuanced theology, but it has undoubtedly reduced the dramatic tension that so fascinated Greene, between the certainty of damnation and the infinite mercy of God.

The Lawless Roads quotes as an epigraph the famous passage in Newman's *Apologia pro Vita Sua* about the problem of evil which concludes: "*If* there be a God, *since* there is a God, the human race is implicated in some terrible aboriginal calamity."[4] This "calamity" of sin became vividly real to Graham Greene as a boarder at the public school of which his father was the headmaster. Later, Catholicism both affirmed and explained the existence of absolute evil; but it was not until 1938, when he went to Mexico to report on the religious persecution raging there, that he "discovered some emotional belief" in Catholicism, as he claimed in the second volume of his autobiography, *Ways of Escape* (1980). In the previous volume, *A Sort of Life* (1971), Greene had explained that, having decided to seek instruction from a priest, as his fiancée Vivien Dayrell-Browning was a devout Catholic convert, he "became convinced of the probable existence of something we call God" and decided to be received into the Church, "not . . . emotionally moved, but only intellectually convinced."[5] Ten years after his reception, he commented: "I had not been converted to a religious faith. I had been convinced by specific arguments in the probability of its creed."[6] Although his friend Evelyn Waugh was certainly convinced intellectually by the arguments of Father Martin D'Arcy, he too did not experience the full reality of Catholicism until he saw the Church in action in the missions. For Greene it was the heroism of the persecuted Mexican Church which inspired the most Catholic period of his life, as well as his fictional masterpiece. Here were to be found both evil and sanctity, both God and the Devil, unlike secular Western countries such as England and America, where "faith" had been replaced by "ugly indifference." Whereas in Mexico there were "idolatry and oppression, starvation and casual violence, but you lived under the shadow of religion—of God or the Devil," North American culture "wasn't evil, it wasn't anything at all, it was just the drugstore and the Coca Cola, the hamburger, the sinless graceless chromium world."[7]

Greene's denial that he had ever believed in hell must have resulted from a lapse of memory or alternatively from a desire to distance himself from his earlier years when he became known as a Catholic novelist. In 1936 he wrote in *Journey without Maps:* "I am a Catholic with an intellectual if not an emotional belief in Catholic dogma; I find that intellectually I can accept the fact that to miss a Mass on Sunday is to be guilty of mortal sin."[8] But, as Greene knew very well, the concept of mortal sin is meaningless if there is no hell. Certainly, his biographer Norman Sherry is in no doubt not only that Greene once himself believed in hell but also that "what attracted him as much as anything to Catholicism was the Church's belief in Hell"; and Sherry quotes a letter to Vivien, written at the end of 1925, a few weeks before he was received, on the subject of hell: "It gives something hard, non-sentimental and exciting."[9] In the same letter he reacts strongly against what he sees as the sentimentalism of Anglicanism. The word *exciting* is, I think, very significant, but for the moment I want to stress the word *hard*, not only because of this strange denial in Greene's conversations with Marie-Françoise Allain, which conflicts with the known facts, but also because of a curious inconsistency between his vaunted liberal Catholicism and his contempt for the Church of England's fuzzy attitude to dogma.

In conversation with Allain, Greene insists on the necessity of dogma—"otherwise one becomes as foggy as the Anglicans"—and speaks of the "absurdity" of Anglican bishops who deny the fundamentals of Christian belief. And yet almost in the same breath he dismisses the Catholic concept of mortal sin, which follows from the doctrine of hell and which underpins one of the seven defined Catholic sacraments, that of penance, which originated from and which depends on the fundamental Christian belief that human beings have been endowed with unconditional free will, which must consequently have the unrestrained capacity to commit such serious sin as ruptures communion with Christ and his Church and therefore demands sacramental reconciliation. "As for mortal sin, I find the idea difficult to accept because it must by definition be committed in defiance of God. I doubt whether a man making love to a woman ever does so with the intention of defying God. . . . The word 'mortal' presupposes a fear of hell, which I find meaningless."[10] Now, not only was Greene instructed by an able and intelligent priest, Father Trollope, to whom he pays tribute in *A Sort of Life*,[11] but he was very literate theologically, with a great admiration, for instance, for Newman, "whose books influenced me a great deal after my conversion,"[12] and indeed with a lifelong interest in theology ("Theology is the only form of philosophy which I enjoy reading").[13] It seems, therefore, extraordinary that he should have thought that the Catholic Church teaches that a person who commits adultery or fornication commits mortal sin because his or her motive for doing so is to defy God! Such a case must be very rare indeed! The Catholic Church, as Greene must have known, is very well aware why people commit what it regards as mortal sins—not in order to defy God, but rather to seek their own pleasure, even though it involves seriously disobeying God. That Greene is obfuscating the issue is anyway clear from his Catholic novels, where the idea of mortal sin in a perfectly conventional sense is used to great dramatic effect.

The reason I have spent so much time on whether Greene ever believed in hell and mortal sin is that, as I have said, the two themes, together with the possibility of forgiveness in confession and the unlimited mercy of God, are integral to his finest writing, which is what makes his denial so paradoxical. But before considering how Greene uses these themes, it is important to see how he blends these most traditional Catholic motifs with two very contemporary influences on the novel to produce an altogether new kind of fiction in the English language. These two related influences, of which Greene was very conscious, are the cinema and the thriller.

As a seventeen-year-old schoolboy, Evelyn Waugh had urged a friend who was an aspiring novelist to "GO TO THE CINEMA": "Try and bring home thoughts by actions and incidents. Don't make everything said. This is the inestimable value of the Cinema to novelists. . . . Make things happen."[14] Certainly Waugh was to use the cinematic shot to great effect in his own Catholic fiction, not least in the gripping repentance scene in *Brideshead Revisited,* when Lord Marchmain finally makes the sign of the cross.

Writing about his early novels, Greene too wrote of how he used to think "in terms of a key scene," a scene such as "halts the progress of the novel with dramatic emphasis, just as in a film a close-up makes the moving picture momentarily pause." He continued to follow this method in his later novels: "It might even be said that I reached the logical climax of the method in *The Honorary Consul* where almost the whole story is contained in the hut in which the kidnappers have hidden their victim."[15] It is significant that Greene mentions this scene, where he is at his most powerful as a novelist, as it perfectly embodies the three key elements of Catholicism, cinema, and thriller. In one of those early novels that Greene mentions, *Stamboul Train* (1932), the best-selling novelist Q. C. Savoury, wondering how he should describe the night scene from the train, reflects that he "must show not all that I see but a few selected sharp points of vision. I must not mention the shadows across the snow, for their colour and shape are indefinite, but I may pick out the scarlet signal lamp shining against the white ground, the flame of the waiting-room fire in the country station."

Savoury also notes how "the films had taught the eye . . . the beauty of land-scape in motion, how a church tower moved behind and above the trees, how it dipped and soared with the uneven human stride."[16]

Samuel Hynes has pointed out not only that Greene was "the first important writer to develop a cinematic technique" but that "his interest in film is paralleled by his interest in, and use of, another popular art form, the thriller."[17] In fact, of course, the film and the thriller are perfectly suited to each other, as Greene himself showed most notably in *The Third Man* (1950), which was written in the first place as a story for a film. There, inter-estingly enough, one of the first cinematic shots at the beginning of the novel is the burial (apparently) of Harry Lime by a priest in Vienna, for, not surprisingly, Harry is a Catholic. He had been Rollo Martins's school-boy hero, but is finally discovered by his admirer to be "evil" in a primeval sense; for his evil is evil as only Catholics are capable of, as Greene had dis-covered in Mexico. Harry's lucrative penicillin racket has, most horribly, led to many children dying or going mad, but in answer to Martins's shocked comment, "You used to be a Catholic," Harry replies with a dev-astatingly cynical theological half-truth: "Oh, I still *believe*, old man. In God and mercy and all that. I'm not hurting anybody's soul by what I do. The dead are happier dead."[18] Although Greene has not yet turned away from the Catholic novel, *The Third Man* does not in any way attempt to develop any kind of Catholic theme. But still it is characteristic of Greene's most original contribution to the English novel that this final denouement of Harry's absolute evil should take place in the car of the revolving Great Wheel high above the city, as Martens confronts the armed Harry Lime: the thriller comes to its climax in a visually terrifying scene made for the cinema camera, but made more sinister still and more spiritually chilling by Harry Lime's perverted Catholic justification of his horrendous crimes.

In his essay "The Lost Childhood" Greene tells us that in his early teens he decided to become a writer after reading Marjorie Bowen's *The Viper of Milan* (1906). It was this book which gave him his "pattern—religion might later explain it to me in other terms, but the pattern was already there—perfect evil walking the world":

> Why did it creep in and colour and explain the terrible living world of the stone stairs and the never quiet dormitory? . . . Goodness has only once found a perfect incarnation in a human body and never will again, but evil can always find a home there. Human nature is not

black and white but black and grey. I read all that in *The Viper of Milan* and I looked round and I saw that it was so.[19]

Greene repeated to Marie-Françoise Allain that it was Marjorie Bowen's novel that "trapped" him into literature: "Her novel had supplied me with my pattern in the carpet—which religion was to explain for me later." He also told Allain that the books he had "liked best in my childhood, those which really influenced me were . . . cloak-and-dagger novels, novels of adventure, and I believe that in a way it's adventure novels I'm writing today."[20] *The Viper of Milan* fell into this category of fiction, but since it also contained a character with a "genius for evil,"[21] it was a thriller with a deeper significance.

In Greene's view the English novel had declined since Henry James because with his death "the religious sense was lost . . . and with the religious sense went the sense of the importance of the human act." This was why for Greene "creative art seems to remain a function of the religious mind": "Rob human beings of their heavenly and their infernal importance, and you rob your characters of their individuality." James, on the other hand, possessed a "sense of evil religious in its intensity," seeing "evil as an equal force with the good." And Greene explains James's attraction to Catholicism as having nothing to do with its "purely aesthetic appeal"— for otherwise he could have joined the superior (at least in the English-speaking world) literary culture of Anglicanism—but rather to do with its "treatment of supernatural evil"—unlike the Anglican Church, which "had almost relinquished Hell." Like Greene himself, James had been taught by experience "to believe in supernatural evil, but not in supernatural good."[22] This sense of evil Greene associates directly with Catholicism, a sense he finds, for example, in Ford Madox Ford, "a Catholic in theory though not for long in practice." This was to be expected in view of the remark of T. S. Eliot, which Greene often quoted, that "[m]ost people are only a very little alive; and to awaken them to the spiritual is a very great responsibility: it is only when they are so awakened that they are capable of real Good, but that at the same time they become first capable of Evil."[23] To Greene, Frederick Rolfe, another Catholic novelist and the author of *Hadrian the Seventh* (1904), "a novel of genius," into which he put "all the good of which he was capable," is "an obvious example" of Eliot's point: "For if ever there was a case of demonic possession it was Rolfe's. . . . The greatest saints have been men with more than a normal capacity of evil, and the most vicious men have sometimes narrowly evaded sanctity. . . . He would be a priest or nothing, so nothing it had to be . . . if he could not have Heaven, he would have Hell."[24]

Another Catholic novelist with whom Greene has often been compared—later, somewhat to his discomfort—was François Mauriac, whose "first importance to an English reader," Greene wrote in 1945 in the midst of his Catholic period, "is that he belongs to the company of the great traditional novelists: he is a writer . . . whose characters have the solidity and importance of men with souls to save or lose." Greene's natural affinity with Mauriac is significantly indicated in a much later essay (1968) on Bernanos, where he even likens Mauriac's art to the cinematic technique that he himself pioneered: "[He] conceals the author's voice in a simile or an unexpected adjective, like a film director who makes his personal comment with a camera angle."[25] But by the time of his conversations with Marie-Françoise Allain (1979), Greene's desire to distance himself from the traditional Catholicism of his most creative period is shown in his criticism of Mauriac "as an example not to follow. I'm a great admirer of some of his books. But his loyalty to the Catholic Church has made him rather too 'scrupulous' a writer—in the theological rather than in the moral sense." But again this is inconsistent with his earlier enthusiastic appreciation of Mauriac as a traditional novelist who treats his characters seriously precisely because he is a genuinely Catholic writer who believes in absolute good and evil by virtue of his believing in heaven and hell. If Mauriac— or the earlier Greene, for that matter—had followed Greene's later prescription that a writer must be "unscrupulous" and ready "to violate his faith,"[26] then it is far from clear that either novelist could have produced their finest fiction.

In *Ways of Escape* Greene noted, "Many times since *Brighton Rock* I have been forced to declare myself not a Catholic writer but a writer who happens to be a Catholic." And he justified this statement by adding, "Newman wrote the last word on 'Catholic literature' in *The Idea of a University*," citing as Newman's words, "[I]f Literature is to be made a study of human nature, you cannot have a Christian Literature. It is a contradiction in terms to attempt a sinless literature of sinful man."[27] He made the same point in conversation with Allain, who reported him as saying: "I refute the term 'Catholic writer.' Cardinal Newman . . . denied the existence of a

'Catholic literature.' He recognized only the possibility of a religious dimension superior to the literary dimension, and he wrote that books ought to deal first of all with what he called . . . 'the tragic destiny of man in his fallen state.'"[28] On both occasions Greene misquotes and distorts what Newman actually said in his essay "English Catholic Literature," in the second part of *The Idea of a University,* which begins with the sentence, "One of the special objects which a Catholic University would promote is that of the formation of a Catholic Literature in the English language." By this, Newman explains, he means not specifically *religious* literature but literature written by Catholics—not just by writers who happen, quite incidentally, to be Catholics, as Greene would have it, but by writers who would write *as Catholics.* English literature for Newman is, with some exceptions, overwhelmingly Protestant—it is a literature, he says, "formed in Protestantism." It is true, however, that Newman also recognizes, apparently somewhat inconsistently, that "human nature is in all ages and all countries the same; and its literature, therefore, will ever and everywhere be one and the same also. Man's work will savour of man; in his elements and powers excellent and admirable, but prone to disorder and excess, to error and to sin. Such too will be his literature." Still, even though Newman regards original sin as affecting all human beings and therefore their literature, he sees writers as being formed by their religious beliefs, or lack thereof; and that is why he calls for "the formation of a Catholic school of writers," with "respect principally to the matter of what is written, and to composition only so far forth as style is necessary to convey and to recommend the matter."[29]

In the case of Graham Greene, Newman would surely have recognized that the "matter" of novels like *Brighton Rock* (1938), *The Power and the Glory* (1940), *The Heart of the Matter* (1948), and *The End of the Affair* (1951) was definitely and specifically Catholic, whatever reservations he might have had about its treatment. As for the "style" of these books, the cinematic technique might have greatly interested him. After all, the Newman who had once written that Catholic children "take in religion principally through the eye"[30] would presumably have been fascinated by the way in which in the twentieth century the technological revolution brought about a new visual culture which favored Catholicism rather than Protestantism. The Reformation could hardly have succeeded without the invention of the printing press and the possibility of mass distribution of the Bible, given the Protestant insistence on Scripture as the sole depository of doctrine and source of devotion. But at the end of the second millennium the wheel came full circle as the power of the printed word gave way to the visual media. Perhaps it was not a coincidence that the most vibrant form of Protestantism, Evangelicalism, came increasingly to emphasize Charismatic or Pentecostal forms of worship, in which physical bodily movements rather than cerebral preaching and reading take center stage. Certainly, however, Catholicism, which had once relied so heavily on visual objects like stained-glass windows, pictures, and statues, now lent itself naturally to the camera which takes so much more easily to the sight of liturgy and ritual than to the spoken word of Bible readings and sermons.

It is not hard, then, to imagine Newman being keenly alive to the new possibilities of communication that the cinema and then television afford Catholicism as opposed to Protestantism. The change of "style," therefore, that Greene pioneered in the written novel, whereby the printed word attempted to adapt itself to the visual cinematic shot, would have seemed to him a highly appropriate development for the "matter" of Catholic fiction. As Greene explained to Allain, "When I describe a scene, I capture it with the moving eye of the cine-camera." The cinema had strongly "influenced" him: "I work with a camera, following my characters and their movements."[31]

Immediately after his repudiation of his reputation as a Catholic writer and his misrepresentation of Newman in *Ways of Escape,* Greene "nevertheless" admitted that "by 1937 the time was ripe for me to use Catholic characters," although he added cautiously, "[T]he ideas of my Catholic characters, even their Catholic ideas, were not necessarily mine." Eleven years had passed since his reception into the Catholic Church, when he had "not been emotionally moved, but only intellectually convinced." However, he acknowledged that he was "in the habit of formally practising my religion, going to Mass every Sunday and to Confession perhaps once a month, and in my spare time I read a good deal of theology . . . always with interest." Even so, "My professional life and my religion were contained in quite separate compartments, and I had no ambition to bring them together." What changed the situation was the politicizing of Catholicism with the communist persecution of the Church in Mexico and the Spanish Civil War. Catholicism no longer seemed merely of aesthetic and intellectual interest; "It was closer now to death in the afternoon."[32] In other words,

Catholicism had suddenly become exciting, or the stuff of which thrillers are made: the four key ingredients of Greene's most creative period could now jell together—evil, Catholicism, the cinema, and the thriller.

The first offspring of this union was Greene's first major novel, *Brighton Rock*—"one of the best I ever wrote." Although he claimed that it was only in Mexico that he had "discovered some emotional belief," nevertheless he had to admit that "probably emotion had been astir before that, or how was it that a book which I had intended to be a simple detective story should have involved a discussion . . . of the distinction between good-and-evil and right-and-wrong and the mystery of 'the appalling strangeness of the mercy of God'—a mystery that was to be the subject of three more of my novels?" Only the "first fifty pages" of *Brighton Rock* may remain of the originally intended detective story, but the novel remains an exciting thriller on both the human and the spiritual levels.[33]

In his earlier thrillers Greene had only introduced Catholic themes incidentally and occasionally. Confession, which was to play a powerful role in the Catholic novels, crops up in his first successful novel, *Stamboul Train*, when Dr. Czinner recalls how there "had been a time when a clear conscience could be bought at the price of a moment's shame," and the vivid image of the confessional scene flashes before him like a cinematic shot: "The priest's face turned away, the raised fingers, the whisper of a dead tongue."[34] In *It's a Battlefield* (1934) the half-French Catholic Jules Briton is always "given confidence, an immense pride, a purpose," when he listens to the inevitable sermon on sin—"in the badly lit church, surrounded by the hideous statues of an uncompromising faith, listening to the certainty of that pronouncement." Similarly, he asks Kay Rimmer, "with comic hopefulness," whether by any chance she is a Catholic: "Easier, then, the formality of marriage, more final the barrier against loneliness, an impregnable dyke till death; otherwise the sea corroded."[35] The relief provided by the certainties of Catholicism was something that had strongly appealed to the author himself, whatever his later denials. In *A Sort of Life* Greene told the story of how he consulted a priest when he was (wrongly) diagnosed as epileptic before his marriage and asked if contraception might therefore be permissible: writing several years after the end of the Second Vatican Council about the uncompromising reply he received, he reflected that no doubt now he would be told to follow his own conscience; but what is so interesting is that he admits that while he was "repulsed" by the "hard answer" he was given then (and could only be given), he "couldn't help admiring" the "unyielding façade" of the Catholic Church.[36] Again, Norman Sherry quotes a letter of 1925 to Vivien in which Greene writes of his interest in becoming a Catholic: "I admit the idea came to me, because of you. I do all the same feel I want to be a Catholic now, even a little apart from you. One does want fearfully hard, something fine & hard & certain, however uncomfortable, to catch hold of in the general flux."[37]

Above all what Greene needed and wanted was a religion that had hard and certain things to say about evil, as an early satirical scene in *Brighton Rock* makes plain. The modernist clergyman who cremates the murdered Fred Hale goes out of his way to deny that there is any such thing as hell:

> "Our belief in heaven," the clergyman went on, "is not qualified by our disbelief in the old medieval hell. We believe," he said, glancing swiftly along the smooth polished slipway towards the New Art doors through which the coffin would be launched into the flames, "we believe that this our brother is already at one with the One." . . . "He has attained unity. We do not know what that One is with whom (or with which) he is now at one. We do not retain the old medieval beliefs in glassy seas and golden crowns. Truth is beauty and there is more beauty for us, a truth-loving generation, in the certainty that our brother is at this moment reabsorbed in the universal spirit."[38]

The Catholic Pinkie who is guilty of Fred's murder has no such illusions. As for the young Greene, the reality of hell is much clearer than that of heaven. When he tells Rose that he doesn't go to mass, she questions him anxiously:

> "But you believe, don't you," Rose implored him, "you think it's true?"
> "Of course it's true," the Boy said. "What else could there be?" he went scornfully on. "Why," he said, "it's the only thing that fits. These atheists, they don't know nothing. Of course there's Hell. Flames and damnation . . . torments."
> "And Heaven too," Rose said with anxiety. . . .
> "Oh, maybe," the Boy said, "maybe."

Rose seems tacitly to accept this pessimistic assumption about what Catholicism essentially consists of when later she remarks bitterly to Pinkie about Ida Arnold, who is in pursuit of Fred's murderer, "You believe in things. Like Hell. But you can see she don't believe a thing." Pinkie refuses the description of religious believer, as facts don't require belief: "I don't take any stock in religion. Hell—it's just there." Pinkie himself "couldn't picture any eternity except in terms of pain": "Heaven was a word: hell was something he could trust."[39]

The secular Ida's determination, by contrast, to find Fred's killer is based on her lack of belief: that is, on her conviction that "death was the end of everything": "Death shocked her, life was so important. She wasn't religious. She didn't believe in heaven or hell. . . . Let Papists treat death with flippancy: life wasn't so important perhaps to them as what came after. . . . She took life with a deadly seriousness . . . the only thing she believed in." As Rose puts it contemptuously to Pinkie, "[S]he doesn't know what a mortal sin is. . . . Right and wrong. That's what she talks about. . . . Right and wrong. . . . Oh, she won't burn. She couldn't burn if she tried." When Rose asks Pinkie if Ida is "good," he laughs, since somebody who isn't capable of going to hell isn't capable of going to heaven either—"She's just nothing." Pinkie, though, has discovered that Rose is "good," while "he was damned: they were made for each other." Ida, on the other hand, "was as far from either of them as she was from Hell—or Heaven. Good or evil lived in the same country, came together like old friends." To Rose's whispered hope that Pinkie may repent and go to confession, Ida contemptuously replies, "That's just religion. Believe me, it's the world we got to deal with." But when Rose responds, "There's things *you* don't know," Ida retaliates with "I know one thing you don't. I know the difference between Right and Wrong. They didn't teach you *that* at school." As for Rose, "[T]he two words meant nothing to her. Their taste was extinguished by stronger foods—Good and Evil. . . . [S]he knew . . . that Pinkie was evil—what did it matter in that case whether he was right or wrong?"[40]

The belief that there are sins called "mortal" which are punished by hell is central to the novel. Rose contemplated going to confession (so as to be "in a state of grace") before her civil marriage to Pinkie but then realized that "[i]t wasn't any good confessing," since they were going to get married outside the Catholic Church—"to do a mortal sin." And Pinkie bitterly relishes the thought that as a result of their invalid marriage "[i]t'll be no good going to confession ever again—as long as we're both alive." Pinkie personifies the Eliot dictum that only people who are properly alive are capable of real evil: "He had no doubt whatever that this was mortal sin, and he was filled with a kind of gloomy hilarity and pride. He saw himself now as a full grown man for whom the angels wept." In bed with Rose, he loses his fear of "damnation—of the sudden and unshriven death"—for now he is in "hell" and there "wasn't anything to worry about: it was just his own familiar room." By losing his fear of hell Pinkie becomes fully alive, as Ida, who is dead to the spiritual, can never even begin to be. Rose, who loves Pinkie, is happy to be with him "in the country of mortal sin. . . . [I]f they damned him they'd got to damn her, too." It is enough for her to have "Pinkie and damnation." Her willingness to commit suicide with Pinkie (as she thinks) involves another mortal sin—the worst of all mortal sins: "It was said to be the worst act of all, the act of despair, the sin without forgiveness." But, not surprisingly, Rose is unable "to realize despair, the mortal sin . . . it didn't feel like despair." Instead, it is her misguided love for Pinkie which makes her want to be damned with him: "She felt responsibility. . . . [S]he wouldn't let him go into that darkness alone." She has to restrain herself from praying, remembering that "she was in mortal sin: it was no good praying." For Rose now to want a "happy death" or "bona mors" would be to be "tempted . . . to virtue like a sin . . . it would be an act of cowardice: it would mean that she chose never to see him again for ever." Rose's conviction that "[t]he evil act was the honest act . . . and the faithful" is the kind of moral or rather spiritual paradox that was to become the hallmark of Greene's Catholic novels.[41] And at the end of the novel she receives unexpected support from the old priest in the confessional, who tells her the story of the French writer Charles Péguy, who, he tells her,

> had the same idea as you. He was a good man, a holy man, and he lived in sin all through his life, because he couldn't bear the idea that any soul could suffer damnation. . . . This man decided that if any soul was going to be damned, he would be damned too. He never took the sacraments, he never married his wife in church. . . . [S]ome people think he was—well, a saint.

The priest confirms too that "a Catholic is more capable of evil than anyone. I think perhaps—because we believe in Him—we are more in touch with the devil than other people."[42]

In *A Sort of Life* Greene speaks of the influence of Robert Browning on him, remarking that if he "were to choose an epigraph for all the novels I have written, it would be from *Bishop Blougram's Apology*:

Our interest's on the dangerous edge of things.
The honest thief, the tender murderer,
The superstitious atheist. . . .
We watch while these in equilibrium keep
The giddy line midway."[43]

In his conversations with Allain, Greene alludes to this passage, commenting: "'The dangerous edge of things' remains what it always has been—the narrow boundary between loyalty and disloyalty, between fidelity and infidelity, the mind's contradictions, the paradox one carries within oneself. This is what men are made of."[44] This "sense of danger"[45] that Greene found in Browning's awareness of the "paradox" of life he experienced even more excitingly in the paradoxical nature of Catholicism's teaching on evil—its insistence on the one hand on mortal sin and the reality of hell and on the other hand on the infinite mercy of God which exceeds human understanding. If, however, as Greene later came to believe, there are no such things as mortal sins because there is no such place as hell, then obviously there is no need for what the priest in the confessional at the end of *Brighton Rock* calls hesitantly "the . . . appalling . . . strangeness of the mercy of God." For, as the priest points out to Rose, the existence of hell does not mean that Catholics are required to believe that "any soul is cut off from mercy," that is, that anyone is actually in hell.[46] But the paradox of Greene's later position is that it eliminates the very paradox which is at the heart of his finest novels and which creates the uniquely thrilling sense of danger that accompanies the fear of eternal damnation. A Calvinist view of the certainty of hell for those predestined to damnation would not remove the fear, but it would lack the thrill of danger involved in the paradox of the Catholic position that certain sins carry the penalty of eternal damnation but that there is no certainty that the penalty will be exacted, as no one can be sure that anyone has paid the supreme price, even if it were possible to judge the secrets of the human heart or to limit the extent of God's mercy—which anyway is guaranteed in sacramental confession.

Pinkie has been criticized as an implausible character on the ground that his background in the back streets of Brighton would hardly enable him to possess the kind of religious knowledge and vocabulary which are attributed to him in the novel.[47] A possible defense of the novelist is to point out that Pinkie is regularly referred to simply as "the Boy," as though he were an archetypal figure of primeval youthful evil rather than a specific individual character. This presumably is what the reader has to do, for example, when Pinkie, after telling Rose that hell is "just there"—"You don't need to think of it—not before you die,"—is confronted by Rose's objection, "You might die sudden." To this Pinkie responds, quite implausibly: "You know what they say—'Between the stirrup and the ground, he something sought and something found.'" No less implausibly, Rose—who is also often called simply "the girl"—replies: "Mercy." She has answered correctly: "That's right: Mercy." Pinkie may regard hell and damnation as inescapable facts, but he also is an orthodox Catholic in knowing that God's mercy cannot be limited, and the thought that "[y]ou could be saved between the stirrup and the ground" recurs more than once in his consciousness. But Pinkie is also aware that, while forgiveness is always available even for the most mortal of sins, repentance is also required—"you couldn't be saved if you didn't repent." But Pinkie hasn't "time" or "the energy to repent"—although he knows that "[b]etween the stirrup and the ground there wasn't time: you couldn't break in a moment the habit of thought." But "[i]t was impossible to repent of something which made him safe." Only "when he was thoroughly secure, he could begin to think of making peace, of going home, and his heart weakened with a faint nostalgia for the tiny dark confessional box, the priest's voice, and the people waiting under the statue, before the bright lights burning down in the pink glasses, to be made safe from eternal pain." The cinematic shot highlights for Pinkie the possibility of escaping damnation, but "he couldn't experience contrition—the ribs of his body were like steel bands which held him down to eternal unrepentance." As Pinkie drives Rose out to the cliffs to carry out their suicide pact—which he has no intention of keeping after Rose has shot herself—he begins "softly to intone" some words from the mass: "'Dona nobis pacem.' . . . He thought: there'll be time enough in the years ahead . . . to repent of this." But even as he thinks that were death to come suddenly there would still be time "between the stirrup and the ground," he realizes that "he wasn't made for peace, he couldn't believe in it. Heaven was a word: hell was something he could trust." At this point Greene suggests that Pinkie is not a fully free agent but the victim of his circumstances: "An awful resentment stirred in him—why shouldn't he have had his chance like all the rest, seen his glimpse of heaven."[48]

The hint that Pinkie's actions did not perhaps have the character of voluntary consent which the Catholic Church lays down as part of the definition of a mortal sin remains undeveloped in the novel. Many years later, however, Greene told Allain: "I don't think that Pinkie was guilty of mortal sin because his actions were not committed in defiance of God, but arose out of the conditions to which he had been born." Maybe that was Greene's later view, but it was not explored in the novel, nor does *Brighton Rock* support the idea that a sin can be mortal only when it is committed in order to defy God. The theology of the book is consistently orthodox in assuming that a sin is mortal if the so-called "matter" is grave and it is committed with full knowledge and consent. But Greene appears confused in his conversation with Allain, as shortly before he made a quite different point about why Pinkie did not necessarily go to hell: "I tried . . . to present the reader with a creature whom he could accept as worthy of hell. But in the end . . . I introduced the possibility that he might have been saved 'between the stirrup and the ground.' I wanted to instil in the reader's mind a fundamental doubt of hell."[49] Not only is this different from the explanation that Pinkie's moral culpability was lessened or even extenuated because of social factors, but it is logically incoherent. If there is no hell, then there is no room for God's infinite mercy offering salvation to Pinkie at the last moment—for what is there to be saved from?

The orthodox Catholic view is to be found in the modern Catechism of the Catholic Church, which states that "although we can judge that an act is in itself a grave offence, we must entrust judgement of persons to the justice and mercy of God."[50] And this is exactly what the priest at the end of *Brighton Rock* tells Rose in the pastoral rather than catechetical context of the confessional: "You can't conceive, my child, nor can I or anyone the . . . appalling . . . strangeness of the mercy of God." It seems extraordinary that Greene could not apparently see that if doubt were in fact cast on the reality of hell (as in liberal Protestantism), or for that matter on the infinite mercy of God (as in Calvinism), then "the dangerous edge of things" would no longer exist, as the paradox of eternal damnation on the one hand and infinite mercy on the other hand of Catholicism would disappear. Indeed, if Greene really had instilled a doubt of hell in the reader's mind, then the spiritual thriller which is *Brighton Rock* would cease to thrill. The book would shoot itself in the foot—rather as the tragedy of *Doctor Faustus* would hardly be tragic if Marlowe had subverted the reality of Mephistopheles and hell. Fortunately, Greene's Catholic novels do hold in balance the two doctrines that the Catholic Church insists on: that human beings have been given unconditional free will to choose (which logically must include the possibility of choosing the absence of God, which is hell) and that God is absolute love who must therefore will all his creatures to be saved. For without the tension between these two doctrines, the novels would not be the spiritual thrillers that they are. Certainly, the cinematic scene at the end of *Brighton Rock* when Rose goes to confession (she "could just see the old head bent towards the grill") would lose its dramatic effect if the priest had suggested to Rose that she should not worry about Pinkie because she need not believe literally in the doctrine of hell. On the contrary, she must "hope and pray" both because there is the possibility of damnation and because God is all-merciful.[51]

Before leaving the novel, it is worth noting one very effective device that Greene uses in several of his most vivid cinematic scenes, where the visual "shot" is accompanied, as it were, by a subtitle on the screen. At the beginning of the book, for example, Pinkie pays a visit to a shooting booth in "the Palace of Pleasure" on Brighton Pier: "The shelves of dolls stared down with glassy innocence, like Virgins in a church repository. The Boy looked up: chestnut ringlets, blue orbs and painted cheeks: he thought—Hail Mary . . . in the hour of our death. 'I'll have six shots,' he said."[52] These snatches of Catholic prayers that rise involuntarily into Pinkie's stream of consciousness add an extra note of spiritual menace to what would otherwise just be typical scenes in a thriller film, as, for instance, when we watch Pinkie uneasily climbing the stairs to his bedroom after a telephone call to Mr. Colleoni ends chillingly with what sounds like the gangster laughing: "'Agnus Dei qui tollis peccata mundi . . .' He walked stiffly, the jacket sagging across his immature shoulders, but when he opened the door of his room—'dona nobis pacem'—his pallid face peered dimly back at him full of pride from the mirror over the ewer, the soap-dish, the basin of stale water."[53]

Later, at the races where Pinkie has arranged for Spicer to be murdered by Colleoni's men, "the Boy sees other images apart from those of the racecourse": "He had started something . . . which had no end. Death wasn't an end; the censer swung and the priest raised the Host, and the loud-speaker intoned the winners: 'Black Boy. Memento Mori. General Burgoyne.'"[54] Spicer succeeds in escaping, so Pinkie returns to the house where the gang live to complete the job himself: "He could hear little creaking leathery movements as the door swung. The words 'Dona nobis pacem' came again to mind; for the second time he felt a faint nostalgia, as if for something he had lost or forgotten or rejected."[55] On the final drive to the cliff, there is a wonderful shot of the car driving through the blinding rain, but there is another force that also seems to be beating on the windscreen trying to get in:

> The car lurched back on to the main road; he turned the bonnet to Brighton. An enormous emotion beat on him; it was like something trying to get in; the pressure of gigantic wings against the glass. Dona nobis pacem. He withstood it with . . . bitter force. . . . If the glass broke, if the beast—whatever it was—got in, God knows what it would do. He had a sense of huge havoc—the confession, the penance and the sacrament—and awful distraction, and he drove blind into the rain.[56]

The reference to Péguy at the end of *Brighton Rock* is picked up again in the epigraph to *The Heart of the Matter* where the radical Catholic writer is quoted as saying in effect that no one is so Christian as the sinner, except the saint. This idea of the "holy sinner" is first explored by Greene in the character of Pinkie, who is Christian in a way that Ida can never be, but it is developed much more compellingly and powerfully in the figure of the priest in *The Power and the Glory*.[57]

The priest, who is never given a name, "carried a wound, as though a whole world had died." He committed the mortal sin of fornication with the peasant woman Maria after falling into the worse sin of "despair—the unforgivable sin." Gradually, he has given up the obligations of the priesthood:

> [F]east days and fast days and days of abstinence had been the first to go: then he had ceased to trouble more than occasionally about his breviary—and finally he had left it behind altogether at the port in one of his periodic attempts at escape. Then the altar stone went—too dangerous to carry with him. He had no business to say Mass without it; he was probably liable to suspension, but penalties of the ecclesiastical kind began to seem unreal in a state where the only penalty was the civil one of death.

As the only priest left in the state who has not either escaped or died or conformed to the atheistic anticlerical government, he is now returning "to the scene of his despair," the village where Maria lives with their illegitimate daughter Brigitta, "with a curious lightening of the heart." For after so many lapses, "he had got over despair too":

> He was a bad priest, he knew it. They had a word for his kind—a whisky priest, but every failure dropped out of sight and mind: somewhere they accumulated in secret—the rubble of his failures. One day they would choke up, he supposed, altogether the source of grace. Until then he carried on, with spells of fear, weariness, with a shamefaced lightness of heart.

The priest "carried on," that is, with his priestly sacramental duties: "Now that he no longer despaired it didn't mean, of course, that he wasn't damned—it was simply that after a time the mystery became too great, a damned man putting God into the mouths of men: an odd sort of servant, that, for the devil."[58] Damned because of his own mortal sins, paradoxically he can bring salvation to others.

The other paradox which lies at the heart of the book is that the priest achieves his own holiness and eventual martyrdom by virtue of, rather than in spite of, his own sins. Again we are "at the dangerous edge of things," and again orthodox Catholic doctrine is the stuff of Greene's drama. In the Exultet, the opening chant of the vigil mass of Easter, the Church celebrates, at its most important liturgical event of the year, the so-called "felix culpa," or "happy fault" of Adam: "O necessary sin of Adam, which gained for us so great a Redeemer!" The original sin of the world can paradoxically be celebrated as the cause of the Incarnation. For the priest of *The Power and the Glory,* too, his sin of fornication paradoxically begins a new life of grace in him. For the "enormous consequences" of his sin involve a child at whose name his "heart jumped," who makes "his heart beat" with a "secret love." And yet the sexual act had apparently no redeeming feature about it: "They had spent no love in her conception: just fear and despair and half a bottle of brandy and the sense of loneliness had driven him to an act which horrified him—and this scared shame-faced overpowering love was the result." As a priest, "he had been responsible for souls, but that was different . . . a lighter thing." But now he "was aware of an enormous load of responsibility: it was indistinguishable from love." The priesthood had cut him off from the deepest kind of human experiences: "This, he thought, must be what all parents feel: ordinary men go through life like this crossing their fingers, praying against pain, afraid. . . . This is what we escape at no cost at all, sacrificing an unimportant motion of the body." Just before his first arrest the priest attempts without success to make "an act of contrition": "He tried to think of his child with shame, but he could only think of her with a kind of famished love." And when he is imprisoned in a cell and hears "the word 'bastard' his heart moved painfully, as when a man in love hears a stranger name a flower which is also the name of his woman. 'Bastard!' the word filled him with miserable happiness. It brought his own child nearer." The priest finds he is unable to repent his "felix culpa": "He couldn't say to himself that he wished his sin had never existed, because the sin seemed to him now so unimportant and he loved the fruit of it."[59]

Yet another paradox is that the priest only really begins to be a true priest, in the sense of "alter Christus," when he is no longer able to exercise his priesthood freely and when he has abandoned the discipline and obligations of the priesthood, along with its security and status. Before the persecution he enjoyed the "good things of life . . . the respect of his contemporaries, a safe livelihood. The trite religious word upon the tongue . . . the ready acceptance of other people's homage." When he says mass in the village, he feels "an immense satisfaction that he could talk of suffering to them now without hypocrisy—it is hard for the sleek and well-fed priest to praise poverty." On the other hand, he now realizes that he no longer has the easy answers he once thought he had: "He was a man who was supposed to save souls. It had seemed quite simple once, preaching at Benediction, organizing the guilds, having coffee with elderly ladies behind barred windows, blessing new houses with a little incense, wearing black gloves. . . . It was as easy as saving money: now it was a mystery. He was aware of his own desperate inadequacy." Once he had seemed to be a successful priest with "ambition," full of building plans for the parish. And when eventually he escapes into the bordering state where the Church is free, it is this old life he is tempted to return to: "He could hear authority, the old parish intonation coming back into his voice, as if the last years had been a dream. . . . He could feel the old life hardening round him like a habit."[60]

In fact, the priest returns at great personal danger to give the last rites to a dying Yankee gangster, only to be betrayed to the police by the mestizo or half-caste. When, near the beginning of the book, the priest was asked to hear confessions, he agreed—but "angrily." However, by the time he goes to Maria's village, he is ready without being asked to say mass even though he is "in a state of mortal sin": it didn't seem "to matter very much, whether he was damned or not, so long as these others . . ." Indeed, he prays to God for "any kind of death—without contrition, in a state of sin—only save this child"—that is, his illegitimate daughter. He "felt the need of somehow ransoming his child. He would stay another month, another year. . . . Jogging up and down on the mule he tried to bribe God with promises of firmness." Finally, at the end of the novel, on the night before his execution he prays: "Oh God, help her. Damn me, I deserve it, but let her live for ever."[61]

But the paradox is that far from being in a state of damnation, the priest is at last discovering what love is, the love he preached about in the old days with confidence but without knowledge. For it is Brigitta, the fruit of his mortal sin, who not only arouses the natural love of a father but also produces the priest's first genuine experience of Christian love, as the sentence that immediately follows the last quotation shows: "This was the love he should have felt for every soul in the world . . ." That is not the end of the sentence, which continues, "all the fear and the wish to save concentrated unjustly on the one child." But the priest is unjust to himself: on the first occasion when he was arrested, he reflected on a paradox: "[I]t sometimes seemed to him that venial sins . . . cut you off from grace more completely than the worst sins of all. Then, in his innocence, he had felt no love for anyone; now in his corruption he had learnt." Without the mortal sin of fornication, he would not have known that "one must love every soul as if it were one's own child. The passion to protect must extend itself over a world."[62]

But this love that the priest now experiences for the first time is not simply human or even Christian love: it has a further dimension because Greene intends us to see this love as the true pastoral love that the priest is meant to have for souls. In the case of Brigitta, this protective love is founded on a special sense of guilt: "[T]he look in the child's eyes . . . frightened him— . . . as if a grown woman was there before her time . . . aware of far too much. It was like seeing his own mortal sin look back at him, without contrition." It is as if Brigitta symbolizes that knowingness which came when Adam and Eve ate from the tree of knowledge in the garden of Eden: "he was appalled again by her maturity, as she whipped up a smile from a large and varied stock . . . enticingly. . . . The world was in her heart already, like the small spot of decay in a fruit. . . . [S]he had no grace." His newfound desire as a priest to save souls springs from the priest's dreadful conviction that the damned Brigitta is made in the image of his own mortal sin, which she reflects: "The knowledge of the world lay in her like the dark inexplicable spot in an X-ray photograph; he longed . . . to save her, but he knew the surgeon's decision—the ill was incurable."[63] It is the sense that he is responsible for the damnation of another person as well as himself that at last unlocks his heart. It is again the Eliot idea that only the one who knows evil is sufficiently alive to know good.

But there is another mortal sin, a much worse sin than the sin of fornication that gave rise to it, which contributes to the priest's growth in holiness: "He had given way to despair—and out of that had emerged a human soul and love." He knows the half-caste is his Judas who will betray him, but "Christ had died for this man too: how could he pretend with his pride and lust and cowardice to be any more worthy of that death than the half-caste? This man intended to betray him for money which he needed, and he had betrayed God for what?" And so he gives the half-caste, sick with fever, his mule to ride on. "'You think you're very fine,' the man said. 'Helping your enemies. That's Christian, isn't it?'" It is indeed, but the genuineness of the priest's humility is expressed in his own absolute acquiescence in the mestizo's accusation:

> This was pride, devilish pride, lying here offering his shirt to the man who wanted to betray him. Even his attempts at escape had been half-hearted because of his pride—the sin by which the angels fell. When he was the only priest left in the state his pride had been all the greater; he thought himself the devil of a fellow carrying God around at the risk of his life.

But if there had been pride before, now there is only humble confession. When he is finally caught by the police lieutenant, he tells him that it was only pride which had made him stay: "Pride's the worst thing of all. I thought I was a fine fellow to have stayed when the others had gone. And then I thought I was so grand I could make my own rules. I gave up fasting, daily Mass. I neglected my prayers—and one day because I was drunk and lonely— . . . I got a child. It was all pride." We are not necessarily meant to take the priest completely at his word as he shows when he corrects, half-contradicts himself: "I wasn't any use, but I stayed. At least, not much use. . . . It's a mistake one makes to think just because a thing is difficult or dangerous . . ." But when he assures the lieutenant that he can preach from the pulpit with complete sincerity about the danger of damnation because he preaches not only from belief but from personal knowledge, we know he is speaking the literal truth as he sees it: "I don't know a thing about the mercy of God: I don't know how awful the human heart looks to Him. But I do know this—that if there's ever been a single man in this state damned, then I'll be damned too."[64]

In fact, Greene depicts the whisky priest as having achieved sanctity through his supposedly mortal sins. On his first imprisonment, the words "God so loved the world" pass through his mind as "he was touched by an extraordinary affection. He was just one criminal among a herd of criminals. . . . He had a sense of companionship which he had never experienced in the old days when pious people came kissing his black cotton glove." Even the pharisaical woman who denounces him receives only compassion: "Hate was just a failure of imagination. He began to feel an overwhelming responsibility for this pious woman. . . . [H]e would have known what to say to her in the old days, feeling no pity at all, speaking with half a mind a platitude or two."[65]

During his first imprisonment before his identity is known, the priest is caught in a cinematic shot carrying the pails from the cells to the cesspool, with the evident allusion to Christ carrying his cross: "The priest bent down and took the pail. It was full and very heavy: he went bowed with the weight across the yard. Sweat got into his eyes. He wiped them free." It recalls the even more cinematic scene of the mass the priest said in Maria's village on a packing-case just before the police arrived, with Indian peasants "kneeling with their arms stretched out in the shape of a cross."[66]

The priest has begun his own *via dolorosa* to martyrdom, very different from that of the hagiographical martyrs whose lives the devout woman reads to her children. It "had never occurred to him—that anybody would consider him a martyr." As he says to his fellow prisoners, "Martyrs are holy men. It is wrong to think that just because one dies . . . no. I tell you I am in a state of mortal sin." And to the lieutenant's furious "Well, you're going to be a martyr—you've got that satisfaction," he replies, "Martyrs are not like me." On the night before he dies, he reflects sadly, "People had died for him, they had deserved a saint, and a tinge of bitterness spread across his mind for their sake that God hadn't thought fit to send them one." When he wakes on the morning of his execution, unlike the nun in "The Wreck of the *Deutschland*," he does not contemplate a "bona mors"—"it was not the good death for which one always prayed." Appropriately, a cinematic shot captures him moments before his martyrdom:

> He caught sight of his own shadow on the cell wall; it had a look of surprise and grotesque unimportance. What a fool he had been to think that he was strong enough to stay when others fled.... [P]erhaps after all he was not at the moment afraid of damnation.... He felt only an immense disappointment because he had to go to God empty-handed, with nothing done at all. It seemed to him, at that moment, that it would have been quite easy to have been a saint. It would only have needed a little self-restraint and a little courage.... He knew now that at the end there was only one thing that counted—to be a saint.[67]

Greene may not have known it when he wrote this passage, but the idea of succeeding through failure, the greatest apparent failure being the crucifixion, was a favorite theme in the writings of his theological mentor Newman.[68]

And so the priest dies, his own martyr's "death-cry" being only "a word that sounded like 'Excuse.'" It is very different from the kind of heroic death scenes of the devout mother's martyrologies, but at the end of the novel she (hesitantly) acknowledges him to be "one of the heroes of the faith," and asks her husband for "a little money . . . to get a relic."[69]

After he escaped to another state where there were still churches and priests, the whisky priest wondered, "What was the good of confession when you loved the result of your crime?" "[T]he child . . . came automatically back to him with painful love."[70] To this the orthodox but paradoxical answer is that one should hate the original sin but love its fruit if it is good. Perhaps the priest is by now too confused to make such distinctions, or rather perhaps the question is a rhetorical one. Be that as it may, the point is that the priest knows that it is through evil—there is no doubt about the sheer evil of the original act—that he has found his humanity and his Christian identity. And, as in *Brighton Rock,* there is a contrast to supernatural good and evil in the form of the Lutheran Lehrs, the American brother and sister who give the priest shelter. For them cleanliness is synonymous with godliness ("'[O]ur water's fresh and clean,' Miss Lehr said primly, as if she couldn't answer for anybody else's") and evil beneath their notice: "Mr Lehr and his sister had combined to drive out savagery by simply ignoring anything that conflicted with an ordinary German-American homestead. It was, in its way, an admirable mode of life." Unsurprisingly, they've "never held, of course, with confession."[71]

In a provocative critical essay on Graham Greene, Terry Eagleton writes of the central "paradox" in his novels whereby, "given a tragic tension between the claims of human relationship and the demands of faith, the rigours of orthodoxy must be guiltily denied in the name of the human." Thus his protagonists

> turn, at the risk of damnation, from a soul-saving theology to the insidious pressures of humanity, but only in the context of a continually undermining disbelief in the final validity of such claims. Orthodox Catholicism is denied in the name of "humanism"; yet that humanism is itself critically qualified by traditional Catholic ways of feeling. The upshot of this is a kind of deadlock: the human value of men like Scobie or the whisky priest lies in their readiness to reject an orthodoxy in which they nevertheless continue to believe; yet to acknowledge the superior truth of that orthodoxy, in the act of refusing it, is to confront the inadequacy of the sheerly human commitments they embrace. . . . The characters' failure to conform to the standard is essential for humane action; their continued acceptance of it is necessary, not only if they are to be distinguished from non-Christian humanists, but if they are to experience that self-deprecating humility of failure which is, for Greene, the condition of holiness.[72]

Applying his thesis to *The Power and the Glory*, Eagleton argues that the priest displays "unorthodoxy" when he refuses to accept the "pious" woman's denunciation of the couple copulating in the cell—"It's mortal sin." But when the priest responds, "We don't know. It may be,"[73] far from making a "criticism of established religion," he is acting entirely in accordance with traditional moral and pastoral theology, not to say in accordance with Christian charity. Apart from the fact that he doesn't know whether the couple are married or not, it is not for him to pronounce that somebody committing what is objectively a mortal sin is necessarily in a state of mortal sin, since for that certain conditions are necessary. But even aside from that, orthodox Christianity has always spoken of hating the sin and loving the sinner, and here the "pious" woman is the kind of uncharitable, proud Pharisee who is a stock figure of condemnation, for instance, in the impeccably orthodox novels of Mauriac.

Eagleton goes on to ask why the priest can be so lenient and liberal toward the sexual sins (if that is what they are) of others but so "extraordinarily astringent with himself."[74] But is he? He has committed the sin of fornication, he has broken his vow of celibacy, he has brought an illegitimate child into the world, and he has caused scandal to the faithful. In the Catholic world of which Greene is writing these were all very serious matters—indeed, Greene himself, in spite of all his later liberal views, continued to believe strongly in the compulsory celibacy of the clergy, telling Allain that "the priesthood must have the attraction of a crack unit . . . which demands self-sacrifice. . . . a difficult and dangerous calling . . . a venture which is total."[75] Right up until the end the priest continues to drink. He has abandoned religious practices incumbent on the priesthood. He has certainly stayed on under persecution, but not in any particularly heroic way—out of "pride. . . . I thought I was a fine fellow to have stayed when the others had gone."[76] Curiously, although the motive the priest attributes to himself fits the picture he gives of himself as having been formerly an ambitious successful priest, Eagleton insists that the "question of motivation is not convincingly established." It seems incredible that Eagleton should so misread the novel as to "conclude that the priest's self-estimation cannot really be true, since it obstinately refuses to accommodate itself to the novel's actual presentation of him."[77] As for the priest being harder on himself than others, that again is not only mere Christian humility but also spiritually quite correct in view of the high theology of the priesthood, which is that of the author and which informs the book. Greene's whole point, so totally missed in Eagleton's specious analysis, is that, flawed as the priest is, nevertheless, through rather than in spite of his faults, he reaches a degree of sanctity and in the end martyrdom.

Eagleton complains that the priest accuses himself of sins such as pride, lust, and cowardice, "which we are forced to take on credence because they are nowhere shown in the novel"—an assertion so strange as to make one wonder whether Eagleton has actually read the novel, which contains, to mention nothing else, the disturbing figure of Brigitta, the fruit of the priest's lust. Eagleton then argues that if, however, "the priest is accurate in his self-evaluation," then "his apparent virtue is cast damagingly into question."[78] But what "virtue" does the priest possess apart from the humility which he has derived from his genuine sorrow over his weaknesses and the love for others which springs from his love for his illegitimate child?

Eagleton, again, claims that the priest's alleged humility "lies largely in infringements of an orthodoxy which he recognizes as actively harmful in the case of the woman prisoner, or, later in the novel, in the bourgeois religion of the hygienically Lutheran Lehrs."[79] Well, the Pharisee in the prison is certainly orthodox—as Pharisees are wont to be—in her condemnation of fornication, but she is also depicted as guilty of the most serious of Christian sins, spiritual pride. If it is potentially "harmful" to be a spiritual person, then, of course, Eagleton is perfectly right, but that is not exactly his point. As for the Lehrs, here Eagleton shows his total misunderstanding of Greene's amused contempt for their lack of any real religion, for their incapacity for and ignorance of evil, and *therefore* of supernatural good— that is, sanctity. They are intended to be counterparts of Ida, although, being American Protestants they still have a veneer of religion, unlike the post-Protestant English dentist Mr. Tench, who, on being asked by the priest if he is a Catholic, replies with complete indifference: "I don't believe in anything like that. It's too hot anyway."[80] Unlike these American and English characters, the Mexican woman in the prison cell is capable of real evil, in this case the most serious sin, spiritual pride, precisely *because* she is a Catholic.

Finally, Eagleton again surely completely misses Greene's point when he claims that in the confrontation between the priest and the lieutenant, "the priest agrees, briefly and unspecifically, with the lieutenant's attack on the established Church, but then affirms the superiority of the Christian faith," since "his humility . . . prevents him from pressing . . . anything which might approach a radical criticism."[81] For in the exchange quoted, the lieutenant is referring to corruptions in the Church—poor people being deemed not "deserving of charity"—and the priest being concerned only with "who had . . . paid his Easter offering." Naturally the priest agrees: "You are so right," adding, "Wrong too, of course"[82]—not because he is backtracking from his criticism but because there is a great deal more to the Church than its corruptions: for all its faults, it is, as *The Lawless Roads* makes clear, the Church of the poor, who are attached to it in a way that they will never be to the anticlerical, atheistic humanism of the lieutenant, however good his intentions. Even the irreligious husband of the devout woman who reads the stories of the martyrs to her children misses the Church: "I was a bad Catholic, but it meant—well, music, lights, a place where you could sit out of this heat."[83] And the novel ends with his son, who hated having to listen to the stories of the martyrs, spitting at the revolver of the lieutenant, whose only desire was to improve the lot of his people, before kissing the hand of another clandestine priest, another potential martyr.

Eagleton's thesis that at the heart of the novel lies an unresolved tension between humanism and orthodoxy is in any case refuted by the evidence of *The Lawless Roads,* where Greene enthusiastically endorses the humanity of Catholicism against the inhumanity of atheistic humanism, which is supposed to be on the side of the poor but in fact is not: "Nothing in a tropical town can fill the place of a church for the most mundane use; a church is the one spot of coolness out of the vertical sun, a place to sit, a place where the senses can rest a little while from ugliness; it offers to the poor man what a rich man may get in a theatre." And Greene insists that the conventional objection to spending money on churches rather than the poor is a fallacy:

> I have no sympathy with those who complain of the wealth and beauty of a church in a poor land. For the sake of another peso a week, it is hardly worth depriving the poor of such rest and quiet as they can find in the cathedral here. I have never heard people complain of the super-cinemas—that the money should be spent in relief—and yet there's no democracy in a cinema: you pay more and you get more; but in a church the democracy is absolute. The rich man and the poor man kneel side by side for Communion; the rich man must wait his turn at the confessional.

Greene shows himself absolutely on the side of the devoutly Catholic Mexican poor and against those like the lieutenant in *The Power and the Glory* who seek to improve their lot while taking away their religion from them.

> And then you go into the cathedral for Mass—the peasants kneel . . . and hold out their arms, minute after minute, in the attitude of crucifixion; an old woman struggles on her knees up the stone floor towards the altar; another lies full length with her forehead on the stones. A long day's work is behind, but the mortification goes on. . . . [Y]ou realize suddenly that perhaps this is the population of heaven— these aged, painful, and ignorant faces: they are human goodness.

Although a "stranger," Greene felt that "it was like going home—a language I could understand." And what "if it were all untrue and there was no God, surely life was happier with the enormous supernatural promise than with the petty social fulfilment." But even on that level Greene says he prefers Catholic social teaching to communism, just as he notes that the socialist schoolmaster, for all his "pity," has no empathy with the Indians ("he . . . knew no Indian dialect at all"), unlike the priests who had been "driven away" but "who had learned the Indian dialects and . . . had shown interest in them as human beings." The church schools, Greene is told, "were far better" than what had replaced them, while the typical kind of school teacher "who tried to take on himself the part the priest would have performed in the old days . . . unlike the priest . . . knew nothing." Such priests as Greene met in Mexico he "really liked."[84]

Far from in any way supporting Eagleton's thesis, *The Lawless Roads* portrays an author truly inspired by the inspiring Catholicism he encountered in Mexico. As he told Allain, "[T]he fidelity of the believers assumed such proportions that I couldn't help being profoundly moved."[85] And without this inspiration Greene could never have written the spiritual thriller (written, incidentally, at the same time that he was writing a much more straightforward thriller, *The Confidential Agent* [1939]) that was to be his masterpiece.

Eight years later Greene published his second most important novel, *The Heart of the Matter*. Like his creator, Scobie finds hell much more real than heaven: "Nobody here could ever talk about a heaven on earth. Heaven remained rigidly in its proper place on the other side of death, and on this side flourished the injustices, the cruelties, the meanness that elsewhere people so cleverly hushed up. Here you could love human beings nearly as God loved them, knowing the worst."[86] But the "capacity for damnation" is reserved for Catholics who don't have the advantage of "invincible ignorance." When the young acting district commissioner Pemberton commits suicide, Scobie declares to Father Clay: "You are not going to tell me there's anything unforgivable there, father. If you or I did it, it would be despair. . . . We'd be damned because we know, but *he* doesn't know a thing." Similarly, when Scobie tells his mistress Helen Rolt about his dilemma of going to mass with his Catholic wife Louise, who will expect him to receive Communion, as he cannot do because he is in mortal sin and because he cannot go to confession, she asks, "You don't really believe in hell?"

Unfortunately, Scobie does. In that case, Helen wonders why he is having an affair with her. "How often, he thought, lack of faith helps one to see more clearly than faith." But if Helen has the perception of common sense, she altogether lacks supernatural sight. She cannot see why Scobie can't just "go and confess everything now? After all it doesn't mean you won't do it again."

> "It's not much good confessing if I don't intend to try. . . ."
> "Well then," she said triumphantly, "be hung for a sheep. You are in—what do you call it—mortal sin? now. What difference does it make?"
> He thought: pious people, I suppose, would call this the devil speaking, but he knew that . . . this was innocence. He said, "There *is* a difference—a big difference. . . . *Now* I'm just putting our love above—well, my safety. But the other—the other's really evil. It's like the Black Mass, the man who steals the sacrament to desecrate it. It's striking God when he's down—in my power."
> She turned her head wearily away and said, "I don't understand a thing you are saying. It's all hooey to me."
> "I wish it were to me. But I believe it."
> She said sharply, "I *suppose* you do. Or is it just a trick?"

In her turn, Louise, when she hears that Helen is her husband's mistress, remarks to her would-be lover Wilson, "But she's not a Catholic. She's lucky. She's free." As Scobie himself laments, "The trouble is . . . we know the answers—we Catholics are damned by our knowledge."[87]

Scobie, of course, has particularly in mind the knowledge of mortal sin. And again it is absolutely essential for the drama of a novel, which is a spiritual as well as an ordinary thriller, that the awful reality of mortal sin should not in any way be impugned—but with one reservation. For the action to be poised "on the dangerous edge of things," it is also necessary that other perfectly orthodox Catholic considerations should come into play. For example, Catholic moral theology recognizes that there can be extenuating circumstances which lessen the guilt of what is objectively a mortal sin. Scobie appears not to know this when he hopes: "And then, against all the teaching of the Church, one has the conviction that love— any kind of love—does deserve a bit of mercy." But two other factors he is aware of—that there is purgatory as well as hell for the punishment of sins and that repentance, however late, secures forgiveness: "One will pay, of course, pay terribly, but I don't believe one will pay for ever. Perhaps one will be given time before one dies."[88]

Like the priest in *The Power and the Glory,* Scobie finds enormous difficulty in repentance, not because he loves the fruit of his sin but because he is not at all a straightforward adulterer. Indeed, a major problem about the novel is that it is very hard to imagine Scobie in bed with Helen, or why his compassion for her has to lead to an affair as opposed to a father-daughter relationship. As one critic has sarcastically put it: "[N]ot on pity alone is adultery committed, in any climate: not, that is, unless by pity something more psychologically complex is intended than *The Heart of the Matter* admits."[89] But, of course, Scobie has to commit adultery because he has to be in mortal sin. However, to be fair to Greene, although pity is the overwhelming motive, the author does make some effort to depict a genuine love affair, as when Scobie imagines the unreality of confessing to so-called "adultery": "to hear Father Rank telling me to avoid the occasion: never see the woman alone (speaking in those terrible abstract terms: Helen—the woman, the occasion, no longer the bewildered child clutching the stamp-album . . . that moment of peace and darkness and tenderness and pity 'adultery')." The word *peace* is certainly significant as Scobie's longing for it ("the most beautiful word in the language") is a pervasive theme of the novel. He had just assured Helen herself, "[I]f I were dying now I wouldn't know how to repent the love." Not since his wife "was young" had he "felt so much at ease with another human being." But Scobie doesn't seem to know whether it was "even love, or was it just a feeling of pity and responsibility?" Does he really "love . . . or is it only that this automatic pity goes out to any human need?" At any rate pity is the dominant emotion: "He knew from experience how passion died away and how love went, but pity always stayed."[90]

Scobie's inexhaustible pity and indefatigable sense of responsibility for those who attract his pity become very tedious. Even he himself seems to realize what a bore he can be in his endless spiritual soliloquies: "'O God, give me death before I give them unhappiness.' But the words sounded melodramatically in his own ears." Greene skates very close to melodrama in each of the Catholic novels, but most of all in *The Heart of the Matter,* where Scobie's endless protective pity has an air of unreality about it—again, as Scobie himself seems to acknowledge: "[W]hy me, he thought, why do they need me, a dull middle-aged police officer who had failed for promotion? I've got nothing to give them that they can't get elsewhere: why can't they leave me in peace? Elsewhere there was a younger and better love, more security. It sometimes seemed to him that all he could share with them was his despair."[91] Quite, the reader is tempted to say. Greene was to claim that "[t]he character of Scobie was intended to show that pity can be the expression of an almost monstrous pride," but, as he admitted, "the effect on readers was quite different." And the reason is that the novel presses us to empathize with Scobie's dilemma, but the trouble is that, at least as far as Helen is concerned, the problem seems more self-inflicted than tragic, since Scobie is aware that she would be better off with a younger man. Not surprisingly, Greene told Allain that *The Heart of the Matter* was "a book I dislike," explaining, "Scobie is torn between pity and pride."[92] If this was the author's intention, it fails to realize itself in the novel.

Yet the book is very far from disastrous and will surely continue to rank as the best of Greene's novels after *The Power and the Glory*—and not only because it is on one level an exciting thriller set in a wonderfully evoked wartime Sierra Leone, but because, in spite of the flawed character of Scobie, it does at least partially succeed as a gripping spiritual thriller, employing the usual Catholic themes. In particular, there is nothing unreal about Scobie's anguished desire to protect his wife from knowledge of his affair with Helen, which involves him in committing a sacrilegious act. Unable to promise Father Rank in confession that he will end the affair with Helen, he is forced to receive Holy Communion in a state of mortal sin when Louise insists that they should go to mass together and receive the sacrament as a sign that they are starting a new life together. By taking the Host not in a state of grace, Scobie damns himself as only a Catholic can. On the first Sunday Scobie pretends to be ill and drinks some brandy, which saves him from the ordeal, as he has broken the strict fasting law. As Scobie watches his wife receive Communion, there is nothing contrived or unreal about this highly cinematic scene in which the camera of the novelist focuses on this drama of "divine materialism."

> Father Rank turning from the altar came to them with God in his hands. Scobie thought: God has just escaped me, but will He always escape? *Domine non sum dignus . . . domine non sum dignus . . . domine non sum dignus . . .* His hand formally, as though he were at drill, beat on a particular button of his uniform. It seemed to him for a moment cruelly unfair of God to have exposed himself in this way . . . a wafer

of bread . . . here in the hot port, there, everywhere, allowing man to have his will of Him . . . to put Himself at the mercy of men. . . . The priest had reached Louise in his slow interrupted patrol, and suddenly Scobie was aware of the sense of exile. Over there, where all these people knelt, was a country to which he would never return.

But there is no escape for Scobie as Louise asks him to go again to mass next morning. There Scobie watches "the priest pour the wine and water into the chalice, his own damnation being prepared like a meal at the altar." The "meal" is now ready as the novelist's camera closes in on the elevation of the Host after the consecration: "*Hoc est enim corpus:* the bell rang, and Father Rank raised God in his fingers—this God as light now as a wafer whose coming lay on Scobie's heart as heavily as lead." This scene, which is one of the finest things Greene ever wrote, comes to a marvelous cinematic climax:

> At the foot of the scaffold he opened his eyes. . . . He rose and followed her and knelt by her side like a spy in a foreign land who has been taught the customs and to speak the language like a native. Only a miracle can save me now, Scobie told himself, watching Father Rank at the altar opening the tabernacle. . . . Father Rank came down the steps from the altar bearing the Host. The saliva had dried in Scobie's mouth. . . . He couldn't look up: he saw only the priest's skirt like the skirt of the mediaeval war-horse bearing down upon him: the flapping of feet: the charge of God. If only the archers would fly from ambush, and for a moment he dreamed that the priest's steps had indeed faltered. . . . But with open mouth (the time had come) he made one last attempt at prayer, "O God, I offer up my damnation to you. Take it. Take it. Use it for them," and was aware of the pale papery taste of an eternal sentence on the tongue.[93]

Having offered up his damnation for Louise and Helen, a kind of infernal parody of the Catholic devotion of offering one's Communion for someone, Scobie has again perforce to go to Communion on the feast of All Saints: "Even this act of damnation could become as unimportant as a habit." As he says to Helen, "I'm damned for all eternity. . . . What I've done is far worse than murder." And so he determines on one final mortal sin which will secure his immediate damnation without any chance of future repentance, his deliberate suicide. Scobie sees it as a "felix culpa," as he tells God: "I've preferred to give you pain rather than give pain to Helen or my wife because I can't observe your suffering. . . . They are ill with me and I can cure them." Anyway, God "can look after" himself: "You survive the cross every day. You can only suffer. You can never be lost. Admit that you must come second to these others." Nevertheless, Scobie claims, his sin against God is really a "felix culpa" from God's point of view too: "I can't go on, month after month, insulting you. . . . You'll be better off if you lose me once and for all. . . . I'm not pleading for mercy. I am going to damn myself. . . . But you'll be at peace when I am out of your reach. . . . You'll be able to forget, God, for eternity."[94]

Scobie, then, dies convinced that his death, though far from a conventional "happy death"—which earlier he called "the most enviable possession a man can own"—is still a "felix culpa" so far as both God and the two women in his life are concerned. But while he chooses damnation, he cannot escape the infinite mercy of God. And in his last moments he tries to make "an act of contrition," although "he couldn't remember what it was that he had to be sorry for." But, as in *Brighton Rock,* God refuses to be shut out: "It seemed to him as though someone outside the room were seeking him, calling him . . . someone wandered, seeking to get in, someone appealing for help, someone in need of him." God is suffering because Scobie is destroying the life God gave him, and as a victim God has an undeniable call on Scobie: "[A]utomatically at the call of need, at the cry of a victim, Scobie strung himself to act. . . . He said aloud, 'Dear God, I love . . . ' but the effort was too great." The novel ends with Father Rank having the last word, a word that is as orthodox and Catholic as Scobie's conviction of damnation and mortal sin. He tells Louise "furiously,"

> "For goodness' sake, Mrs Scobie, don't imagine you—or I—know a thing about God's mercy."
> "The Church says . . ."
> "I know the Church says. The Church knows all the rules. But it doesn't know what goes on in a single human heart."

Certainly, Scobie has committed the ultimate mortal sin of despair—yet, "It may seem an odd thing to say—when a man's as wrong as he was—but I think, from what I saw of him, that he really loved God."[95]

The paradox of the "felix culpa" is carried to its extreme in *The End of the Affair,* when Sarah confides to her journal the thought that her and Maurice's adulterous passion was paradoxically intended to bring them close to God.

> Did I ever love Maurice as much before I loved You? Or was it really You I loved all the time? Did I touch You when I touched him? Could I have touched You if I hadn't touched him first, touched him as I never touched . . . anybody? And he loved me and touched me as he never did any other woman. But was it me he loved, or You? For he hated in me the things You hate.

One might well think that in a passage like this Greene is no longer "on" but over "the dangerous edge of things." The paradoxical is now verging on caricature, self-parody: "For he gave me so much love, and I gave him so much love that soon there wasn't anything left, when we'd finished, but You. . . . But even the first time, in the hotel near Paddington, we spent all we had. You were there, teaching us to squander, like you taught the rich man, so that one day we might have nothing left except this love of You."[96]

Less extreme, more realistic than the idea that God encourages their extravagant fornication so that he can enter the void left when their passion is consumed and exhausted is the paradox that Maurice's hatred and jealousy of God, who now has Sarah to himself for eternity, is an expression of belief in a self-professed atheist: "I hate You if you exist. . . . We have got on for years without You. Why should You suddenly start intruding into all situations like a strange relation returning from the Antipodes?" His "jealousy had not finished," like her husband Henry's, "with her death. It was as if she were alive still, in the company of a lover she had preferred to me." "How" he "wished" he "could send" the private detective, Parkis, whom he had hired to spy on her, "after her to interrupt their eternity." By the end of the novel, Maurice can say to the God who has taken away Sarah, "I hate You, God, I hate You as though You existed." To Sarah he says, "I believe you live and that He exists, but it will take more than your prayers to turn this hatred of Him into love. He robbed me and . . . I'll rob Him of what he wants in me." But Maurice is well aware of what his hatred implies: earlier he thought, "I mustn't hate, for if I were really to hate I would believe, and if I were to believe, what a triumph for You and her."

But Maurice knows that it is not so much hate that he feels as fear—"for if this God exists . . . and if even you—with your lusts and your adulteries and the timid lies you used to tell—can change like this, we could all be saints by leaping as you leapt, by shutting the eyes and leaping once and for all: if *you* are a saint, it's not so difficult to be a saint." The last sentence of the book shows Maurice accepting that God exists, a God to be loved: "O God, You've done enough, You've robbed me of enough, I'm too tired and old to learn to love, leave me alone for ever." Maurice has traveled some way from his frame of mind at the beginning of the novel, when, rather like the young Greene who found hell much easier to believe in than heaven, he indicated that the existence of the Devil presented no problems to him: "I have never understood why people who can swallow the enormous improbability of a personal God boggle at a personal Devil. I have known so intimately the way that demon works in my imagination."[97]

Sarah herself travels a similar path, from refusing to believe, while at the same time expressing a desire to "hurt" God, "to rob" him "of what you love most in me," "to do something that I enjoy and that will hurt you. Otherwise what is it but mortification and that's like an expression of belief." She tells the militant atheist Richard Smythe, "I'm not sure that I don't believe. But I don't want to." And then she finds herself "praying to the God he was promising to cure me of, 'Let me be of use to him.'" She walks into a church and realizes that it is

> a Roman church, full of plaster statues and bad art, realistic art. I hated the statues, the crucifix, all the emphasis on the human body. I was try-ing to escape from the human body and all it needed. I thought I could believe in some kind of a God that bore no relation to ourselves, some-thing vague, amorphous, cosmic. . . . One day I too would become part of that vapour—I would escape myself for ever.

Her husband Henry explains that Catholicism is "a very materialistic faith." And then Sarah realizes that only a "divine materialism" can account for her desire to hate God: "[H]ow can one hate a vapour? I could hate that figure on the Cross with its claim to my gratitude . . . but a vapour . . ." But if she "could really hate God, what would that mean?" After all she had hated Maurice—"but would I have hated him if I hadn't loved him too?" As she walks out of the church, she is caught at a moment of con-version in a cinematic shot reminiscent of the Lord Marchmain scene in

Brideshead Revisited: "[I]n defiance of Henry and all the reasonable and the detached I did what I had seen people do in Spanish churches: I dipped my finger in the so-called holy water and made a kind of cross on my forehead."[98]

The priest in *The End of the Affair,* Father Crompton, represents that hard rigidity of pre–Vatican II Catholicism which so impressed and attracted the young convert Greene: "A priest sat rigidly on the edge of an armchair in the study: a man with a sour gaunt face, one of the Redemptorists probably who served up hell on Sundays in the dark church" which Sarah had frequented. Belonging to an order that was famous or notorious for its hellfire sermons, Father Crompton is well able to produce the kind of cut-and-dried definitions that so drew Waugh to the Catholic Church: "Father Crompton produced a formula. He laid it down like a bank note." To the unbelieving Maurice, "He had the answers too pat." But his uncompromising orthodoxy does not prevent him from recognizing "what a good woman" Sarah actually was, in spite of all her sins.[99]

The End of the Affair is the last of Greene's quartet of Catholic novels. He was never to write again with such power as during these years when his Catholicism was a vibrant force in his life. As his faith lessened, or at least became less real to him, so his creative inspiration seemed to flag. Although the human need to believe in something—"We have lost the power of clear action because we have lost the ability to believe," he laments in *Ways of Escape*[100]—is a recurring theme even in the later novels,[101] the attraction of the hard edges of Catholicism lessened for Greene. In *A Burnt-Out Case* (1960), which has a distinctly autobiographical resonance, Querry, the famous architect who has lost all interest in his work, as well as his Catholic faith, tells Marie Rycker the story of the jeweler of a distant king, whom nobody has ever seen, and in whose existence the jeweler himself ceases to believe; but the jeweler has "moments when he wondered if his unbelief were not after all a final and conclusive proof of the King's existence," for "[t]his total vacancy might be his punishment for the rules he had wilfully broken."[102] As Greene himself privately acknowledged in 1984: "I have a continuing faith that I am wrong not to believe and that my lack of belief stems from my own faults and failure in love." It was the end of a process which he had admitted in a passage in *A Sort of Life,* where he describes his reception into the Catholic Church and refers obliquely to his own adulterous affairs:

Later we may become hardened to the formulas of confession and sceptical about ourselves: we may only half intend to keep the promises we make, until continual failure or the circumstances of our private life, finally make it impossible to make any promises at all and many of us abandon Confession and Communion to join the Foreign Legion of the Church and fight for a city of which we are no longer full citizens.[103]

Greene did not leave the Church or cease to be a Catholic, but clearly the growing inability even to repent and confess the sexual transgressions which his Church taught were mortal sins involved a lessening absorption in that moral drama of Catholicism which had so excited him and which had inspired his best novels. Thereafter Greene wrote many more accomplished novels, all highly readable, but the triumph of *The Power and the Glory* was never to be surpassed or even equaled. Greene must have been very conscious of this, as he liked to think that *The Honorary Consul* (1973) was his best book, or at least "[m]y favourite book, the one that bothers me the least," "perhaps the novel I prefer to all the others." But the reason he gives is "[b]ecause I've succeeded in showing how the characters change, evolve."[104] Yet even if that is so, the fact remains that Greene himself once wrote that with the loss of the religious sense "went the sense of the importance of the human act," as well as the "individuality" of the novel's characters, robbed "of their heavenly and their infernal importance." And this is true of *The Honorary Consul*, which, while interestingly it harks back to the old Catholic themes, nevertheless lacks the old excitement and thrill—that is, at the spiritual rather than at the human level of the terrorist thriller.

Unlike the priest in *The Power and the Glory*, not only is Father Leon Rivas an ex-priest, who has married, but, more significantly, he only half-believes. When Doctor Plarr asks him if he believes in God, he replies: "In a way. Sometimes. It is not so easy as all that to answer yes or no. Certainly he is not the same God as the one they taught us at school or in the seminary." So far as Rivas does believe, his conception of God is scarcely orthodox: he doesn't "blame" God for the pain of the world—"I pity Him." He claims that he "could never believe in Satan. It was much easier to believe that God was evil." And this is the less-than-orthodox way in which Rivas accounts for the evil in the world: "I believe in the evil of God, but I believe in His goodness too." Some will think that this simplifies the theological problem, others that it makes it more interesting, but what is certain is that this paradoxical explanation is *not* "at the dangerous edge of things." Instead, hell and Satan are abolished in an evolutionary process—"I believe God is suffering the same evolution that we are, but perhaps with more pain"—an evolution, however, that is destined to "end in a goodness like Christ's."[105] There may be a painful struggle, but there is no longer any real danger, as there is no longer any prospect of hell, just as there is no longer any absolute evil, as God is evil, as well as good.

Greene no doubt wants to make Father Rivas a more complex, interesting character than the whisky priest, more, in fact, like his own later self. And so there is another, more orthodox side to him, as when he scruples to say mass because he has excommunicated himself by marrying: "Perhaps they are not scruples—only superstitions. You see if I took the Host I would still half believe I was taking His body." Begged by his wife Marta "to speak to God for us," he agrees to celebrate mass—but "Suppose what they say is true and I am damning myself?" As for the Church's claim to be "Christ on earth—I still half believe it even now." Nor has he ever left her, because "[t]here is only one way any of us can leave the Church and that is to die. Not even then, if what we sometimes believe is true." He tells Doctor Plarr that he is only separated, not divorced, from the Church: "I shall never belong wholly to anyone else." And in the end he not only says the mass but persuades his hostage Charley Fortnum, whom he intends to kill, to go to confession to him—while acknowledging that it is a "mortal sin. The best I can do is to ask for God's mercy." He is one of those, he says, who "are condemned to belief. . . . They have no choice. No escape." But it is a half-belief, a less-than-orthodox belief. Asked by Fortnum whether he believes "in anything at all," Plarr first replies, "No," and then adds, "I don't think so." "Nor do I—" answers Fortnum.[106]

More or less like Greene himself, the characters in *The Honorary Consul* are "burnt-out" Catholics. And it is significant that the Spanish priest, Father Leopoldo Duran, who became a close friend and confidant of Greene, records that, while the novelist thought that *The Honorary Consul* was "perhaps his best novel" because of the characterization, probably *The Power and the Glory* "in his subconscious at least . . . was the novel that meant most to Graham among all his books." But when Greene wrote that novel, he was not the "burnt-out" Catholic that he professed himself to be to Duran in 1984: "I am to a certain extent an agnostic Catholic. I am quite unable to believe in Hell." Duran does not make the connection; but he does pay tribute to Vivien, the wife Greene abandoned, who was "the cause of Graham becoming the great writer he was. I mean the writer who decided to make theology the backbone of virtually everything he wrote. Thanks to Vivien, Graham became a convert to Catholicism."[107] The conclusion Duran fails to draw is that, if he is right, then it is Greene's most Catholic and theological novels which are his greatest achievement.

There is, by way of a postscript, an amusing story recounted by Christopher Sykes in his biography of Evelyn Waugh, of an encounter between the two novelists in 1953. To Greene's announcement that he was contemplating writing a political novel ("It will be fun to write about politics for a change, and not always about God"), Waugh wittily responded: "I wouldn't give up writing about God at this stage if I was you. It would be like P. G. Wodehouse dropping Jeeves half-way through the Wooster series."[108] Like Waugh, Greene had an "enormous respect" for Wodehouse, and the warning should not have been lost on him.[109]

CHAPTER 6

Evelyn Waugh

The Priest as Craftsman

1

Novelists who want to create realistic fictitious characters are usually cut off from the actual world which they seek to recreate in their books by one very significant factor: work. After all, writing is hardly a "job" as the vast majority of people, who have to spend a very large part of their waking hours working for their living, would understand the word. It is not surprising, then, that most novelists show little interest in or empathy with what in fact occupies their fellow human beings for so much of their time—except, of course, when one of the characters is actually a writer. There are exceptions: Conrad was a merchant seaman before he was a novelist, and this knowledge is used to creative effect in his books; Hardy, too, knew about the work of the agricultural laborer. But for the most part novelists are separated from "real life" by the fact that they do not have to do a "normal" job. Jane Austen is the most obvious example, although, given the environment in which she lived, where leisure itself was a way of life, her writing distinguishes her as definitely one of the workers. True, strenuous work in the shape of the navy is very much a reality in her books, but it is always off rather than on stage. She is an extreme example, but the fact is that for the vast majority of novelists the jobs of their characters are significant only in so far as they determine their social status or affect or reflect their personality or influence the plot. The actual job in itself that forms so large a part of the character's life is not normally part of the writer's interest.

There is one great exception noted by C. S. Lewis, when he writes how before Kipling poets and novelists had largely avoided the subject of work: "They had dealt almost exclusively with men in their 'private hours.'" Thus for Jane Austen, Scott, Dickens, and Thackeray, the working lives of their characters for the most part take place "offstage." "With a few exceptions imaginative literature in the eighteenth and nineteenth centuries had quietly omitted, or at least thrust into the background, the sort of thing which in fact occupies most of the waking hours of most men." It was, Lewis claims, Kipling who "first reclaimed for literature this enormous territory."[1]

It is this same territory of work that is so important also for Evelyn Waugh, whose novels to a considerable extent revolve around the jobs his characters do (or fail to do). While Kipling's interest centered on the discipline required for learning and practicing a profession or trade, Waugh was fascinated by the craftsmanship involved in a job well done. Just as in real life, so in Waugh's fiction the question of a job looms large, not least the question of trying to find a job. This is not very surprising when one realizes not only that Waugh tried his hand at a good number of jobs but that the job of being a writer—and here he is surely different from almost every other writer—was not at all the job that first appealed to him but was the job he finally resorted to only when all else had failed.

After leaving Oxford without a degree, Waugh enrolled at an art school in September 1924 but left before Christmas, having decided that he could not draw well enough to become a professional painter. He then thought of apprenticing himself to a private printing press in Sussex but withdrew when he discovered that the methods involved were not as artistic as he had hoped. The prospect seemed very bleak, as Waugh's ambition was to be a graphic, not a literary, artist. He had no desire at all to follow in the footsteps of either his father, Arthur, a literary critic as well as publisher, or his brother, Alec, who had precociously begun a lifelong career as a novelist with the publication at the age of seventeen of his notorious best-seller *The Loom of Youth* (1917). As he says in his unfinished autobiography *A Little Learning* (1964), it was a long time before he gave up the idea of being a draftsman: his ambition lay in drawing, decorating, designing, and illustrating, and, while completely happy when working with the brush, he was much less at ease with the pen.[2]

It is true that in his early boyhood Waugh had appeared to be following in the family tradition, trying his hand at fiction as well as poetry. Later at Lancing, he tried to write his first novel but found the work too hard and uncongenial. He wrote both verse and a satirical play about public school life which was performed in front of the school, as well as editorials for the school magazine of which he became editor.[3] But his real love lay elsewhere, in his passion for book illumination and calligraphy. During his first year at Lancing, his father had taken him to visit Edward Johnston, the calligrapher and, with Eric Gill, the most important member of the Ditchling community. Over forty years later, he vividly recalled the occasion when Johnston took the fourteen-year-old boy into his workroom and, cutting a turkey quill into a pen, showed him how he used it to produce his distinctive script: "I treasure that piece of writing. But still more I treasure the memory of the experience of seeing those swift, precise, vermillion strokes coming to life. It was a moment of revelation. . . . It was the awe and exhilaration of the presence of genius."[4] A couple of years later, Waugh's housemaster, who possessed a small printing press, which Waugh, already an enthusiastic bibliophile, helped to run, introduced the youth to a local illuminator called Francis Crease, who had been shown an illustrated missal with which Waugh had won first prize in a school art exhibition. Next term Waugh was allowed to visit Crease for weekly lessons in calligraphy, and the influence which the middle-aged craftsman exerted for several months on the adolescent[5] can be felt in the preface Waugh wrote several years later to a book of Crease's designs: "He taught me with the utmost patience how to cut a quill pen. Everything about his rooms was tranquil and beautiful."[6] These two interests, illuminating and printing, both feature in the autobiographical fragment "Charles Ryder's Schooldays," written in 1945 (but not published posthumously until 1982), which sketches the background to the narrator of *Brideshead Revisited* (1945) and was intended to be the beginning of a novel about school life.[7]

At Oxford we see the same pattern. Heavily involved in undergraduate journalism, Waugh was a prolific writer of articles and stories;[8] but his real interest, and indeed talent, lay in his artwork, which he took much more seriously; it included cartoons, cover designs, and column headings for student journals and newspapers, as well as the book jackets for his father's firm, Chapman and Hall, which he had begun doing while still at school, and also prints for the *London Mercury*.[9]

After the failure to take up the apprenticeship at the printing press in Sussex for which his father had already paid the premium, Waugh felt that his last hope of becoming a draftsman or graphic artist had disappeared, and, as he put it amusingly in a magazine article in 1937, there were only two sorts of job left open to him "under the English social system—domestic service and education." Not having "the right presence for a footman," Waugh opted to become a master at a preparatory school. The article which recounts how Waugh was "[d]riven into writing because I found it was the only way a lazy and ill-educated man could make a decent living" is disingenuous to the extent that it fails to admit that without this rude exposure to economic necessity it is hard to imagine Waugh ever becoming the novelist that he became.[10] Indeed, one can only regret that he did not also try his hand at domestic service, as the fictional fruits would surely have been hardly less glorious than those of his foray into the "hilarity" of schoolmastering! The irony is not only that had he succeeded in becoming a professional graphic artist he might never have bothered to write a novel but that it is hard to see where the initial comic inspiration could have come from in a life of solid craftsmanship, since Waugh certainly never imagined himself as an original painter ("a Titian or a Velasquez"), only as a draftsman.[11]

In January 1925 Waugh managed, through a scholastic agency, to get a job at a boarding preparatory school in Wales. His biographers are quick to point out that Arnold House bore little actual resemblance to the Llanaba Castle of *Decline and Fall*.[12] Certainly, it was the desperate need to find relief by making a grotesque joke out of the unhappy experience of feeling totally out of place in what was in fact an above-average preparatory school that sowed the seeds for the famous novel that was to make his name. But when we allow for all the fantastic exaggerations of Waugh's imagination, the fact is that fate could hardly have chosen better than to place Waugh in such an utterly dispiriting but also potentially creative setting, since, however comparatively respectable in practice the school may have been, the uniquely peculiar world of the traditional English boarding prep school, a small claustrophobic community of small boys, taken away from family and home, and mainly bachelor masters, who at their best were often eccentrics or misfits like Waugh, and at their (not uncommon) worst pedophiles like the real-life Mr. Young and the fictitious Captain Grimes, was a world that was practically made to order for the purposes of Waugh's anarchic comic imagination.

In the Easter holidays following Waugh's first term at Arnold House, his brother Alec told him that he might be able to get a job in Italy as the secretary to Charles Scott Moncrieff, the translator of Proust. During the summer term he heard from Alec that the job was his and promptly gave in his notice. A few weeks later his hopes were dashed when he heard that Scott Moncrieff was not after all looking for a secretary, "least of all one with my deficiencies."[13] Shortly before, he had received from his old Oxford friend, Harold Acton, a damning verdict on the first few chapters of a novel he had begun, called "The Temple at Thatch." Waugh promptly consigned the chapters he had written to the furnace of the school boiler. It looked "rather like being the end of the tether," he wrote in his diary.[14] And he recounts how he went down to the beach and swam out to sea with thoughts of drowning himself, only to find, after encountering a jellyfish, that suicide, too, was beyond his capability.[15]

After leaving Arnold House at the end of the summer term, Waugh again tried to find a niche in the art world, this time writing round in vain to galleries and art magazines. Once again, he had to endure what was for him the ignominy of another undistinguished teaching job, this time at a cramming establishment at Aston Clinton, near Aylesbury. It was a more congenial post than the one in Wales, and therefore by the same token less stimulating creatively. Before the new term began, Waugh completed a long, experimental story called "The Balance," which was published in 1926 in an anthology; its originality was recognized, and another, but less promising story, as it turned out, was commissioned for another anthology.[16] But still there was no suggestion that a literary career was feasible, or even desirable, especially after the publishers Kegan Paul turned down a short book, in which they had expressed interest, called "Noah; Or the Future of Intoxication." This was in January 1927. In February Waugh was summarily dismissed by the headmaster at Aston Clinton for harassing the new matron after an alcoholic evening at the local pub. Incongruously, he had been investigating the possibility of becoming a clergyman, but, unsurprisingly, his vocation was dismissed as frivolous.

He left Aston Clinton the day after being given notice, and wrote in his diary the next day: "I have been trying to do something about getting a job and am tired and discouraged. . . . It seems to me the time has arrived to set about being a man of letters."[17] But in the meantime he was forced to take a "quite awful" temporary teaching post at a state school in Notting Hill for the rest of the term.[18] However, in April 1927 he got a very different kind of job as a gossip columnist on the *Daily Express,* another job that was to prove a source of creative inspiration. Six weeks later he was given the sack, with only one piece published, a story that was rumored to have been stolen from another newspaper. Once again he began applying for jobs: these included "a singularly repulsive job," apparently at Golders Green—was this a job his subsequent fiction might have benefited from?—and "a fantastic job about toothbrushes which I don't suppose will come to anything." It did not, which was no doubt a pity from the point of view of what it might have inspired in fictional terms. He even applied, in desperation, for yet another teaching post, but "it fell through after a prolonged and rather painful interview with the headmaster."[19]

Meanwhile, a privately printed essay of Waugh's on the Pre-Raphaelites had secured a commission from a publisher to write a biography of Dante Gabriel Rossetti in time for the centenary of Rossetti's birth in 1928. The book was successfully completed by the spring of the following year. As Waugh's biographer, Martin Stannard, has pointed out,[20] the study is in many ways a remarkable self-portrait, not least in the author's judgment that Rossetti was ultimately a failure as an artist: "There is . . . a sense of ill-organisation about all that he did."[21] This was very much how Waugh saw his own failure as a graphic artist.

But he was not proud of the book,[22] and yet again he tried to become a handcraftsman, this time as a carpenter or cabinetmaker. At the end of October 1927 he started classes at the Central School of Arts and Crafts. As one who wanted to be a craftsman rather than an artist, he not unsurprisingly much preferred the carpentry to the carving.[23] He was introduced to a cabinetmaker with a workshop at Christchurch, a premium was paid, and it was agreed that Waugh should begin an apprenticeship in January 1928. Years later Waugh recorded how watching the cabinetmaker "cutting concealed dovetails gave me the thrill which, I suppose, others get from seeing their favourite batsman at the wicket or bullfighter in the ring." He was forced to abandon the idea by the consideration that it would be years before he could even qualify for a small wage, whereas he wanted soon to marry. Humorously, he describes how he was literally forced to become a writer:

> Some dreary weeks followed during which, though I cannot claim to have trudged the streets without food, I certainly made a great many fruitless and rather humiliating calls on prospective employers. Dickens held it against his parents that they tried to force him into a blacking factory instead of letting him write. The last firm at which I solicited a job was engaged, among other things, in the manufacture of blacking. I pleaded desperately. If I wasn't employed there I should be driven to Literature. But the manager was relentless. It was no use my thinking of blacking. That was not for the likes of me. I had better make up my mind and settle down to the humble rut which fate had ordained for me. I must write a book.

The biography of Rossetti was not a book in the literary sense; it was not even a literary biography; rather, it was a critical life of a craftsman, with little literary merit. Having, then, "held out" until he was twenty-four, he was finally "sucked under."[24] By the beginning of September 1927 he had begun work on the "comic novel" that was to become *Decline and Fall.*[25]

II

Decline and Fall (1928) opens with a scene in which two fellows of an Oxford college gloat over the impending fines (which, on reaching a certain level, permit the introduction of a prized vintage port into the senior common room) soon to be incurred by the excesses of the annual Bollinger Club dinner. The other dons who fled Scone College for the evening convene next day to count the fines and to expel for indecent behavior the diligent, industrious student Paul Pennyfeather, who was debagged in the quad the previous night by the drunken revelers. The academic profession is the first of many to be satirized in the course of the novel. And it is symbolic in the imaginative world of Waugh that these cynical dons, more interested in port than scholarship, should welcome and enjoy the fruits of anarchy and chaos. As he leaves the college, Paul encounters the chaplain, who congratulates him on discovering before it is too late his unfitness to take Holy Orders and warns him that he will now have to think of another "profession."[26] The college porter receives his tip with the prophecy that, like most other undergraduates sent down for indecent behavior, Paul will take to schoolmastering. In a Carlylean vein, Paul's guardian pronounces that he must find work, if only to prevent him from brooding.

Paul's introduction to the world of schoolmastering is at a scholastic agency where he is assured that his lack of experience and testimonials and his ignorance of German and cricket, all stated requirements in the advertisement, are in fact no barriers at all to his applying for the job, which "might have been made" for him: "It's wonderful what one can teach when one tries." This assurance the headmaster of the school concerned confirms, remarking that Paul's inexperience "is in many ways an advantage. One too easily acquires the professional tone and loses vision." As for Paul's disgrace, that is no bar: "I have been in the scholastic profession long enough to know that nobody enters it unless he has some very good reason which he is anxious to conceal."[27] At Waugh's own interview for the job at Arnold House, the headmaster merely asked if he possessed a dinner jacket. The marvelous satire on private school teaching that follows and that makes up the best half of the novel is similarly founded on, even if it quite transcends, Waugh's own experience at Arnold House. Thus Paul finds himself on arrival in charge of games, carpentry, and the fire drill, as well as having to give private organ lessons. To Paul's terrified inquiry as to what he should teach his first class, Captain Grimes coolly replies, "Oh, I shouldn't try to *teach* them anything, not just yet, anyway. Just keep them quiet." To this another colleague, Mr. Prendergast, sighs, "Now that's a thing I never learned to do." The chaotic scene that follows as Paul enters the classroom for the first time not only is extremely funny but, for all its exaggeration, succeeds in conveying exactly the feel of what it is like to face a classroom of unruly yet diabolically cunning children and to try hopelessly to keep order. Paul's inspired offer of half a crown for the longest essay on self-indulgence is the kind of master stroke that would occur only to a novelist who not only knows from the inside what teaching is like but also is fascinated by the "craft" of the job.[28]

According to Waugh's (somewhat exaggerated) account, he "was from the first an obvious dud" at schoolmastering.[29] Paul at any rate is not an unmitigated disaster; he sometimes talks to the boys about their lessons and sometimes sets them work, some of which is done, and in return the rest of the time the boys can do what they like provided they don't disturb Paul's reading or writing of letters. But both he and Prendergast are mere amateurs, amateur teachers among professionals—not, needless to say, professional teachers but professional frauds and rogues.

The headmaster, Dr. Fagan, with his bogus doctorate in philosophy, presides over the school with effortless assurance. There is no disorder when at the beginning of term prayers he opens the Bible at random and smoothly reads out "a chapter of blood-curdling military history" before announcing that the Fagan cross-country running challenge cup will not be offered this year on account of the floods ("'I expect the old boy has popped it,' said Grimes in Paul's ear") and that the Llanaba Essay Prize will not be offered either ("'On account of the floods,' said Grimes"). The imperturbable calm with which he presides over the annual sports day, always an utter disaster—"One way and another, I have been consistently unfortunate in my efforts at festivity. And yet I look forward to each new fiasco with the utmost relish"—contrasts strikingly with its chaos and disorder in what is perhaps the greatest comic scene in the whole of Waugh.

The problem of the wrong or nonexistent equipment for the various sports events is solved "imperturbably" by the Doctor: "Previously competed for." Never mind that there are no running tracks, the competitors have the whole park to run over, and, the Doctor notes "sagely," "the longer the race the more time it takes." But if the sports are all bogus, the seats for the parents and tubs of palms and flowering shrubs for display are there and "must be set in order," the Doctor characteristically directs.[30]

For order, not disorder, it is important to note, characterizes Dr. Fagan, since, in the world of Waugh, order as opposed to disorder accompanies a job well done, a job executed with the precision of the skilled craftsman. And that is what Dr. Fagan is—not, of course, as a schoolmaster but as the fraudulent proprietor of a bogus educational establishment. He is as serenely in command as the most masterly craftsman is of his materials: his response to Lady Circumference's rage that a boy who has run only five laps should be judged the winner of a six-furlong race because he is (naturally) ahead of the other boys at the winning post is quite effortless: "'Then they,' said the Doctor imperturbably, 'are first, second, third, fourth, and fifth respectively in the Three Miles.'" The only occasion when the order of Dr. Fagan's world is disturbed is when another master of his craft, Grimes the pederast, gets himself engaged to the Doctor's elder daughter in order to avoid getting the sack for one of his usual misdemeanors with one of the boys—for the Doctor merely "a minor question. I have quite frequently met with similar cases during a long experience in our profession."[31] Actually, Llanaba Castle is only one of Dr. Fagan's various "enterprises," and at the end of the novel we meet the Doctor again, this time not as a Ph.D. but as an M.D. and the superintendent of a private sanatorium, where a drunken surgeon signs a certificate to say that Paul died during an operation. Dr. Fagan presides over Paul's faked death as effortlessly as he did over the spurious sports day, while the substantial fee he receives for the bogus operation enables him to retire from one of his admittedly less successful enterprises and to "start lightheartedly on a new manner of life."[32]

Philbrick, the butler at Llanaba Castle, like his employer is another accomplished confidence man, whose speciality is false pretenses and impersonation. He tells Paul how, after retiring from a profitable career as a burglar, he became the landlord of the "Lamb and Flag" pub, south of Waterloo Bridge. Known to "the boys" as Sir Solomon Philbrick, he turns his thoughts to a new trade, that of kidnapping—hence his pretending to be a butler at Llanaba Castle—when his wife dies, whom he put in to run the pub for him. A better proposition now presents itself in the form of Dr. Fagan's younger daughter, Diana (known to the boys as Dingy), whose parsimonious housekeeping deeply impresses Philbrick: "Real business woman, just what I need at the Lamb." According to Philbrick, it is Dingy who proposes marriage after hearing that he owns the cinema next to the Lamb and Flag. Forced by a warrant for his arrest to retire from butlering at Llanaba Castle, Philbrick next turns up as the purchaser of Llanaba Castle: "I have had an offer from a cinema company, the managing director of which, oddly enough, is called Sir Solomon Philbrick, who wish to buy the Castle," Dr. Fagan informs Paul in a letter after he has left the school. "They say that its combination of medieval and Georgian architecture is a unique advantage. My daughter Diana is anxious to start a nursing-home or an hotel."[33] Philbrick makes his final appearance in Blackstone Gaol, where, as an old hand, he secures the best job as reception cleaner, but one feels his career is hardly over, only momentarily checked: "he still wore an indefinable air of the grand manner," and he successfully convinces the other inmates that he is the Governor's brother, "Sir Solomon Lucas-Dockery. . . . 'Ere for arson. Burnt a castle in Wales. You can see he's a toff." This information is given to Paul by another convict, for whom prison not only is a way of life but also involves a regular job: "I'm known here, so I always gets made 'landing cleaner.' . . . The warders know me, see, so they always keeps the job open for me if they hears I'm coming back."[34]

Paul is in prison after conviction as a white slaver, having been successfully conned by Margot Beste-Chetwynde into helping her (unknowingly) with her flourishing trade. Invited to stay at her country house, King's Thursday, as a holiday tutor for her son Peter, Paul finds himself being offered a new job:

> I'm sure I can find you a better job. It's absurd you're going back to Wales. I still manage a great deal of my father's business, you know, or perhaps you didn't. It was mostly in South America in—in places of entertainment, cabarets and hotels and theatres, you know, and things like that. I'm sure I could find you a job helping in that, if you think you'd like it.

Like Dr. Fagan, Margot is the mistress of her craft, as Paul discovers when Margot (reluctantly) allows him to sit in on one of her interviewing sessions for girls destined for Margot's "South American business": "Paul sat in the corner ... enraptured at her business ability."[35] Although warned (by Philbrick, whom Paul bumps into in an expensive Mayfair restaurant) that his fiancée is being investigated by a League of Nations Committee, Paul unsuspectingly agrees to go to Marseilles, where Margot's agent has suddenly resigned, to expedite the passage of the girls selected by Margot for work in Rio. Touched by Margot's concern for the safety of the girls, whom he finds in the red light district, Paul solves the problem of their passports by arranging at considerable cost to have them signed on as stewardesses on the ship bound for Brazil. Margot, of course, has chosen her man well: Paul is much too gentlemanly to attempt to incriminate her and for his pains receives a lecture from the judge at his trial on his effrontery in planning to degrade by marriage a lady of impeccable virtue.

The prison chaplain, Paul finds, is none other than his former colleague, Mr. Prendergast. Like Paul, he was an unwilling schoolmaster, having felt obliged to resign his living in the Church of England after experiencing "Doubts." His bishop couldn't answer his question why God had made the world at all—but "[h]e said that he didn't think the point really arose as far as my practical duties as a parish priest were concerned."[36] Such clergy of the Established Church as appear in Waugh's novels are always more or less figures of fun: he would have agreed with the sarcastic remark of Jeremy Bentham that so upset the hero of *Loss and Gain*, for, after all, what does an Anglican clergyman *do*, what is his *craft*? But, Prendergast happily discovers, there is a new kind of clergyman who does not even pretend to profess—that he has anything to profess, that is, that he has any real profession or craft—the "Modern Churchman" who "[d]raws the full salary of a beneficed clergyman and need not commit himself to any religious belief."[37]

Such a bogus clergyman, as described by Dr. Fagan in his letter to Paul, would no doubt have struck the doctor as a fellow practitioner of the successful art of fraud if he had not been preoccupied with the loss of Prendergast, who has no more thought of fraud in his new role as prison chaplain than Paul had of practicing white slavery but who characteristically finds that he is as incompetent as he had been as a schoolmaster: "[c]riminals are just as bad as boys, I find. They pretend to make confessions and tell me the most dreadful things just to see what I'll say, and in chapel they laugh so much that the warders spend all their time correcting them." Unfortunately, as it turns out for Prendergast, the governor, Sir Wilfred Lucas-Dockery, a progressive penologist, "is very modern too."[38] But penology—in Waugh's satirical vision an obviously bogus craft—does not harmonize very well with the job of being a prison governor. This point becomes vividly clear when Paul's companion in the exercise yard, "a carpenter by profession . . . a cabinet-maker," but now in prison for life, having committed murder as a result of a vision, is brought before the governor on charges of breaking off a piece of wood from the stool in his cell and abusing the Chief Warder in colorful biblical terms. To Sir Wilfred the cause of the offenses is clear: a "case of frustrated creative urge. . . . You have been used to creative craftsmanship . . . and you find prison life deprives you of the means of self-expression." Furnished again with the tools of his trade, the religious carpenter saws off Mr. Prendergast's head. It is unlikely that he knew what a Modern Churchman was, but he knew that the chaplain was "no Christian" because he had no visions.[39] Insane the carpenter may be, but he is as genuine a carpenter as in his madness he knows that the chaplain is a bogus clergyman.

In the next prison to which Paul is sent, he finds another old colleague, Captain Grimes, who tells Paul that he intends to give up schoolmastering when he gets out. He had told Paul when they first met at Llanaba Castle that he didn't think he had been "meant by Nature to be a schoolmaster"—"temperament and sex" being the problem. This looked as if it would be the first end of term he had seen for two years, as he usually landed in the soup after about six weeks. Asked by Paul if it was "quite easy to get another job after—after you've been in the soup?" Grimes explained that he was at a public school, and "[t]hat means everything." He was expelled from Harrow at the age of sixteen for reasons that do not need explaining; but his housemaster provided him with a testimonial, and he went into business until the war when he "got into the soup again" and was threatened with court-martial by the army, only to be saved by a fellow old Harrovian who found him a "cushy" job in Ireland. Since then he admitted he had been "in the soup pretty often," but always, thanks to the old boy network, something turned up.[40] Faced with dismissal from Llanaba Castle, his less-than-voluntary engagement to Miss Flossy Fagan was "the best thing that could have happened. I think I've about run through the schoolmastering profession. I don't mind telling you I might have found it pretty hard to get another job. There are limits. Now I'm set up for life, and no more worry about testimonials."[41]

Not that Grimes was not a professional compared with Paul and Prendergast in the schoolmastering world of Llanaba Castle: faced, for example, with the problem posed by the fact that Mr. Prendergast had failed to get the boys to run the preliminary heats for the sports day, Captain Grimes imperturbably welcomed the lack of any outcome: "Quite right . . . you leave this to me. I've been in the trade some time. These things are best done over the fire. We can make out the results in peace."[42] Thanks to his timely adjudication as referee at the sports day when Percy Clutterbuck won the six-furlong race although he had run only five furlongs, Grimes was offered a job at the Clutterbuck brewery. Deciding that it could only be a joke and that anyway it was too late now to escape from marriage with Flossy, Grimes feigned suicide. The next time we encounter him is at Margot's, where he tells Paul that the police are after him, as his real wife has turned up. Fortunately, he has bumped into an old colleague from Ireland days who is looking for a couple of "chaps who could control themselves where women were concerned" to help him manage a chain of "sort of" nightclubs in South America owned by a syndicate in England belonging to the Beste-Chetwynde family.[43] Margot gives him the job, but he is arrested on his return to England and sent to prison for bigamy, which is where Paul encounters him for the last time. After Grimes escapes from prison, his hat is found floating on Egdon Mire, but "Paul knew that Grimes was not dead. . . . Grimes . . . was of the immortals. He was a life force."[44]

To say that the lesson of *Decline and Fall* is that vice, not virtue, pays in this life is no doubt true enough, but what the book also shows is that it is the villains who are skilled at their craft and the innocent who are the amateur bunglers at their jobs. To be successful means to be good at one's job. And craftsmanship means order, even if perverted order, as opposed to chaos, albeit well-meaning chaos. It is significant that, as Paul leaves behind him the chaos of schoolmastering at Llanaba Castle and drives down the chestnut avenue to Margot's country house, he muses: "Surely, these great chestnuts in the morning sun stood for something enduring and serene in a world that had lost its reason and would so stand when the chaos and confusion were forgotten?"[45] The irony of the scene is obvious enough, given that King's Thursday rests on the white slave trade, but still it is true that Margot is as imperturbably serene as Fagan, Grimes, and Philbrick and in her fraudulence does represent a kind of order in the midst of a world of confusion. Margot herself is, as it were symbolically, absent from the chaotic weekend house party that follows Paul's arrival: she "kept to her room."[46] King's Thursday itself would have had to leave the family's possession had not Margot, on the proceeds of her infamous trade, bought it from her brother-in-law, Lord Pastmaster. Her enterprise contrasts with "the poverty and inertia of this noble family," which "had preserved its home unmodified by any of the succeeding fashions that fell upon domestic architecture." Unspoilt domestic Tudor the house may be, but it has become completely impractical and can no longer be kept up. At least the property can now remain with the family, even if it is to be rebuilt on "clean and square" lines by Margot's progressive protégé architect, Professor Silenus, also apparently involved in the white slave trade.[47]

The motto of *Decline and Fall* might be the gospel saying that the children of this world are more astute than the children of light. But in Waugh's next novel, *Vile Bodies* (1930), there is not much astuteness in evidence, and almost the only craft practiced is the craft of the partygoer. The book reflects the collapse of Waugh's own private world following the breakup of his marriage after the adultery of his first wife, with the dominant note one of anarchy and chaos and the breakdown of all discipline and order:

> "[W]hat a lot of parties."
> (. . . Masked parties, Savage parties, Victorian parties, Greek parties, Wild West parties, Russian parties, Circus parties, parties where one had to dress as somebody else, almost naked parties . . . parties in flats and studios and houses and ships and hotels and night clubs, in windmills and swimming-baths . . . all that succession and repetition of massed humanity . . . Those vile bodies . . .)[48]

Like *Decline and Fall*, *Vile Bodies* begins with chaos, although not the chaos of drunken revelry but the chaos of a bad sea crossing and general seasickness. However, the first two characters we meet before the gale are both skilled practitioners in their respective—ostensibly religious—crafts, who significantly remain imperturbable in the face of the bad weather—unlike the "Bright Young People," whose stomachs feel "just exactly like being inside a cocktail shaker." Father Rothschild, S.J., with "[s]ix important new books in six languages" and "a false beard" in his suitcase, is meant to be the archetypal Jesuit, whose business it is "to remember everything that could possibly be learned about everyone who could possibly be of any importance." With his "Asiatic resignation" ("no passage was worse than any other"), he is as much a match for the weather as the American evangelist, Mrs Melrose Ape, who advises her "angels": "If you have peace in your hearts your stomach will look after itself, and remember if you *do* feel queer—*sing*." (One of these "angels," called "Chastity," later leaves Mrs. Ape when she is recruited by Margot, now Lady Metroland, for "a job in South America.")[49]

When they arrive at customs, Father Rothschild has only to flutter a diplomatic *laissez-passer* before being whisked away in a large car. Adam Fenwick-Symes, on the contrary, the "hero" of the novel, who has his recently completed autobiography seized as indecent by customs officers, after vainly protesting his innocence pleads to no avail: "But do you realize that my whole livelihood depends on this book?"[50] Adam remains unemployed until he gets a job as the gossip columnist on the *Daily Excess.* Here his power to invent fictitious characters does wonders for the Mr. Chatterbox column; but his invention of nonexistent fashions includes that of the bottle-green bowler hat, which leads to his dismissal by the proprietor, Lord Monomark. The effectiveness of Waugh's satire here stems from his own firsthand (albeit brief) acquaintance with this particular journalistic craft. Similarly, the filmmaking at Colonel Blount's estate, one of the more humorous scenes in a novel that is more bitter than funny, reflects the author's own interest in the craft of the cinema; at Oxford he wrote not only film reviews which showed a keen interest in cinematic technique but also a film called *The Scarlet Woman* for an undergraduate production, which satirized an unsuccessful attempt to convert the Prince of Wales to Roman Catholicism.[51]

When he wrote *Vile Bodies,* Waugh was not yet a Catholic, and afterwards he regretted his fictional stereotype of the "sly Jesuit."[52] The stagy priestcraft he satirized in Father Rothschild was certainly very different from the priestcraft that he came to know and that came to mean so much to him:

> The Great Men withdrew to Lord Metroland's study. Father Rothschild closed the door silently and looked behind the curtains.
> "Shall I lock the door?" asked Lord Metroland.
> "No," said the Jesuit. "A lock does not prevent a spy from hearing; but it does hinder us, inside, from catching the spy."
> "Well, I should never have thought of that," said Mr Outrage in frank admiration.

While they are thus "plotting" in Lord Metroland's study, Father Rothschild suddenly switches off the light—"Quick, get behind the curtains."[53] The scene is funny only because it is so absurdly stereotyped; for although Waugh was to be received into the Catholic Church by a famous Jesuit, at this stage he knew no more about Jesuits and their "craft" than what popular mythology told him. Later in the novel, Father Rothschild comes out with a very odd sententious little speech about contemporary young people, which includes the following sentence: "They say, 'If a thing's not worth doing well, it's not worth doing at all.'"[54] Later, Waugh is supposed to have said that he regretted this piece of incongruous sermonizing and thought it very silly.[55] Certainly, it appears to have little or nothing to do with the character of Father Rothschild, the wily and worldly Jesuit. This suggests that it may be something of an authorial intrusion, and this is supported by the sentence quoted above, which has the hallmark of a Waugh dictum: in the meaningless world of the Bright Young People nothing is worth doing well, and therefore nothing is worth doing. There is one other novel of Evelyn Waugh where jobs hardly feature, *Brideshead Revisited,* but there, as we shall see, it is for a very different reason. In *Vile Bodies,* the corollary to anarchy, chaos, and disorder is the absence of the order that accompanies the job or the craft well done, however fraudulent. For unlike in *Decline and Fall,* even the bogus "craftsmen"—the gossip columnist, the American evangelist, the wily Jesuit—play only a limited part in a much more hopeless world where the aimless, drunken party is the normal way of life. *Bogus* is the word that Father Rothschild notes is on the lips of all the Bright Young People ("They won't make the best of a bad job now"); indeed, as one of them exclaims, "[T]his really is all too bogus."[56] If everything is bogus, then the genuinely bogus no longer merits attention: it no longer matters that the fraudulent job is well done, while the honest craft is badly practiced.

In Waugh's first travel book, *Labels* (1930), published later in the same year as *Vile Bodies,* he notes near the beginning that *bogus* is a word that is "used a great deal," and certainly the concept of "bogosity" appears a number of times in *A Mediterranean Journal,* the subtitle of the book.[57] Even after two highly successful novels, it is striking that the author claims that he "[s]till regarded" himself "less as a writer than an out-of-work private schoolmaster."[58] There is a hint of the reason Waugh later gives for his conversion in the respect he expresses for the "Irish monk" he encounters in the Holy Land, after visiting the caves at Nazareth alleged to be the sites of the Annunciation and Joseph's workshop:

> He was as sceptical as ourselves about the troglodytic inclinations of the Holy Family. The attitude of my fellow travellers was interesting. This sensible ecclesiastic vexed them. They had expected someone very superstitious and credulous and medieval, whom they would be able to regard with discreet ridicule. As it was, the laugh was all on the side of the Church. It was we who had driven twenty-four miles, and had popped our tribute into the offertory box, and were being gently humoured for our superstition.[59]

The priest may not yet be seen as exactly a craftsman, but he is discovered to be quite down-to-earth, sensibly realistic, the practitioner of a very other-worldly religion which, however, also paradoxically belongs very much to this world. As so often in this book, the this-worldly aspect of Catholicism strikes the Protestant imagination, which expects superstition and "priest-craft," with particular force.

Waugh's next book was another travel book, *Remote People* (1931), which recounts his experiences as a special correspondent for the *Times*, sent to cover the coronation of the emperor of Ethiopia, Haile Selassie I, as well as subsequent travels in other African countries. *Remote People* was to make possible Waugh's next novel, *Black Mischief* (1932), and once again it is a new job which stimulates the author's imagination. As "a fully accredited journalist," he discovers the fraudulent nature of his new profession: "I found the Press reports shocking and depressing," dictated as they were by the "two dominating principles of Fleet Street"—to get a scoop and to give the public what it wants.[60]

Waugh had been received into the Catholic Church at the end of September 1930, shortly before departing for Africa. And some of the most memorable pages in *Remote People* are the description of a visit to the monastery of Debra Lebanos, the spiritual center of the Ethiopian Coptic Church. Confronted by the "[s]ecret and confused character" of the liturgy, something he had "hitherto associated with the non-Christian sects of the East," Waugh now sees Western Christianity, which, "alone of all the religions of the world, exposes its mysteries to every observer," in a quite new light. Instead of imagining "the growth of the Church as a process of elabo-ration—even of obfuscation" from the early Church (seen "as a little clus-ter of pious people reading the Gospels together, praying and admonishing each other with a simplicity to which the high ceremonies and subtle the-ology of later years would have been bewildering and unrecognizable"),

> I suddenly saw the classic basilica and open altar as a great positive achievement, a triumph of light over darkness consciously accom-plished, and I saw theology as the science of simplification by which nebulous and elusive ideas are formalized and made intelligible and exact. I saw the Church of the first century as a hidden and dark thing. . . . And I began to see how these obscure sanctuaries had grown, with the clarity of the Western reason, into the great open altars of Catholic Europe, where Mass is said in a flood of light, high in the sight of all, while tourists can clatter round with their Baedekers, incurious of the mystery.[61]

It would be easy to conclude from this passage that Waugh's later vio-lent objections to the liturgical reforms of the Second Vatican Council, with their stress on intelligibility, simplification, and openness, were thoroughly inconsistent with this earlier understanding and were merely the nostal-gic conservatism of an old man. But this would be to miss the essential point he is making here about defined order. Once again, it is the vision of a craftsman seeking definite and specific shape and form: compared with the exact, unvarying Tridentine rite, the new order of the mass intro-duced in the 1960s struck Waugh as incoherent, formless, and shapeless, as introducing chaos and uncertainty. The more informal liturgy reflected a eucharistic theology that sought to emphasize other aspects of the mass apart from the priestly and sacrificial; but the price paid was a loss of the absolutely clear-cut nature of the Tridentine sacrifice of the mass. The unpleasant impression of the disorderly nature of the Ethiopian liturgy is reinforced when Waugh and his companion are allowed a brief glimpse of the secret, curtained sanctuary. To Waugh's astonishment he finds in the "Holy of Holies" a "hopeless confusion": "[I]n deep dust, for the sanctuary is rarely, if ever, swept out, lay an astonishing confusion of litter. . . . I noticed a wicker chair, some heaps of clothes, two or three umbrellas, a suitcase of imitation leather, some newspapers, and a teapot and slop-pail of enamelled tin."[62]

The tension, so evident in both Waugh's writings and his life, between a fascination with anarchy and disorder and at the same time a craving for discipline and order[63] explains why he can both be repelled by this kind of slovenly disorder and yet at the same time write that "an essential part" of the "character and charm" of the Ethiopians lies precisely in the "irregularity" of their "proceedings," in their "unpunctuality," in the fact that "everything was haphazard and incongruous."[64] This delight in disorder finds ample scope for expression in the inevitable chaos of traveling in both Abyssinia and the other African countries Waugh visited, most memorably perhaps in his description of the lake crossing from Kigoma to the Belgian Congo, which takes up the first half of the penultimate section of the book, called "Second Nightmare." The brief concluding "Third Nightmare" depicts the rowdy chaos of a fashionable "supper-restaurant" which Waugh visits on his return to England—London, he discovers, can "knock spots off the Dark Continent."[65] But Africa also has an advantage over London: for there the order and discipline so loved by the craftsman in Waugh can manifest itself even more strikingly than would be possible in Europe, as a visit to a convent in Uganda illustrates:

> It does not sound very remarkable to a reader in Europe; it is astounding in Central Africa—this little island of order and sweetness in an ocean of rank barbarity; all round it for hundreds of miles lies gross jungle, bush, and forest, haunted by devils and the fear of darkness, where human life merges into the cruel, automatic life of the animals; here they were singing the offices just as they had been sung in Europe when the missions were little radiant points of learning and decency in a pagan wilderness.[66]

A similar kind of scene is found at the beginning of *Black Mischief*, when the mercenary General Connolly leads his rabble of an army victoriously into Matodi and there, amid the chaos, finds an oasis of order and peace, the White Fathers' mission:

> Here he encountered a vast Canadian priest with white habit and sun-hat and spreading crimson beard, who was at that moment occupied in shaking almost to death the brigade sergeant-major of the Imperial Guard. At the General's approach the reverend father released his victim with one hand—keeping a firm grip in his woollen hair with the other—removed the cheroot from his mouth and waved it cordially.

". . . I came in from Mass and found him eating my breakfast." A tremendous buffet on the side of his head sent the sergeant-major dizzily across the road. "Don't you let me find any more of your fellows hanging round the mission today or there'll be trouble." . . . "I've got a lot of our people camped in here so as to be out of harm's way, and I am not going to have them disturbed."

As Newman would have said, this is a very natural as well as a very supernatural religion: the White Father is as real as the American Protestant archbishop is a "fraud."[67] Here Waugh adds another distinctly dynamic dimension to the concept of the priest as one who does rather than merely says that has been a recurring theme of this study.

A major part of the comedy in the novel is provided by the satirical treatment of a job in which Waugh had no actual personal experience but which he knew at firsthand from his journalistic observation as well as from his close Oxford friend Alastair Graham, who had gone into the diplomatic service and with whom Waugh had stayed in Athens a few years before when Graham was in the embassy there. The world of journalism is glanced at, but its full satirical treatment had to wait till *Scoop* (1938). On the other hand, the different kinds of diplomacy practiced respectively at the British and French embassies provide one of the funniest elements in the book. The British diplomats are characterized by their total lack of interest in the affairs of the country to which they are accredited, Sir Samuel Courteney's "most nearly successful achievement" being an ultimately ineffectual attempt to have the more or less impassable road, or rather track, to the legation repaired. However, the resulting "isolation" of the compound has its advantages, as it enables the Courteneys and their staff to confine themselves to uninterrupted domesticity.[68] By contrast, the business of the French legation is seen as, if anything, even more absurd: Gallic intelligence and logic, without pragmatic common sense, lead the minister and his first secretary into the absurd illusion that the inertia and lethargy of the British must mask the most cunning diplomacy, which threatens to outwit the French and against which they must maintain constant surveillance of Sir Samuel and deploy every stratagem possible. The implication is that since diplomacy is a bogus job, then Sir Samuel is well advised, as the Bright Young People would say, not to attempt to do a job which is not worth doing, so that it is M. Ballon who is effectively outwitted.

Waugh's next travel book, *Ninety-Two Days* (1934), again paves the way for his next novel, *A Handful of Dust* (1934). This account of his travels in Guiana and Brazil contains a loving portrait of an English Jesuit missionary priest whom the novelist encountered out in the desolate loneliness of the savannah and who gave him help and hospitality. Father Mather is also a highly symbolic figure for understanding Waugh as a Catholic novelist. For Father Mather was not only a priest but also an extremely accomplished craftsman. In Waugh's fond description we can read an implicit apology for the absurd Father Rothschild, S.J.:

> He was at work in his carpenter's shop when we arrived and came out to greet us, dusting the shavings off his khaki shirt and trousers, and presenting a complete antithesis of the "wily Jesuit" of popular tradition. . . . He is a skilled and conscientious craftsman; everything he does, from developing films to making saddles, is done with patient accuracy. Most of the simple furniture of the living-room was his work—firm, finely jointed and fitted, delicately finished, a marked contrast to the botched makeshift stuff that prevailed even in Georgetown.[69]

There is a striking note of hero worship in Waugh's depiction of this unsophisticated missionary priest, a very different kind of Jesuit from the brilliant Father Martin D'Arcy, who had received Waugh into the Catholic Church at the fashionable Mayfair church in Farm Street. D'Arcy's later written account of the instructions he gave Waugh emphasized both how "matter of fact" he was in his approach to Catholicism and also how he "never spoke of experience or feelings," being simply interested in the exact doctrines he was required to believe.[70] As a theological "craftsman," D'Arcy's careful outline of Catholicism would have been superior to anything Father Mather could have offered. But Mather had one considerable advantage over his learned colleague—he was literally a craftsman, with a "workshop where every kind of odd job in leather, iron and wood was brilliantly performed." Considering the boredom and depression that beset Waugh's adult life, one is tempted to speculate whether those days with Father Mather in his mission were not among the happiest of his life: "They were peaceful and delightful days. Mass at seven . . . then Father Mather would go off to his workshop. . . . Breakfast at noon and then Father Mather returned to his business."[71] Where a craft or job is well done, there will be order (of a sort) in Waugh's world, but there is nothing sinister about this order: not only is Father Mather an accomplished craftsman with his hands, doing thoroughly worthwhile practical jobs, but he is also a craftsman in his little church at the altar, punctiliously performing the job that (in Waugh's view) is the highest of all jobs, which again not only involves using his hands at the crucial point of the consecration but proclaims meaning and order in a world created and redeemed by Christ. Waugh does not say so, but Father Mather, who represents Christ ("alter Christus") at the altar, also practices the trade of carpentry which the divine craftsman himself practiced before beginning his work of redemption. And then finally there is the order of routine where every day follows a prescribed pattern: "I have a longing," Waugh had written three years before, "for some kind of routine in my life."[72]

In 1948 Waugh recalled: "It took me years to begin to glimpse what the Church was like . . . and it was chiefly missionaries who taught me."[73] Perhaps indeed it was the unknown Father Mather rather than the renowned Father D'Arcy who was Waugh's real instructor in the faith. And perhaps it was the sight of Father Mather in his little church made of tin and thatch, with his scanty congregation kneeling on the mud floor, rather than the splendid liturgy of fashionable Farm Street that made the deepest impression on the young convert. For as Waugh explained in a letter to a Catholic newspaper at the time of the liturgical changes of Vatican II,

> I was not at all attracted by the splendour of her great ceremonies—which the Protestants could well counterfeit. Of the extraneous attractions of the Church which most drew me was the spectacle of the priest and his server at low Mass, stumping up to the altar without a glance to discover how many or how few he had in his congregation; a craftsman and his apprentice; a man with a job which he alone was qualified to do. That is the Mass I have grown to know and love.[74]

It seems that *Ninety-Two Days,* one of Waugh's least-read books, contains the key to understanding his Catholicism—or at least how it affected his imagination and shaped his later novels. But if it was in Guiana that he really discovered his vision of the priest as a craftsman, he also admittedly did not find there quite the kind of order which had so impressed him about Catholicism in the midst of the chaos of Africa: "St. Ignatius was very unlike the missions I had seen there—the crowded compounds, big school houses with their rows of woolly black heads patiently absorbing 'education'; the solid presbyteries and packed, devout congregations; the native priests and nuns, methodical in white linen and topees; the troops of black children veiled for their first Communion; the plain chant and the examination papers."[75] But still the Church represented order, even if on a less impressive scale, as Waugh found to his relief when he reached the run-down, ramshackle town of Boa Vista in the Brazilian savannah, where the only buildings of any substance were those of the Benedictine mission, with its "symmetrical" garden beds, its rooms "geometrically regular in arrangement" with "[d]evotional oleographs symmetrically balanced; a table in the exact centre . . . everything showing by its high polish of cleanliness that nuns had been at work there." From the ordered life of this lonely outpost of the Church, where he took refuge, Waugh was finally able to escape "the forces of chaos" which threatened his return to civilization.[76]

In Guiana and Brazil Waugh was rather more than a travel writer looking for material; he was something of a real explorer in that unchartered desolation. On arrival in Georgetown he had met a Dr. Roth, who offered to take him to an Indian settlement not yet touched by civilization. In the end, Waugh decided not to take up the offer, having been told that Roth had "no sense of time or money" and neglected "rudimentary precautions." But this "opinionated and rather disagreeable old man," who was said to be an "irresponsible traveller,"[77] no doubt suggested the character of the explorer Dr. Messenger in *A Handful of Dust.* Messenger is not a fraud, but his self-confident assertions are belied by events on the disastrous expedition he and Tony Last undertake in the Brazilian jungle. Professing to be an explorer, Dr. Messenger turns out to be less than a professional at his job. Disaster strikes when the clockwork mice, which he has brought as the ultimate bribe for Indians, far from persuading the Macushis to guide them into the country of the Pie-wies, lead to the Indians fleeing in terror and abandoning the two English explorers to their respective fates—for Dr. Messenger, drowning in the rapids while trying to get help for Tony, now delirious with fever; and for Tony, rescue at the hands of Mr. Todd, an elderly half-breed who lives in a small settlement of Pie-wies, most of whom turn out to be his children—"That is why they obey—for that reason and because I have the gun." Mr. Todd has many books, but unfortunately he cannot read, so Tony, who prides himself on his reading aloud, gladly agrees to read Dickens to him. Unlike his wife Brenda, who could not stand being read to, Mr. Todd is most appreciative: "You read beautifully."

What Tony does not at first realize is that this job he does so well is intended to be literally a job for life, a singularly steady job of "unvarying routine."[78] For without Mr. Todd's help and a boat there is no escape, and his host has no intention of allowing such a good reader to escape.

The sinister irony of the situation is that Tony does at least find a job at which he is very proficient and which is accompanied by order, as opposed to the chaos of his life after Brenda left him for another man, when he found himself "in a world suddenly bereft of order; it was as though the whole reasonable and decent constitution of things, the sum of all he had experienced or learned to expect, were an inconspicuous object mislaid somewhere on the dressing table; no outrageous circumstance in which he found himself, no new, mad thing brought to his notice, could add a jot to the all-encompassing chaos that shrieked about his ears." The civilized, traditional world to which Tony Last was heir "had come to grief."[79] The disciplined order and routine which should have belonged to it is now only to be found in the sinister domain of Mr. Todd, literally beyond the pale of civilization. Five years earlier Waugh had written that modern society needed "the imposition by rigid discipline . . . of the standards of civilization," as "[f]reedom produces sterility."[80] Tony had enjoyed that very freedom together with the sterility; now the discipline of barbarism is imposed on him, but instead of his "creative impulses" being directed and tempered by "the restraint of a traditional culture," he has to suffer the restraint of reading endlessly the fruits of somebody else's creative impulses. Tony had hoped that the "Gothic world" he had lost could be rediscovered in the lost "City" that Dr. Messenger was trying to find: "He had a clear picture of it in his mind. It was Gothic in character . . . a transfigured Hetton." In the delirium of fever Tony seemed to see the "City" before him, the way carpeted by blossom petals, "as, after a summer storm, they lay in the orchard at Hetton." Tony was partly right: there was lying ahead a kind of barbaric "citadel" in the form of Mr. Todd's farm, behind "the ramparts and battlement" of which he was effectively to be imprisoned.[81]

There had been order and routine in the old days at Hetton Abbey. It was most noticeable, significantly, on a Sunday, when Tony, dressed in a dark suit and a stiff white collar, went to church and sat in the family pew; he always read the lessons on Christmas Day and Harvest Thanksgiving; and when the service was over chattered with the villagers before returning home, when he always picked a buttonhole, "[s]topped by the gardeners' cottages for a few words . . . and then, rather solemnly, drank a glass of sherry in the library. That was the simple, mildly ceremonious order of his Sunday morning. . . . Brenda teased him whenever she caught him posing as an upright, God-fearing gentleman of the old school . . . but this did not diminish the pleasure he derived from his weekly routine."[82]

Brenda is a less regular church attender and much less enamoured of Hetton Abbey, which is ugly Victorian Gothic. Although Brenda is one of the most hateful characters in Waugh, at least she cannot be blamed for rejecting a genuinely true tradition. Now while critics have noticed that the author made plain his dislike of the late Victorian Gothic revival architecture of Hetton Abbey in his original manuscript (and in American editions) by openly calling it "stodgy," they seem not to have appreciated the significance of the fact that the house is called Hetton *Abbey*, although in the manuscript it was called Hetton Castle.[83] For just as the house, in the words of the guidebook, had been "one of the notable houses of the county" but was now "[d]evoid of interest," so too it is no longer a real abbey, having brazenly retained the name of the dissolved monastery out of whose ruins and spoils it had originally been built. Similarly, the medieval parish church is no longer Catholic, with a priest-craftsman performing the sacraments, but is now characterized by the squire's box-pew equipped with a fireplace and a poker which Tony's father "used to rattle when any point in the sermon excited his disapproval," and the "brass eagle" from which the lessons were read. "Things" are no longer done here, but even the words that are preached are not preached by a craftsman who knows his job. For, in spite of his "noble and sonorous voice," the vicar, Mr. Tendril, had composed his sermons "for delivery at the garrison chapel," but

> he had done nothing to adapt them to the changed conditions of his ministry and they mostly concluded with some reference to homes and dear ones far away. The villagers did not find this in any way surprising. Few of the things said in church seemed to have any particular reference to themselves. They enjoyed their vicar's sermons very much and they knew that when he began about their distant homes, it was time to be dusting their knees and feeling for their umbrellas.

As usual in Waugh, the Anglican clergyman is portrayed as totally ineffectual: he doesn't have a proper job to do, like a Catholic priest, and what he does attempt to say accomplishes nothing. Tony himself remains quite unmoved by the service he is so punctilious in attending, performing "the familiar motions of sitting, standing and leaning forward," while "his thoughts drifted from subject to subject." Not surprisingly, when Tony's son John is killed in a riding accident and Mr. Tendril calls, Tony tells Mrs. Rattery that he only wants to see him about the funeral arrangements: "[A]fter all the last thing one wants to talk about at a time like this is religion."[84] Mrs. Rattery is a divorced American blonde who "played big bridge, very ably, for six or seven hours a day." A houseguest at the time of the fatal accident, she is at least a skilled card player and keeps Tony company after the death: "intent" at her game of patience, she moved "little groups of cards adroitly backwards and forwards about the table. . . . [U]nder her fingers order grew out of chaos; she established sequence and precedence; the symbols before her became coherent, interrelated."[85]

Tony's occupation is that of the landed gentleman, but his failure to maintain family prayers in the chapel in Hetton Abbey and a fire in the squire's pew are signs that old traditions are not being kept up. Unlike Mrs. Rattery, he enables chaos to overtake order by his weakness in allowing Brenda to rent a flat in London, where she is able to pursue her affair with Mr. Beaver. In Waugh's view, Brenda has a duty to obey her husband and Tony has a duty to control his wife, as his patriarchal role demands. Unable to draw from a deeper traditional order, such as the pre-Reformation abbey at Hetton would have provided, in order to withstand the chaotic modern world, he remains naively ignorant of Brenda's adultery and fails to protect his marriage.

The flat where the adultery takes place is provided by Beaver's mother, a very modern person and a very successful interior designer who specializes in converting old properties into very modern, very convenient, characterless, identical flats. She is also commissioned by Brenda to convert an "appalling room" at Hetton into a small sitting room for Brenda's use. Limited by the shape of the room, Mrs. Beaver proposes "to disregard it altogether and find some treatment so definite that it *carried* the room, if you see what I mean . . . supposing we covered the walls with white chromium plating and had natural sheepskin carpet." Soon her workmen are busy "tearing down the plaster tracery."[86]

Mrs. Beaver, of course, stands for everything that Waugh hates; but like Mr. Todd in his little empire, she is successful in her field of operation. For, as in *Decline and Fall,* it is the fraudulent, the villainous, and the suspect characters (like Mrs. Rattery) who achieve a kind of order, or, as in the case of Mrs. Beaver, uniformity, through successfully practicing their craft or trade, while it is the honest characters like Tony and Dr. Messenger and Mr. Tendril who cause or abet chaos through failing in their avocations.

In 1935 Waugh returned to Abyssinia, this time as a war correspondent for the *Daily Mail*, sent to cover the impending Italian invasion. He already knew about being a journalist, but he "[d]id not know the first thing about being a war correspondent."[87] He soon found out, and again the experience inspired not only another travel book, *Waugh in Abyssinia* (1936), but also his next novel, *Scoop*, subtitled *A Novel about Journalists* (1938).

Waugh thought the press bureau in Addis Ababa "might well have been classed among the places of entertainment in the town." Protesting to the Abyssinian authorities about various grievances seemed to be the war correspondents' "chief function," with the result that "the protesting habit became automatic," with "[s]mall groups and pairs protesting to one another, cabling their protests to London and Geneva, scampering round to the Palace and protesting to the private secretaries of the Emperor at every turn of events." The correspondents were apt to file their reports on events before they actually took place, and when the hostilities commenced it was easier to report "the war at leisure from their imaginations" in the comfort of their hotel rooms. There was, however, he discovered,

> a slight difference in the professional code of European and American journalists. While the latter will not hesitate, in moments of emergency, to resort to pure invention, the former must obtain their lies at second hand. This is not so much due to lack of imagination, I think, as lack of courage. As long as someone, no matter how irresponsible or discredited, has made a statement, it is legitimate news, but there must always be some source . . . on which the blame can later be laid.

But all the war correspondents were agreed that "[a]n exclusive lie was more valuable than a truth which was shared with others."[88]

A return visit to Abyssinia enabled Waugh to reflect further on the difference between this ancient Eastern Christian society and Western Christianity, especially as "aesthetic feelings found expression" only in the Coptic Church, since the Abyssinians otherwise "had no crafts" and had "produced so little." But "[c]ompared with the manifestations of historic Christianity in any other part of the world, West or East, the decoration was shoddy, the ceremony slipshod, the scholarship meagre," although "at least, it was something unique in the life of the people." After witnessing the feast of Maskal, "the highest expression of historic Abyssinian culture," "the Church's most splendid and solemn occasion," Waugh could not help contrasting its "artificial silk and painted petrol cans" with an equivalent ceremony in medieval Europe in "a culture which had created an object of delicate and individual beauty for every simple use; metal, stone, ivory and wood worked in a tradition of craftsmanship which makes succeeding generations compete for their humblest product." In contrast to the Abyssinian capital, the Arabian city of Harar was distinguished for its "fine craftsmanship" and "formal and intricate" dancing. If even a Moslem culture is superior—and for Waugh the crucial criterion is, as usual, craftsmanship—to that of the heretical, schismatic Coptic culture, then the comparison with the Catholic culture of the Italian invaders is overwhelming. The undisciplined Abyssinian soldiers ("all were in a delirious condition, hoarse, staring, howling for blood") are pictured, in one vivid scene, packed into a cattle truck on their way to the front, while "[i]n the next coach sat a dozen Italian nuns on the way to the coast; fresh faced, composed, eyes downcast, quietly telling their beads." Again, while "the whole structure of order" is "fragile" in Abyssinia, it is the Italian invaders who bring "order" through the great highway they build in place of the "pathetic tracks" made by the natives. But for Waugh order goes hand in hand with craftsmanship, and so it is only natural to find that the Italian workmen embellished the road as they progressed with "ornamental devices," the product of their "fine workmanship."[89]

Like Hetton Abbey, or, more pertinently, like the bizarre Doubting Hall in *Vile Bodies*, Boot Magna Hall in *Scoop* is intended to represent a world of order, although a degenerate one. The Boot family mansion is certainly not afflicted by "change," as "decay" is its characteristic. The trees in the park are all suffering from "old age," the lake either "[s]ank to a single, opaque pool" or "rose and inundated five acres of pasture," as the only man who knew its workings has been dead fifteen years. The eight members of the Boot family, together with their retainers, who inhabit the house resemble these natural surroundings. Like the lake, Uncle Theodore occasionally breaks out, making "[d]isastrous visits to London," but the rest of its inhabitants are sedentary or bedridden.[90] After his adventures in Ishmaelia, William Boot returns with relief to the antique order and routine of Boot Magna Hall.

When, through a mistake of identity, William is summoned to Copper House, the Megalopolitan building, numbers 700–853, Fleet Street, home of *The Beast,* he is "rudely shocked" by the frenetic activity: "Six lifts seemed to be in perpetual motion. . . . 'Going up,' they cried in Punch-and-Judy accents and, before anyone could enter, snapped their doors and disappeared from view." This anarchic world of journalism, where "on a hundred lines reporters talked at cross-purposes; sub-editors busied themselves with . . . reducing to blank nonsense the sheaves of misinformation which whistling urchins piled before them," inevitably lacks any semblance of order, as the job involved is in Waugh's view completely bogus. The proprietor, on the other hand, who is a businessman, not a journalist, is very good at making money out of his paper, so in the midst of all this meaningless hubbub we should not be surprised to find a kind of serenity in the person of Lord Copper: "At the hub and still centre of all this animation, Lord Copper sat alone in splendid tranquillity. His massive head, empty of thought, rested in sepulchral fashion upon his left fist. He began to draw a little cow on his writing pad." Here order, accompanied naturally by craftsmanship (drawing), is comical, not sinister, as Lord Copper is too stupid to be quite aware of the "bogosity" of *The Beast.* Indeed, the ordered future to which he looks forward is something "no sane man seriously coveted—of long years of uninterrupted oratory at . . . banquets . . . of yearly, prodigious payments of super-tax crowned at their final end by death duties of unprecedented size; of a deferential opening and closing of doors."[91]

There are a few glorious pages of satire on the diplomatic profession, which William has first to encounter in order to obtain his visa for Ishmaelia and later meets in the person of the British Minister in the capital, Jacksonburg, who proclaims his lack of interest in "any politics" as well as the affairs of the country to which he is accredited.[92] But the main interest of the novel is the "craft" of the journalist, particularly that of the foreign correspondent, to which William is introduced when he meets on board ship, bound for Ishmaelia, Corker of the Universal News Agency, who explains to him that "personally" he "can't see that foreign stories are ever news—not *real* news of the kind U.N. covers." To William's inquiry as to why special correspondents have to be sent when all the newspapers also receive reports from three or four news agencies—"if we all send the same thing it seems a waste"—Corker explains that the papers prefer to get "different news": "It gives them a choice. They all have different policies, so of course, they have to have different news." William clearly has "a lot to learn about journalism . . . News is what a chap who doesn't care much about anything wants to read. And it's only news until he's read it. After that it's dead." Apart from news—"If someone else has sent a story before us, our story isn't news"—there is always "colour. . . . It's easy to write and easy to read, but it costs too much in cabling, so we have to go slow on that." Waugh actually uses the word *craft* when he writes that Corker tells William "a great deal about the craft of journalism": of "classic scoops and hoaxes; of the confessions wrung from hysterical suspects; of the innuendo and intricate misrepresentations . . . of the positive lies," of the famous scoops written by journalists who had never actually witnessed the events described (that is, if they ever even happened). As a veteran journalist who has "loitered . . . on many a doorstep and forced an entry into many a stricken home," Corker also explains to William the art of laconic cabling, which saves the effort of elaborate analysis or description, and which William uses to legendary effect when he types his first news story, about the revolution in Ishmaelia—a scoop that is to become legendary in the annals of Fleet Street and that, on receiving a cable of dismissal from *The Beast,* he leaves unfinished, with the postscript: "SACK RECEIVED SAFELY THOUGHT I MIGHT AS WELL SEND THIS ALL THE SAME." Popularity, too, he learns from Corker, is an aspect of the job: "Ring people up any hour of the day or night, butt into their homes uninvited, make them answer a string of damn fool questions when they want to do something else—they like it."[93]

In *Work Suspended* (1942), a fragment of a novel which was never finished, Waugh moved away from his usual satirical style and tried his hand at a very different kind of first-person narrative, which he was to develop in *Brideshead Revisited* (1945). The narrator, John Plant, explains at the very beginning that at the age of twenty-one he decided to be a writer—that is, a writer of detective stories as that seemed one of the few ways in which to "make a decent living" by writing without being "ashamed." It was also "an art which admitted of classical canons of technique and taste." In short, it was a genuine craft: "[t]o produce something, saleable," something which had "a use."[94] Speaking autobiographically, the author of *The Ordeal of Gilbert Pinfold* (1957) says that the middle-aged novelist "regarded his books as objects which he had made, things quite external to himself to be used."[95] Plant's father, who was a representational painter, had a less than "reputable" but very lucrative side to his "business," "what was called 'restoration,'" which involved the successful imitation of the great English portrait painters, and which his father defended on the ground that it was better for people to look at "beautiful pictures," even if they were not the originals, than "to make themselves dizzy by goggling at genuine Picassos."[96] This represents a kind of reversion of Waugh's usual theme: the bogus becomes the genuine craft and the genuine the bogus.

Work Suspended, first published in a limited edition, did not reach a wider audience till 1943, when it was published in a collection called *Work Suspended and Other Stories*. One of these stories, "Excursion in Reality" (1934), again satirized the chaotic, frenetic world of the film studio, particularly in the person of the film director, Sir James Macrae, one of Waugh's most splendid minor characters. This story had first appeared in a prewar collection called *Mr. Loveday's Little Outing and Other Sad Stories* (1936). The story which gives its name to the book contains a brief satirical hit at a new profession, that of the psychiatrist, but the two most interesting stories are "Excursion in Reality" and "Out of Depth" (1933), which Waugh never republished but which is important for understanding him as a Catholic writer.

The story tells of how a lapsed Catholic is catapulted by a magician into the twenty-fifth century in London, where primitive whites are now ruled over by superior blacks. But one thing has survived: "a shape in chaos. . . . Something was being done that Rip knew; something that twenty-five centuries had not altered. . . . In a log-built church . . . [t]he priest turned towards them his bland, black face. 'Ite, missa est.'"[97] Here Waugh conveniently forgets that the mass was originally in Greek and altered considerably over nineteen centuries, but what is important to note is the idea that the mass is "a shape in chaos" and that the priest who performs the rite is a craftsman who does a job—his color, his personality are entirely irrelevant.

Put Out More Flags (1942) was the fruit of a month's voyage in a troopship in 1941. The advent of war was highly significant for Waugh's writing, if only because it brought him into close contact with two new professions, the civil service and the army. The bureaucratic world of memoranda and red tape is memorably satirized in the form of the Ministry of Information. What does the job consist of? "Well, mostly it consists of sending people

who want to see me on to someone they don't want to see," Geoffrey Bentley explains to Ambrose Silk. Apart from journalists, the chief difficulty of
"bureaucratic life" turns out to be the civil servants: without them "everything would be perfectly easy." The memoranda particularly make the job
"uphill work," as Mr. Bentley demonstrates to Ambrose:

> He showed Ambrose a long typewritten memorandum which was
> headed *Furniture, Supplementary to Official Requirements, Undesir-
> ability of.* "I sent back this." He showed a still longer message headed
> *Art, Objets d', conducive to spiritual repose, Absence of in the quarters of
> advisory staff.* "To-day I got this." *Flowers, Framed Photographs and
> other minor ornaments, Massive marble and mahogany, Decorative fea-
> tures of, Distinction between.*[98]

Ambrose himself ends up in the religious department of the ministry as
the representative of atheism.

Basil Seal, who "had never had much difficulty in getting jobs," only in
"keeping them," finds with the outbreak of war that everyone is "busy getting a job"; not only that, but having been used to an "orderly . . . world in
which to operate," Basil finds himself at a disadvantage in this new "chaotic
world." However, he recovers his equilibrium as a district billeting officer,
a job he turns into a lucrative "racket." Having passed his "trade" on to the
neighboring billeting officer, Basil turns to a new "career" in the intelligence
branch of the War Office, where he finds that "denunciation" of suspects is
also a profitable job, as it lands him the hapless Ambrose Silk's flat.[99]

Actual soldiering doesn't feature very much in the novel, although
Waugh had by now himself experienced active service. Instead, the book
deals with the so-called "Phoney War," when hostilities had not properly
begun. However, the sheer chaos of trying to transport an army is evoked
in a scene of embarkation when a regiment finds itself in the wrong ship, a
commandeered civilian liner, where by contrast the ship stewards carry on
their regular routine in the exact order they would in peacetime, regardless
of the new conditions: a kind of absurd order in the midst of chaos.

A visit to California in 1947 brought Waugh into contact not only with
Hollywood but also with the world of another kind of profession calculated
to stimulate his keenest satirical art. Seeing the capital of the film industry at close quarters enabled him to focus his satirical eye more sharply

on the fraudulent world of filmmaking; but *The Loved One* (1948) was inspired chiefly by his delighted discovery of the Californian burial industry. Now, most novelists would have been content just with satirizing the amazing "Whispering Glades" cemetery, but Waugh was fascinated not only by the external appearance of this remarkable burial ground but also, characteristically, by the craftsmen working behind the scenes. Any novelist would have been proud to create the character of Mr. Joyboy, the senior mortician, but Waugh was not satisfied even by that. For what grips his imagination is the actual craft which Mr. Joyboy practices with such skill: "He had only to be seen with a corpse to be respected." As Miss Aimée Thanatogenos, the junior cosmetician, remarks to him, "[F]or you the Loved Ones just naturally smile." Certainly for Aimée's own "handi-work" Mr. Joyboy always ensures that "the dry and colourless lips" of the corpse have "a nice bright smile."[100] In a letter written during his stay in California, Waugh remarked that he was "on easy terms with the chief embalmer. . . . It is . . . the *only* thing in California that is not a copy of something else."[101] In other words, it was at least a genuine craft.

III

The publication of *Brideshead Revisited* in 1945 preceded that of *The Loved One,* but it is more convenient to discuss it in connection with Waugh's other specifically Catholic novels, those of *The Sword of Honour* trilogy, which is, along with Eliot's *Four Quartets,* the finest work of English literature to come out of the Second World War. In retrospect, it, along with *Brideshead Revisited,* can now be seen as Waugh's greatest achievement, even though at the time prejudice against their Catholicism as well as postwar indignation against the author's well-publicized political and social views meant that the critical response was not as favorable as it should have been.

Brideshead Revisited begins with the narrator, Charles Ryder, expressing his disillusion with the "job" of soldiering. The prologue to the book contains an authentic picture of army life, but Waugh's personal experience of the job of soldiering did not engage his full creative powers till the trilogy. By profession, Ryder is himself a craftsman who finds his true metier as an architectural painter. The author shows his own fascination with craftsmanship in evoking Ryder's delight in having his "finger in the great, succulent pie of creation." And, as always in Waugh, there is the sense of sheer "job satisfaction" when the job is a genuine "craft" and done with "technical skill": "My work upheld me, for I had chosen to do what I could do well, did better daily, and liked doing."[102]

As I have already pointed out, as in *Vile Bodies*, although for a quite different reason, jobs or crafts do not feature very much in *Brideshead*. The don makes a reappearance in the person of Mr. Samgrass, a "fake," an "intellectual-on-the-make." The "author of several stylish little books," he is a genealogist who "claimed to love the past, but I always felt that he thought all the splendid company, living or dead, with whom he associated slightly absurd; it was Mr Samgrass who was real, the rest were an insubstantial pageant." A very significant part of his bogusness is that "he knew more than most Catholics about their Church; he had friends in the Vatican and could talk at length of policy and appointments"—indeed, "he had everything except the Faith."[103]

At the heart of *Brideshead* is this "Faith," or the business of being a Catholic. For it is the profession of Catholicism which dominates the book, and it is the job of being a Catholic, or rather of doing Catholic "things," which eclipses all other jobs. Charles Ryder is the typical Englishman with "no religion," although he was taken to church weekly as a child and attended chapel daily at school. The idea that "the supernatural" might be "the real" comes as a considerable surprise to him. He at first assumes that Sebastian Flyte's Catholicism which keeps surfacing in his conversation is "a foible, like his teddy-bear." But when he asks Sebastian if being a Catholic "makes much difference" to him, he is told, "Of course. All the time." Without any sense of the supernatural, Charles assumes that religion is synonymous with morality:

> "Well, I can't say I've noticed it. Are you struggling against temptation? You don't seem much more virtuous than me."
> "I'm very, very much wickeder," said Sebastian indignantly.[104]

As Waugh himself claimed in an article about his conversion, Catholics "are notable for their ability to pray without any feeling of affectation," for "prayer is not associated in their minds with any assertion of moral superiority," and they go to church because they are not good rather than because, like Protestants, they are good. It is also a natural part of their daily life: they "use their churches. It is not a matter of going to a service on Sunday; all classes at all hours of the day can be seen dropping in on their way to and from their work."[105]

Charles gets more and more confused: when he asks if Sebastian is required to "believe an awful lot of nonsense," he receives another mysterious reply: "Is it nonsense? I wish it were. It sometimes sounds terribly sensible to me." When Charles comments that Catholics "[s]eem just like other people," he is again sharply corrected by Sebastian: "[T]hat's exactly what they are not—particularly in this country, where they're so few. . . . [T]hey've got an entirely different outlook on life; everything they think important is different from other people." Whereas for an Englishman like Charles, religion is not something to talk about, for the Flyte family, he discovers, "It's a subject that just comes up naturally."[106]

The idea that religion is a natural part of life, not something to be brought out solemnly on Sundays, is a recurring theme of this study, and nowhere is it conveyed more amusingly and extravagantly than in *Brideshead,* in particular through the character of the youngest member of the Flyte family, Cordelia. On first meeting her, Charles hears that her last school report said that she was the worst girl in the memory of her convent school: "That's because I refused to be an Enfant de Marie. Reverend Mother said that if I didn't keep my room tidier I couldn't be one, so I said, well, I won't be one, and I don't believe our Blessed Lady cares two hoots whether I put my gym shoes on the left or the right of my dancing shoes." This natural matter-of-factness in Catholics which so impressed Newman is also linked with the reservation of the Blessed Sacrament: "'We must have the Blessed Sacrament here,' said Cordelia. 'I like popping in at odd times; so does Mummy.'" When Charles admits to the family that he is an agnostic, Cordelia (who has "made a novena for her pig") promises to pray for him: "I can't spare you a whole rosary you know. Just a decade. I've got such a long list of people. I take them in order and they get a decade about once a week." As Newman discovered, Catholicism is a businesslike religion, highly concrete and practical. It certainly astonishes Charles ("You know all this is very puzzling to me"), who, on remarking that it is more than he deserves, is assured by Cordelia, "Oh, I've got some harder cases than you." But Charles's agnosticism disappoints Cordelia in practical terms, as otherwise she would have asked him "for five shillings to buy a black goddaughter. . . . It's a new thing a missionary priest started last term."[107]

The job to which all the Flyte family are called is the practice of Catholicism, but they practice or fail to practice in different ways. Sebastian's elder brother, Bridey, nearly became a Jesuit, and he is represented as "Jesuitical" in his insistence on precise definitions.[108] This was an important aspect of Catholicism for Waugh, as it indicated a "world-order in which words have a precise and ascertainable meaning and sentences a logical structure," as opposed to the "chaos" of modern life. To a literary friend he once wrote that "God's order is manifest everywhere" and that as writers they were "entitled to see it specially in writing," so long as they recognized that writing differed "not at all from gardening or needlework or any other activity." Waugh despised any romantic notion about the writer, who for him was simply a craftsman in words, as he insisted to Thomas Merton: "[y]our monastery tailor and boot-maker would not waste material. Words are our materials." Words had to be crafted, but they also had to be ordered by reason. He told John Betjeman that logic was "the architecture of human reason," and, since his Anglo-Catholicism was "entirely without reason," it was not "genuine": he did not mind what he called "Barchester Towers" Protestants so much as Anglo-Catholics who "ape the ways of Catholics." He had earlier brutally informed poor Betjeman: "Many things have puzzled me from time to time about the Christian religion but one thing has always been self-evident—the bogosity of the Church of England."[109]

According to Cordelia, Bridey "thinks he has a vocation and hasn't." The narrator makes a point of emphasizing that Bridey has never had a job: "He had been completely without action in all his years of adult life; the talk of his going into the army and into parliament and into a monastery, had all come to nothing. All that he was known with certainty to have done . . . was to form a collection of match-boxes." But, of course, Bridey does have a job, and a very important one, that of being a Catholic. On his mother's side he is an old or recusant Catholic: his "grim mask" of a face is that of "a man of the woods and caves, a hunter . . . the repository of the harsh traditions of a people at war with their environment." Bridey knows all about fighting for the Faith, and he acts as the theologian of the family. Disapprove he may of Sebastian's drunkenness, but he knows perfectly well that "God prefers drunkards to a lot of respectable people." At the climax of the novel, when the question arises of whether to call a priest to Lord Marchmain's deathbed, Bridey explains to Charles "at some length" and in "quite logical" terms why this is necessary.[110]

Lady Marchmain is "popularly believed to be a saint," but she is more pious than holy, for holiness depends on love. Cordelia confesses to Charles that she never

> really loved her. Not as she wanted or deserved. It's odd I didn't, because I'm full of natural affections. . . . I sometimes think when people wanted to hate God they hated Mummy. . . . [Y]ou see, she was saintly but she wasn't a saint. No one could really hate a saint. . . . They can't really hate God either. When they want to hate him and his saints they have to find something like themselves and pretend it's God and hate that.[111]

If Lady Marchmain is a bogus saint, it is the alcoholic Sebastian who lapsed at Oxford who ends his days in a monastery. Sent from England to bring him back to see his dying mother, Charles finds him in a Franciscan hospital in Casablanca. There the lay brother tells Charles that Sebastian is "so patient . . . so kind . . . A real Samaritan." The "poor German boy," called Kurt, a former Foreign Legionary, with syphilis and a bad foot, whom Sebastian found starving in Tangier and took in, may be a "thoroughly bad hat," but he offers Sebastian something he never had before: "[I]t's rather a pleasant change when all your life you've had people looking after you, to have someone to look after yourself." Eventually, he ends up in a monastery at Tunis, where he has applied to be taken on as a missionary lay brother. Turned down for the order because of his drinking, he is nevertheless given a monastic cell with the idea that he should become "a sort of under-porter; there are usually a few odd hangers-on in a religious house . . . people who can't quite fit in either to the world or the monastic rule." Nanny Hawkins is astonished to hear from Cordelia that Sebastian is now "very religious"—"Brideshead was one for church, not Sebastian." Cordelia explains to Charles that Sebastian has now achieved "holiness'":

> I've seen others like him, and I believe they are very near and dear to God. He'll live on, half in, half out of, the community, a familiar figure pottering round with his broom and his bunch of keys. He'll be a great favourite with the old fathers, something of a joke to the novices.

Everyone will know about his drinking; he'll disappear for two or three days every month or so. . . . One can have no idea what the suffering may be, to be maimed as he is—no dignity, no power of will. No one is ever holy without suffering.[112]

When Charles first knew Sebastian, he equated religion with morality, but he now has to understand that holiness is not the same as moral virtue. In *The Sword of Honour* Waugh would attempt a much more ambitious portrait of holiness.

On his first introduction to the Flyte family, Charles learned that Lord Marchmain, far from being an old Catholic, was a convert at marriage but had lapsed: "Well, he's had to in a way; he only took to it when he married Mummy. When he went off, he left that behind with the rest of us." When the dying Lord Marchmain returns to Brideshead and to his family, he can regain the faith he left behind. The doctor tells Charles that Lord Marchmain is being worn down by his "fear of death." He asks Cordelia what has happened to the chapel which he had had built for his wife: "They locked it up, papa, when Mummy died." When Lord Marchmain loses consciousness and appears to be dying, Julia sends for the priest. Father Mackay, a "genial Glasgow-Irishman," whose brogue Cordelia enjoys imitating, was previously invited to breakfast after mass in order to try and bring Lord Marchmain back to the Church. The priest "made a hearty breakfast, glanced at the headlines of the paper, and then said with professional briskness: 'And now, Lord Brideshead, would the poor soul be ready to see me, do you think?'" Unsuccessful in his first visit ("I have not been a practising member of your Church for twenty-five years"), Father Mackay now returns, only to meet opposition from Cara, Lord Marchmain's mistress, and from Charles.

> He turned his bland, innocent, matter-of-fact face first on the doctor, then upon the rest of us. "Do you know what I want to do? It is something so small, no show about it. I don't wear special clothes, you know. I go just as I am. . . . I just want to ask him if he is sorry for his sins. I want him to make some little sign of assent; I want him, anyway, not to refuse me; then I want to give him God's pardon. Then, though that's not essential, I want to anoint him. It is nothing, a touch of the fingers, just some oil from this little box. . . ."

Julia, the older Flyte girl, who has also lapsed and become Charles's mistress, insists that Father Mackay be allowed to see her father.

> "Now," said the priest, "I know you are sorry for all the sins of your life, aren't you? Make a sign, if you can. You're sorry, aren't you?" But there was no sign. "Try and remember your sins; tell God you are sorry. I am going to give you absolution. While I am giving it, tell God you are sorry you have offended him." He began to speak in Latin. I recognized the words *"ego te absolvo in nomine Patris . . ."* and saw the priest make the sign of the cross. . . .
>
> The priest took the little silver box from his pocket and spoke again in Latin, touching the dying man with an oily wad; he finished what he had to do, put away the box and gave the final blessing. Suddenly Lord Marchmain moved his hand to his forehead. . . . [T]he hand moved slowly down his breast, then to his shoulder, and Lord Marchmain made the sign of the cross.

Charles has become sufficiently Catholic to think that the priest—who once outside the room reverts to his usual "simple, genial" self—should be "paid for his services."[113]

It would have been inconceivable for Tony Last to offer in effect a tip to Mr. Tendril when he called after his son's death, but then Mr. Tendril had no services *in that sense* to offer, only pious words. Father Mackay, on the other hand, makes no attempt to preach a sermon or to express religious sentiments to Lord Marchmain; he merely tells Lord Marchmain to do two things, to make an act of contrition and to make a sign. Similarly, the priest merely pronounces the Latin formulas which accompany the sign of absolution and the anointing. There are other aspects of Father Mackay which distinguish him from the Anglican clergyman. He is a social inferior but he is totally at ease; he is entirely human, even worldly; he doesn't use any special kind of religious voice; indeed, he does things rather than utters words; he is businesslike, matter-of-fact, and practical. And yet, unlike Mr. Tendril, the simple things he does—with his hands—are supernatural, for he is a divine craftsman: he knows his trade and does what he has to do in accordance with its rules, simply and without fuss. For, it should also be noted, Father Mackay exudes serenity, the serenity of certainty that this life has a meaning and a purpose and this world a divine order, and that he is a practitioner of a craft which can bring order into moral chaos by means of his artifacts, the sacraments. Charles noticed in his earlier days at Brideshead "how unlike" the priest who came to say mass in the chapel was "to a parson." Not because he seemed more religious, but apparently the reverse: "Father Phipps was in fact a bland, bun-faced man with an interest in county cricket."[114] Waugh's repeated use of the word *bland* to describe a Catholic priest is probably influenced by two factors: the desire, first, to stress that the job the priest does has nothing to do with his own personal charisma, as the personality of the craftsman is irrelevant to the execution of his craft, and, second, to suggest the self-confidence that results from the serenity of knowing that there is an order in the world and knowing what it is.

Sebastian originally told Charles that he and Julia were "semi-heathens." For Julia, as a debutante looking for an eligible husband, "her religion stood as a barrier between her and her natural goal," since the kind of eldest son she was looking for was not available to a Catholic. She felt trapped by the logic of her faith: "If she apostatized now, having been brought up in the Church, she would go to hell, while the Protestant girls of her acquaintance, schooled in happy ignorance, could marry eldest sons, live at peace with their world, and get to heaven before her." Forbidden by Lady Marchmain to marry Rex Mottram, she starts sleeping with him; but when she goes to see an old Jesuit at Farm Street, he tells her to go to confession: "'No thank you,' she said, as though refusing the offer of something in a shop." And from "that moment she shut her mind against her religion." When Lord Marchmain gives permission for the marriage, the suspicious Bridey discovers that Mottram has already been married, so he and Julia get married in a Protestant church. Cordelia assures Charles that neither Sebastian nor Julia will be "let . . . go" for long by God, and he quotes Chesterton's Father Brown as "saying something like 'I caught him' [the thief] with an unseen hook and an invisible line which is long enough to let him wander to the ends of the world and still to bring him back with a twitch upon the thread." Julia may reject the "thing" the priest in Farm Street offers her, but she will not escape a God whose priest is a divine fisherman. When she meets Charles again onboard ship, she tells him of her unhappy life with Rex. She has been "punished a little" for marrying him: "You see, I can't get all that sort of thing out of my mind, quite—Death, Judgement, Heaven, Hell . . . and the catechism. It becomes part of oneself." She knows what she is doing with Charles—"living in sin": she knows because, as she cries bitterly to Charles, you can get it "in black and white," buy "it for a penny, in black and white, and nobody to see that you pay; only an old woman with a broom at the other end, rattling round the confessionals, and a young woman lighting a candle at the Seven Dolours. Put a penny in the box, or not, just as you like; take your tract. There you've got it, in black and white." This is a world of clear definitions, a world of order as opposed to the moral chaos of Julia's world. When Charles urges that her feeling of guilt is only caused by "preconditioning from childhood," she replies, "How I wish it was!" And she angrily turns on Charles for trying to turn her "conscience" into a "pre-Raphaelite picture." She breaks off the affair: "[T]he worse I am, the more I need God. I can't shut myself out from his mercy."[115]

The first hint of Charles's conversion occurs when he is reunited with his wife, Celia, after his American travels. She remarks that he does not seem to have "changed at all":

> "No, I'm afraid not."
> "D'you want to change?"
> "It's the only evidence of life."[116]

This is an unmistakable echo of Newman's famous dictum that "to live is to change." And, interestingly, there is another distinct echo of Newman when, in her farewell to Charles, Julia says, "One can only hope to see one step ahead"—a clear allusion to Newman's "one step enough for me" in his poem "The Pillar of the Cloud," more commonly known as the hymn "Lead, Kindly Light."[117] The wider significance of these references will soon become apparent.

During the deathbed scene, Charles "suddenly felt the longing for a sign, if only of courtesy, if only for the sake of the woman I loved . . . praying, I knew, for a sign. . . . I prayed . . . simply; 'God forgive him his sins' and 'Please God, make him accept your forgiveness.'" And when Lord Marchmain does make the sign of the cross, "Then I knew that the sign I had asked for was not a little thing, not a passing nod of recognition, and a phrase came back to me from my childhood of the veil of the temple being rent from top to bottom." The book concludes with Charles, now a Catholic convert, returning to the chapel at Brideshead, where "the *art-nouveau* lamp burned once more before the altar. I said a prayer, an ancient, newly-learned form of words." There, "burning anew among the old stones," was "a small red flame—a beaten-copper lamp of deplorable design relit before the copper-beaten doors of a tabernacle; the flame which the old knights saw from their tombs, which they saw put out; that flame burns again for other soldiers, far from home."[118] The red light which burns before the tabernacle is that same light which so thrilled Newman after his conversion when he discovered that there Christ was present, sacramentally, perpetually in every Catholic church.

In the prologue to the novel, Hooper, Charles's subordinate officer, reported that the great house where they had been billeted, none other than Brideshead, had "a sort of R.C. Church attached. . . . [T]here was a kind of service going on—just a padre and one old man." What Hooper did not know was that he was witnessing a priest and his server at mass, "a craftsman and his apprentice," to use Waugh's words, about their business. On his first visit to Brideshead, Charles noted particularly the sanctuary lamp in the chapel, "bronze, hand-beaten." Much later, Cordelia describes to Charles how the chapel was closed after Lady Marchmain's death: "[T]he priest . . . blew out the lamp in the sanctuary, and left the tabernacle open and empty, as though from now on it was always to be Good Friday"— when the Blessed Sacrament is removed from the tabernacles in Catholic churches—"and then, suddenly, there wasn't any chapel there any more, just an oddly decorated room."[119] As Newman said, it was the presence of the reserved Sacrament which made a Catholic church a different kind of building from any other in the world. Or, as Waugh himself put it in his biography *Edmund Campion* (1935), at the Reformation the village churches of England became "empty shells."[120] The point that there is nothing special, humanly speaking, about a Catholic priest is made again when the Quartering Commandant tells Charles that the "blitzed R.C. padre" is "a jittery old bird. . . . He's opened the chapel; that's in bounds for the troops; surprising lot use it, too."[121] The personality of the craftsman is strictly irrelevant to his craft: a "jittery" priest can produce just as any other priest the same divine artifacts, "things" that are useful, that people need and want, to echo Waugh's view of the job of a writer.

In his historical novel, *Helena* (1950), Waugh did not attempt to introduce anachronisms such as tabernacles, any more than did Newman in *Callista*. But like Newman's novel, so Waugh's treatment of the finding of the true Cross by the Empress Helena, mother of Constantine, reflects his own sense of what he loved and valued in Catholicism—even though the Christianity of the third century was hardly Tridentine Catholicism and even though, as he once put it with provocative disregard for history, "For me Christianity begins with the Counter-reformation."[122]

In the newspaper article in which he explained his conversion to Roman Catholicism in 1930, Waugh maintained that the loss of faith in the modern world was "the active negation of all that western culture has stood for. Civilization . . . has not in itself the power of survival. It came into being through Christianity. . . ."[123] Before her conversion to Christianity, Helena wonders whether the wall of the Roman Empire, representing "order," that "single great girdle round the civilized world," might one day no longer be needed: "[W]on't Rome ever go beyond the wall? into the wild lands? Beyond the Germans, beyond the Ethiopians, beyond the Picts, perhaps beyond the ocean there may be more people and still more, until, perhaps, you might travel through them all and find yourself back in The City again."[124] This vision of order spreading throughout the barbarian world with the spread of Christianity reflects the author's own view that "the essential issue" for Europe was "no longer between Catholicism, on the one hand, and Protestantism, on the other, but between Christianity and Chaos"—with Christianity existing "in its most complete and vital form in the Roman Catholic Church."[125]

Unaware of the concrete objectivity of sacraments, Helena neverthe-less tests any religion that comes her way by asking whether it is factually true. Her husband, Constantius, who belongs to the cult of Mithras, is disgusted when she presses him as to the historical facts of the tale of Mithras—"a very childish question." Similarly, the Gnostic lecturer regards her question "When and where did all this happen? And how do you know?" as "a child's question." Replying that "[i]f I ever found a teacher it would have to be one who called little children to him," she then asks Lactantius if his Christian god had a historical existence: he answers that there are both written records and continuous oral tradition about Christ's birth and death. That is all Helena has ever asked, she tells Lactantius, "a straight an-swer to a straight question.'" She demands to know where the cross is on which Christ died, a question Pope Sylvester says nobody has ever asked before. "'Just at this moment when everyone is forgetting it and chattering about the hypostatic union, there's a solid chunk of wood waiting for them to have their silly heads knocked against. I'm going off to find it,' said Helena." Find it she does—and "she was as practical about arrangements as though some new furniture had been delivered at her house." Not a crafts-man, nevertheless Helena had a job to do which she did: "Her work was finished."[126] As Waugh wrote to Betjeman, the point of the novel is that Helena "just discovered what it was God had chosen for her to do and did it": she went "straight to the essential physical historical fact of the redemption."[127]

We come, finally, to Waugh's masterpiece, the *Sword of Honour* trilogy (1966), comprising *Men at Arms* (1952), *Officers and Gentlemen* (1955), and *Unconditional Surrender* (1961). At the outbreak of World War II, Waugh recorded in his diary: "My inclinations are all to join the army as a private. . . . Nothing would be more likely than work in a government office to finish me as a writer; nothing more likely to stimulate me than a complete change of habit."[128] In fact, a civil service job would surely have led to a marvelous satire on the world of bureaucracy; but Waugh was to have enough contact with the workings of Whitehall in his search for an army posting to provide him with the materials he needed. The army was a different matter: to learn what it is to be a soldier involves being one. And Waugh's choice was certainly inspired, as soldiering appealed more powerfully than perhaps any other job could have done to the two opposing sides of his personality. For on the one hand, nothing could be more disciplined, more ordered, more routine bound, than drilling on the parade ground; whereas, on the other hand, nothing was more anarchic and chaotic than a defeated army in headlong retreat. Both these aspects of army life were to be described from within and from personal experience in the trilogy.

On joining the Halberdiers, Guy Crouchback immediately falls in love with their ordered traditions and formalities. At dinner in the mess, he is fascinated by exactly the kind of detail which thrilled the craftsman in Waugh: "The removal of the cloth was a feat of dexterity which never failed to delight Guy. The corporal-of-servants stood at the foot of the table. The mess orderlies lifted the candlesticks. Then with a single flick of his wrists the corporal drew the whole length of linen into an avalanche at his feet." The trilogy abounds in such detailed descriptions of army life—again, reminding one of Kipling. Waugh positively revels in the esoteric, monotonous, mechanical maneuvers of the parade ground: "The odd numbers of the front rank will seize the rifles of the even numbers of the rear rank with the left hand crossing the muzzles, magazines turned outward, at the same time raising the piling swivels with the forefinger and thumb of both hands." Closely juxtaposed to this display of military craft by Guy is the visit he makes at the end of the parade to a Catholic church in Alexandria, where exactly the same sort of abrupt routine characterizes his going to confession:

> A bearded face was just visible through the grille; a guttural voice blessed him. He made his confession and paused. The dark figure seemed to shrug off the triviality of what he had heard.
> "You have a rosary? Say three decades."
> He gave the absolution.
> "Thank you, father, and pray for me."[129]

The craftsman has done his job according to the rubrics; that is all that matters, as Waugh emphasizes by indicating that the priest is a spy who, with his job done, tries to start up a conversation with Guy in the confessional.

Waugh imaginatively delights in the "alternating chaos and order" of soldiering. The visit to the church places Guy under suspicion as having had contact with a spy; a report clearing him, together with the original report, is then "photographed and multiplied and distributed and deposited in countless tin boxes" until it reaches military intelligence in London, where Colonel Grace-Groundling-Marchpole directs it should be filed under three different names, all connected in the mind of this intelligence officer. "'It all ties in,' he said gently, sweetly rejoicing at the underlying harmony of a world in which duller minds discerned mere chaos." The bogosity of the military bureaucrat as opposed to a genuine fighting soldier succeeds in first inventing disorder and then reducing it to a spurious order. Not that the order of the real army is impregnable, at least in wartime. Thus the regular soldiers "were survivals of a happy civilization where differences of rank were exactly defined and frankly accepted." And not only in battle is "the world of good order and military discipline" threatened by chaos: outside the strict parameters where routine reigns, military organization is always on the point of breaking down.[130]

Waugh rejoices in the bogosity of those in desk jobs in London, the military equivalent of civil servants. Major-General Whale, known as "Sprat" to a few old friends, is Director of Land Forces in Hazardous Offensive Operations. But he knows that his real hazardous and offensive operations are against his enemies in the War Office: "He need not name the enemy. No one thought he meant the Germans. 'There's only one thing for it. We must mount an operation at once and call in the press.'" A bogus operation called "Popgun" is mounted, which Ian Kilbannock, formerly of Fleet Street, now General Whale's press office, is instructed to write up, with "a little colour" added for the press release. The acclaimed "hero" of the operation ("our sole contribution to the war effort to date") is the bogus Trimmer, now called Colonel McTavish, whom Ian Kilbannock introduces to the American press corps as "a portent—the new officer which is emerging from the old hide-bound British Army." In his portraits of Ian, who has the "gift of tongues," varying his language according to whom he is speaking, and the American reporters Scab, Bum, and Joe, Waugh is back in a very familiar satirical world. Although General Whale forfeits the name "Sprat" in favor of "Brides-in-the-bath," "for the reason that all the operations he sponsored seemed to require the extermination of all involved," Hazardous Offensive Operations Headquarters expands from its "modest offices," now fully occupied by Ian Killbannock's press office, to "numerous mansions from Hendon to Clapham," filled with "experts" of all kinds, including "a Swahili witch-doctor . . . engaged to cast spells on the Nazi leaders."[131]

Unfortunately, the bogus, Waugh painfully discovered, is not restricted to those military personnel in desk jobs. Guy first saw his fellow officer, Ivor Claire, "putting his horse faultlessly over the jumps, concentrated as a man in prayer." Such a man "was the fine flower of them all. He was quintessentially England, the man Hitler had not taken into account." But Ivor is more than an equestrian craftsman. He also has a skill in redefining terms like *honor*, Guy discovers to his horror during the rout in Crete, when, with the British forces in full retreat, Ivor disobeys his orders and deserts his men, arguing that "in the next war, when we are completely democratic, I expect it will be quite honourable for officers to leave their men behind. It'll be laid down in King's Regulations as their duty—to keep a *cadre* going to train new men to take the place of prisoners." When Guy demurs, pointing out that soldiers "wouldn't take kindly to being trained by deserters," Ivor has his answer ready: "Don't you think in a really modern army they'd respect them the more for being fly?"[132]

Guy, then, discovers that soldiering involves chaos as well as order, the bogus as well as the genuine. But Guy also lives in another world, which throughout the novels exists alongside the world of war. In the prologue to *Men at Arms*, we learn that Guy belongs to an old Catholic family, with an ancestral home at Broome. It is now let to a convent school, but "the sanctuary lamp" in the chapel "still burned at Broome as of old." Like the sanctuary lamp at Brideshead, it is not "a thing of great antiquity," just "something" Guy's grandmother picked up in Rome. It is in this sense that the "phrase, often used of Broome, that its sanctuary lamp had never been put out" is only "figurative." But while it is not literally the same lamp that burned through penal times, the point that the Broome chapel has never been devoid of the Blessed Sacrament is the literal truth and not at all "figurative." It is not the artifact of the lamp, or even the tabernacle, that counts—it is almost appropriate that they should be things of little value—when the "artifact" that they indicate and contain is the real artifact that alone matters—the handiwork of the priest-craftsman.[133]

Men at Arms opens with Guy going to confession in Italy before leaving for England to join up in the war: "On an impulse, not because his conscience troubled him but because it was a habit learned in childhood to go to confession before a journey." What would seem to many to be mechanical and superficial strongly appeals to Waugh's imagination: routine prescribes a clear-cut job to be done, and the job is done without fuss but according to rule:

> There was no risk of going deeper than the denunciations of his few infractions of law, of his habitual weaknesses. Into that wasteland where his soul languished he need not, could not, enter. He had no words to describe it. There were no words in any language. . . .
>
> The priest gave him absolution and the traditional words of dismissal . . . and he answered. . . . He rose from his knees, said three "aves" . . . and passed through the leather curtain into the blazing sunlight.

There is the matter-of-factness too of Catholic practice, which contrasts in a later scene, when Guy is staying with his sister, Angela, with the Protestantism of his brother-in-law:

> "Mass is at eight," said Angela. "We ought to start at twenty to. . . ."
> "Oh I say, isn't there something later? I was looking forward to a long lie."
> "I thought we might all go to communion tomorrow. Do come, Tony."
> "All right, Mum, of course I will. Only make it twenty-five to in that case. I shall have to scrape after weeks of wickedness."

Box-Bender looked self-conscious, as he still did, always, when religious practices were spoken of. He did not get used to it—this ease with the Awful.

Similarly, Guy's father, Mr. Crouchback, "went to mass every day, walking punctually down the High Street before the shops were open; walking punctually back as the shutters were coming down, with a word of greeting for everyone he passed."[134]

It is not just that religion is a normal part of daily life, part indeed of the mundane routine, but that it provides a kind of eternal rhythm to the passing days and to their ephemeral events. Thus the winter months' training, when the "curriculum followed the textbooks, lesson by lesson, exercise by exercise," is suddenly set against a quite other world, but one which also has its year and its seasons: "On the morning of Ash Wednesday Guy rose early and went to mass. With the ash still on his forehead he breakfasted and tramped up the hill" back to the depot. A little later, St. Valentine's day comes round, when Guy "whenever possible went to mass." On leave during Holy Week, Guy visits his father: "Dawn was breaking that Good Friday when Guy arrived at the little church. . . . His father was alone, kneeling stiff and upright. . . . He turned to smile at Guy and then resumed his prayer." Months later on All Souls' Day, when Guy "walked to church to pray for his brothers' souls," an elderly convert, "Mr. Goodall was there, popping in and up and out and in again assiduously, releasing . . . soul after soul from Purgatory. 'Twenty-eight so far,' he said. 'I always try and do fifty.'"[135]

But it is not only the Catholic characters who live their lives against the order of this eternal calendar, or *ordo,* as the liturgical calendar, which is kept in every Catholic sacristy, is indeed named. Just when General Whale's enemies at the War Office "closed in for the kill," at that very time, "[o]utside, in the cathedral, whose tower could be seen from the War Office windows; far beyond in the lands of enemy and ally, the Easter fire was freshly burning." Defeated at the meeting, Spratt "returned to his own office. All over the world, unheard by Spratt, the *Exultet* had been sung that morning"—that is, the opening chant of the vigil mass of the Resurrection: "It found no echo in Spratt's hollow heart." Again, in the opening scene of *Officers and Gentlemen,* the sight of an air raid over London and firemen fighting the flames "reminded" Guy "of Holy Saturday at Downside . . . the doors wide open in the . . . Abbey . . . the glowing brazier and the priest with his hyssop, paradoxically blessing fire with water."[136]

Due to fly to Croatia, Guy once again goes to confession in Italy. The dialogue between priest and penitent is intentionally comical, but it is not satire on Waugh's part. What he knows will shock his Protestant readers is by the same token what he so much admires—the matter-of-fact, indeed the mechanical, the concrete, the punctiliously exact, the cut-and dried nature of Catholicism, which brings divine order into the chaos and uncertainty of human life:

> "Father, I wish to die."
> "Yes. How many times?"
> The obscure figure behind the grille leant nearer. "What was it you wished to do?"
> "To die."
> "Yes. You have attempted suicide?"
> "No."
> "Of what, then, are you accusing yourself? To wish to die is quite usual today. It may even be a very good disposition. You do not accuse yourself of despair?"
> "No, father; presumption. I am not fit to die."
> "There is no sin there. This is a mere scruple. Make an act of contrition for all the unrepented sins of your past life."
> After the Absolution he said: "Are you a foreigner?"
> "Yes."
> "Can you spare a few cigarettes?"[137]

Two things should be noted about the request of the priest: first, it illustrates again the way in which the mundane and natural coexist so easily with the supernatural; and second, while the priest shows himself a thoroughly skilled craftsman in the business of hearing confessions, he remains utterly human, even sinful, in spite of the nature of his artifact (divine absolution), in exploiting the sacramental occasion for his own material gain—but his character remains entirely irrelevant to his competence in his craft. Similarly, not only is the Irish priest in the town where the Halberdier barracks, to which Guy is first sent, is situated unenthusiastic about the Allied cause, but after mass he accosts Guy to get a list of the Catholic soldiers, ostensibly for the bishop but in fact, as Guy icily observes, because in the absence of a Catholic chaplain the parish priest gets a capitation grant from the War Office.

Meanwhile, in London at Westminster Cathedral, Guy's divorced wife Virginia, who has decided to become a Catholic in the hope that Guy will take her back, is also going to confession at about the same time. It is her first confession: "She told everything; fully, accurately, without extenuation or elaboration." This is exactly the kind of convert Waugh approved of— not emotional but matter-of-fact and to the point, like himself. "The recital of half a lifetime's mischief took less than five minutes. 'Thank God for your good and humble confession,' the priest said. She was shriven." Virginia herself was furious with Guy when, during an encounter much earlier, he suggested that, since in the eyes of his Church they were still hus- band and wife, there would be nothing wrong in their sleeping together: "I thought you'd chosen me specially, and by God you had. Because I was the only woman in the whole world your priests would let you go to bed with. That was my attraction. You . . . pig.'"[138] Such a legalistic Catholicism might appall a later generation of Catholics, but Waugh loves the precise definitions of this kind of theological formalism.

During the early training, when the Halberdiers are thrown into "chaos" by the sudden need in 1940 to send a battalion of regulars imme- diately to reinforce the retreating British forces in France, order is, as it were, restored on Sunday mornings when a priest, "untroubled by the 'flap,'" comes to say mass, "and for three-quarters of an hour all was peace." In *Unconditional Surrender,* by contrast, we are presented with the modern secular humanist, Everard Spruce, the founder and editor of *Survival,* who, "despite the title of his monthly review," believed "that the human race was destined to dissolve in chaos"; the magazine is professedly "devoted 'to the Survival of Values,'" but for Waugh such abstractions as values are the inevitable recipe for chaos, unlike the sacrifice of the mass, where some- thing happens, something is done by a craftsman who through his actions restores order and peace. Even when the secular world is offered something to worship like the sword made at the King's command as a gift to the people of Stalingrad for their heroic resistance to Hitler, "exposed for ado- ration" in Westminster Abbey "between two candles, on a table counter- feiting an altar," to be "venerated" by the people, they unhappily "knew no formal act of veneration . . . and passed on." By now, Guy, like his creator, has become thoroughly disillusioned, having originally enlisted in what he saw as a just war, indeed a holy crusade against the unholy alliance of the two godless tyrannies of Nazi Germany and communist Russia—"the Modern Age in arms."[139]

While Guy is still in Croatia, Virginia is killed in an air raid, so Guy goes to church with a tin of bully beef and bars of chocolate taken from army stores, which he presents to the priest—his offering for a mass to be said for her soul. Waugh, like Belloc, is proud, not ashamed, of this very concrete, earthy side of Catholicism, of the way in which financial goods are offered in exchange for spiritual works. This is not something familiar or acceptable to the English religious sensibility, as Guy discovered far earlier at the Halberdier barracks when he "earnestly" asked the Church of England padre:

> "Do you agree that the Supernatural Order is not something added to the Natural Order, like music or painting, to make everyday life more tolerable? It *is* everyday life. The supernatural is real; what we call 'real' is a mere shadow. . . . Don't you agree, Padre?"
>
> "Up to a point."
>
> "Let me put it another way . . ."
>
> The chaplain's smile had become set.

The chaplain was no doubt surprised to hear that the church service on Sunday was intended to make everyday life "more tolerable," but he would certainly have been taken aback to hear that Sunday service was just part of everyday life. But then his religion was very different from that of those Italians among whom Guy had lived, "to whom the supernatural order in all its ramifications was ever present and ever more lively than the humdrum world about them."[140]

Virginia wants to go back to Guy because she is with child by Trimmer, who has gone to America. Guy decides to sacrifice himself because he feels he has never done any purely unselfish deed in his life, and here is "something most unwelcome, put into my hands"—a soul, an unwanted child. Unable to explain to Kerstie Kilbannock what difference it makes saving one unwanted child who is no business of his, Guy seems to remember that somebody said: "All differences are theological differences." He is right: it was the dictum of Cardinal Manning which so impressed Hilaire Belloc. In Croatia Guy tries vainly to do another work of mercy by securing the evacuation of some Jews: "in a world of hate and waste, he was being offered the chance of doing a single small act to redeem the times." And so Guy's "crusade," during which he was involved in only one small ill-fated operation on the coast of Dakar apart from the rout in Crete, finds its "consummation in one frustrated act of mercy."[141] The job of soldiering has proved ultimately unsuccessful, but the job of being a Catholic, of doing Catholic things, remains. At the end of his life Waugh wrote (characteristically) in his diary that "[o]ne of the rarest experiences" is "to find a man or woman in any position capable of the job." "Growing up and growing old" are seen as "a continuous process of learning what one cannot do well." A member of an old faithful Catholic family, Guy at last discovers the job he can do because of his faith, a faith which a modern humanist like Kerstie does not possess.

The writer himself had written to a friend "very early in the war to say that its chief use would be to cure artists of the illusion that they are men of action"; it had "worked its cure" with him, for he knew now that he didn't "want to be of service to anyone or anything. I simply want to do my work as an artist." He now finally knew the nature of his true craft. All his life Waugh had wanted nothing else but to be a craftsman. When he had visited the Wembley Empire Exhibition in 1924, he had exclaimed ecstatically: "I saw sculpture and desired with all my heart to become a sculptor and then I saw jewels and wanted to be a jeweller and then I saw all manner of preposterous things being done in the Palace of Industry and wanted to devote my life to that too."[142] In *A Little Learning*, he recorded that he had "[a]lways . . . delighted in watching things being well done," feeling "a veneration for . . . artists, and a scorn for the bogus."[143] In the diary entry of 1964 where he explained sadly, in the midst of the liturgical changes of the Second Vatican Council, that what had attracted him to the Church was "the spectacle of the priest as a craftsman," he actually wrote: "Compare the Mass to the hunting-field. The huntsman's (priest's) primary task is to find and kill foxes. He is paid for this."[144] It was for this sacrifice of the mass that Guy gave the Croatian priest bully beef and chocolate.

In *Brideshead Revisited*, Waugh had attempted the extremely difficult task of describing holiness in the brief sketch of Sebastian in the monastery. The fact that Sebastian is still a flawed character, liable to drinking bouts, makes it easier for the author to avoid any trace of priggishness or sanctimoniousness. In *The Sword of Honour*, Mr. Crouchback is without faults and yet remains intensely human, indeed extremely lovable. Waugh, incredibly, never hits the wrong note. When Mr. Crouchback's grandson,

Tony, is reported missing and presumed dead, there is no trace of false piety in his brief, simple note to Guy: "He was always a good and happy boy and I could not ask a better death for anyone I loved. It is the *bona mors* for which we pray." The key to Waugh's triumph is that he makes Mr. Crouchback's faith entirely real and convincing, so that the holiness is not perceived as coming from *his* virtue or *his* efforts—it is not *his* (irritating) achievement, but God's.[145]

Nor is there any false asceticism: when Lent is over, Mr. Crouchback returns to his customary wine and tobacco:

> At luncheon Mr Crouchback drank a pint of burgundy. It was what his merchant cared to send him, not what he would have ordered, but he took it gratefully. After luncheon he filled his pipe. Now that he had no sitting-room, he was obliged to smoke downstairs. That afternoon seemed warm enough for sitting out. In a sheltered seat above the beaches, he lit the first pipe of Easter, thinking of that morning's new fire.

Waugh succeeds in conveying in this kind of quiet description the order and peace of the supernatural world, which the mass above all brings, and which puts the surrounding chaos and disorder into its proper perspective *sub specie aeternitatis*. Given the author's own notoriety as a snob, it is remarkable how careful he is in the opening characterization of Mr. Crouchback to stress that "[a]ll his pride of family was a schoolboy hobby compared with his religious faith." And when Ian Kilbannock's publicity skills ensure that Captain McTavish's exploits are fully reported in the newspapers, Mr. Crouchback doesn't falsely try to conceal his awareness of Trimmer's social background but at the same time comments admiringly: "He looks what he is—a hairdresser's assistant. And all honour to him. I expect he's a very shy sort of fellow. Brave men often are." He is as charitable as his son Guy will prove to be after a less publicized exploit of Trimmer gives Guy an unexpected heir. But by then Guy has had the advantage of this advice from his father (a letter he "carried always in his pocket book"): "The Mystical Body doesn't strike attitudes and stand on its dignity. It accepts suffering and injustice. It is ready to forgive at the first hint of compunction." Unaware of the future application of his words, Mr. Crouchback adds that "[i]f only one soul" were to be "[s]aved that is full compensation for any amount of loss of 'face.'"[146]

One obvious way of conveying holiness in fiction is to hint at a certain naïveté—one has to be a little naive to be quite so good—but that, of course, undermines the holiness, and Waugh has no intention of taking that easy way out. Far from it, he insists on the self-awareness of Mr. Crouchback: "As a reasoning man Mr Crouchback had known that he was honourable, charitable and faithful; a man who by all the formularies of his faith should be confident of salvation." But that doesn't lead to pride because "as a man of prayer he saw himself as totally unworthy of divine notice." And when we are told that "[t]o Guy his father was the best man, the only entirely good man, he had ever known," we don't feel we are being manipulated because that is how we feel too. The mercenary proprietor of the boardinghouse where Mr. Crouchback lives as a permanent resident, who knows as little or less than Kirstie about holiness, can only conclude in his "invincible ignorance": "He's a deep one and no mistake. I never have understood him, not properly. Somehow his mind seems to work different than yours and mine." His wife knows from the many grateful letters she has seen in his room that Mr. Crouchback "*gives* it away, right and left," handouts which include "a weekly allowance to an unfrocked priest." When Mr. Crouchback dies, it seems entirely appropriate that his solicitor should observe that, although none of Mr. Crouchback's furniture is "of any value," nevertheless "[i]t was all well made."[147] A man who has done the job of being a Catholic, of doing Catholic things, so perfectly would naturally also have well-crafted furniture.

Waugh died in 1966, a year after the Second Vatican Council concluded its proceedings. "The buggering up of the Church," he wrote to Nancy Mitford, "is a deep sorrow to me."[148] It was a tragedy that he should have lived to see a Council which in effect brought the Counter-Reformation to an end and which consciously sought to free the Church from the straitjacket of the rigidities of the Tridentine Church. For that routine, even mechanical, practice of Catholicism, that moral and canonical inflexibility, that cut-and-dried theology, that *ex opere operato* sacramentalism which insisted so peremptorily on the objectivity of the sacrament regardless of the character of the minister, and which above all stressed the sacrifice of the mass over all other eucharistic and liturgical considerations, were the very aspects of Catholicism which the Council sought to modify or reform but which were dear to Waugh's heart. For indeed it was these very factors which had not only drawn Waugh to the order of the Church as against the chaos of the modern world but contributed so significantly to the creation of some of the best novels of the twentieth century.

CONCLUSION

We saw in the Introduction how misplaced Newman's pessimism was about the possibility of an English Catholic literature. However, when we looked at the exceptions to the general rule that modern English literature is inevitably Protestant rather than Catholic, both those which Newman mentions and those which he doesn't, we could see that before the Catholic revival in the nineteenth century, there was no body of Catholic literature, in Newman's sense of literature, by writers who wrote as Catholics. Thus Crashaw was no more Catholic than Milton in writing in an Italian baroque style. Like Crashaw, Southwell did not write explicitly Catholic poetry. The most that can be said is that for Southwell, Alabaster, and Crashaw, lachrymal or "tears-poetry" was particularly appropriate for a Catholic poet to write because tears signify devotion and love as opposed to the Protestant stress on justification by faith. Dryden's one Catholic work used materials drawn from Protestant poetry and polemic. Pope did produce one poem which looks very Catholic in its ethos and form, but even so it is highly enigmatic in its sentiments.

It was not until the nineteenth century that the kind of Catholic writer envisaged by Newman begins to appear. An explicitly Catholic literature starts emerging, but the interesting thing is that the sort of obvious Catholic elements and themes which we would expect are more or less confined to the lesser writers, while the six principal Catholic writers who wrote *qua* Catholics and whom we have been examining in this book do not in fact conform to the expected pattern. The kind of motifs we would anticipate finding in such writers, especially when they are converts, as all but one of these six writers were, are surely the sort of things that are normally assumed to attract people to the Roman Catholic Church: aestheticism, a love of ritual, ceremony, tradition, the appeal of authority, a romantic triumphalism, the lure of the exotic and foreign, a preoccupation with sin and guilt.

Instead, the surprising discovery is to see how Catholicism influenced and shaped their writings in quite unexpected ways. It would be hard to imagine that the poet who is often called the first modern, twentieth-century poet would be affected by the demotic language of the popular devotions of English Catholicism in his attempt to bring English poetry closer to the rhythms and sounds of the spoken idiom. We also saw how Hopkins was influenced by the fact that a Catholic priest is a professional who does things with his hands, who indeed is a craftsman, and therefore whose work can form the subject of truly pastoral, in the sense of priestly, poetry. Newman was very aware too of this difference from the amateur, educated, gentlemanly Anglican clergyman. And both Newman and Hopkins made a special Catholic contribution to the Victorian literature of death. For Newman, the practical character of the priesthood was only a part of the sheer ordinariness of a religion that, paradoxically, impressed itself on him as being at the same time much more supernatural than Protestantism. His discovery of the naturalness of Catholicism, the way in which it was not separate from but a part of day-to-day life, the way in which, in a Catholic culture, the sacred mingles so easily with the secular, has been a continuing theme of this book. The objectivity of Catholicism came as a liberation after the subjectivity of Protestantism, and the freedom from the prison of one's own personal beliefs and opinions that a dogmatic religion sure of its own certainties provided was inseparable from the straightforward, businesslike nature of a religion which the believer could "practice" externally rather than merely hold internally.

This concreteness of faith and worship that so delighted Newman was at the very heart of Belloc's conception of Catholicism and his endeavor to make Catholicism real to the Protestant imagination. The Newmanian antithesis of objective and subjective becomes in Belloc the difference between the self-isolation of an individualistic religion, imprisoned in its own self-absorption, and the concrete reality of what he called the Catholic "thing"—not a mere theory or "ism," but the Church. Again, the matter-of-factness, the naturalness of a religion that is very much part and parcel of ordinary life, is a constant refrain in Belloc. His love of the hard-and-fast definitions of a Church so definite about its identity and beliefs is also present in Chesterton. For Chesterton, doctrinal definitions were only one form of the limitations which he thought were essential to life, since, paradoxically, there can be no space where there are no limitations. His own love of the ordinary and commonplace he saw reflected in Catholicism, which was not solemn like Protestantism but a popular religion which happily allowed grotesque gargoyles on its cathedrals and churches and whose holy days were also holidays.

Greene gives the usual Catholic sense of evil his own special flavor with his preoccupation in his Catholic novels with hell and mortal sin. Like Waugh, he saw that the novelist could make use of the new art form of the cinema—a visual medium more congenial to Catholicism than Protestantism—and in his best—Catholic—novels he combines this with the contemporary thriller to create an altogether new kind of Catholic fiction, the spiritual thriller. The idea of the priest as a craftsman, which we encounter in Chesterton as well as Newman and Hopkins, is central to Waugh's imaginative vision of a world sunk in chaos. Only the certainties of Catholicism can provide the necessary antidote to this universal anarchy. And at the heart of this divine order which only Catholicism can impose is the mass, which can come into being only through the action of the priest-craftsman. Once again, Catholicism is both otherworldly and at the same time utterly matter-of-fact, not least because of the mechanical sacramental routine, which imposes order on human life.

Of these six writers, two probably have found their definitive place in the canon: Hopkins and Belloc. If I have not actually stated it, I hope I have implied that Newman's literary, as opposed to theological, strengths could still be better and more widely appreciated. Chesterton, I have argued, is the most undervalued, simply because his nonfiction prose classics which mark him as the successor of the great Victorian "sages" have been so underplayed compared to his fiction and verse, which alone would categorize him as a minor writer. Greene's reputation, which I believe is inflated because of interest in his colorful private life and because several of his novels were so topical at the time in their setting, will, I'm convinced, gradually fade in comparison with that of Waugh, whose unfashionable views and cultivated eccentricities have helped to conceal his greatness as a novelist.

But whatever the future reputations of the writers in question, one thing is certain: Newman could hardly have been more wrong than when he sadly pronounced on the self-evident inability of Catholics to "form an English literature." For this they have done—and in the full sense in which he understood the idea of a "Catholic literature."

NOTES

Introduction

1. T. S. Eliot, *On Poetry and Poets* (London: Faber and Faber, 1957), 53–71. See John Henry Newman, *The Idea of a University,* ed. I. T. Ker (Oxford: Clarendon Press, 1976), p.641, n. 267, line 24.

2. Newman, *Idea,* 254, 263, 270, 271.

3. Newman, *Idea,* 262.

4. See Peter Milward, S.J., *The Catholicism of Shakespeare's Plays* (Southampton, England: St. Austin Press, 1997), with a bibliography of both biographical and literary studies.

5. Park Honan, *Shakespeare: A Life* (Oxford: Oxford University Press, 1998), 64.

6. Alison Shell, *Catholicism, Controversy and the English Literary Imagination, 1558–1660* (Cambridge: Cambridge University Press, 1999), 57, 62, 88, 93–94, 97, 101–2.

7. See James Anderson Winn, *John Dryden and His World* (New Haven, Conn. and London: Yale University Press, 1987), 380.

8. Newman, *Idea,* 255; Winn, *John Dryden,* 414, 423, 425–26.

9. Newman, *Idea,* 262–63.

10. Maynard Mack, *Alexander Pope: A Life* (New Haven, Conn. and London: Yale University Press, 1985), 326–28.

11. See Thomas Woodman, "Pope: The Papist and the Poet," *Essays in Criticism,* 46 (July 1996): 219–33. See also Mack, *Alexander Pope,* 337–39.

12. Newman, *Idea,* 263.

13. See James Boswell, *The Life of Samuel Johnson* (London: David Campbell, 1992), 1141. See also 377–79, 412, 482, 640.

14. *Apologia pro Vita Sua,* ed. Martin J. Svaglic (Oxford: Clarendon Press, 1967), 94.

15. Thomas Woodman, *Faithful Fictions: The Catholic Novel in British Literature* (Philadelphia: Open University Press, 1991).

16. Woodman, *Faithful Fictions,* 24.

17. Ford Madox Ford, *The Good Soldier* (Harmondsworth, England: Penguin Books, 1972), 117, 222.

18. Woodman, *Faithful Fictions,* 24.

19. See Woodman, *Faithful Fictions,* 67–69.

20. See Woodman, *Faithful Fictions,* 23–24.

21. See Woodman, *Faithful Fictions,* 32–33, 147.

CHAPTER 1. *John Henry Newman's Discovery of Catholicism*

1. John Henry Newman, *The Letters and Diaries of John Henry Newman,* ed. Charles Stephen Dessain et al., vols. 1–7 (Oxford: Clarendon Press, 1978–95), 11–22 (London: Nelson, 1961–72), 23–31 (Oxford: Clarendon Press, 1973–77), 23:288. Hereafter cited as *LD.*

2. *LD* 5:124.

3. Letter to H. E. Manning, 16 Nov. 1844, quoted in Ian Ker, *John Henry Newman: A Biography* (Oxford: Clarendon Press, 1988), 293.

4. John Henry Newman, *Apologia pro Vita Sua,* ed. Martin J. Svaglic (Oxford: Clarendon Press, 1967), 176. Hereafter cited as *Apo.* See also Ker, *John Henry Newman,* 254.

5. *LD* 1:131.

6. *Apo.* 41, 58–59.

7. *LD* 3:227, 230–32, 240–41.

8. *LD* 3:258.

9. *LD* 3:265.

10. *LD* 3:268.

11. *LD* 3:273–74, 227.

12. *LD* 3:277.

13. *LD* 3:280.

14. *LD* 3:289.

15. *Apo.* 43.

16. John Henry Newman, *Verses on Various Occasions,* 153. All references to Newman's works, except otherwise stated, are to post-1890 impressions of the uniform edition published by Longmans, Green, and Co. of London between 1868 and 1881, the rest of which underwent revisions up to the death of Newman in 1890.

17. John Henry Newman, *Certain Difficulties Felt by Anglicans in Catholic Teaching,* 1:371, 379; 2:24. Hereafter cited as *Diff.*

18. *LD* 24:325.

19. *LD* 11:131.

20. *LD* 11:129.

21. *LD* 11:65, 102; 12:336; 11:146.

22. *LD* 11:252–53.

23. *LD* 12:168.

24. *LD* 11:253.

25. John Henry Newman, *Discussions and Arguments on Various Subjects,* 388. Hereafter cited as *DA.*

26. *LD* 12:224.

27. *LD* 12:234.

28. *LD* 26:115.

29. See Ker, *John Henry Newman,* 364–72.

30. John Henry Newman, *Lectures on the Present Position of Catholics in England,* 253. Hereafter cited as *LPP.*

31. *DA* 295.

32. John Henry Newman, *Essays Critical and Historical,* 1:313, 333–34; 2:53.

33. Letter to M. Holmes, 6 Sept. 1841, quoted in Ker, *John Henry Newman,* 230.

34. *Apo.* 40.

35. John Henry Newman, *Loss and Gain: The Story of a Convert,* 28. Hereafter cited as *LG.*

36. *LPP* 253.

37. *Diff.* 1:276, 283.

38. *Diff.* 1:284–87.

39. *Diff.* 2:89.

40. Letter to F. Rogers, 10 Jan. 1841, quoted in Ker, *John Henry Newman,* 191.

41. *LD* 20:220, 339.

42. *Diff.* 1:288.

43. *Diff.* 1:289–90.

44. *LG* 426–27.

45. *LD* 14:322.

46. *LD* 28:5.

47. *LG* 28.

48. Charles Dickens, *Great Expectations,* chap. 4.

49. *LG* 327–29.

50. *LG* 427.

51. John Henry Newman, *Parochial and Plain Sermons,* 2:171 (hereafter cited as *PPS*), and *Lectures on the Doctrine of Justification,* 330.

52. John Henry Newman, *Callista: A Tale of the Third Century,* 219–20, 265, 292.

53. *PPS* 5:316, 318, 324.

CHAPTER 2. *From Oxford to Liverpool*

1. Geoffrey Hill, *The Lords of Limit: Essays on Literature and Ideas* (London: André Deutsch, 1984), 100–102.

2. Eric Griffiths, *The Printed Voice of Victorian Poetry* (Oxford: Clarendon Press, 1989), 267, 286, 294, 321.

3. Griffiths, *Printed Voice,* 313, 344, 323–24.

4. John Henry Newman, *The Letters and Diaries of John Henry Newman,* ed. Charles Stephen Dessain et al. (Oxford: Clarendon Press, 1978–95), 6:47–48; hereafter cited as *LD;* John Henry Newman, *The Via Media of the Anglican Church,* 1:121, n. 9.

5. G. K. Chesterton, "The Thing: Why I Am a Catholic," in *The Collected Works of G. K. Chesterton* (San Francisco: Ignatius Press, 1986–), 3:285.

6. John Henry Newman, *Loss and Gain: The Story of a Convert,* 425. Hereafter cited as *LG.*

7. John Henry Newman, *Meditations and Devotions of the Late Cardinal Newman* (London: Longman, Green, 1893), 225. Hereafter cited as *MD.*

8. *MD* 241–43.

9. See *Epitome Societatis Jesu* (Rome, 1689).

10. "A Devout Method of Hearing Mass," in *The Catholic Manual of Instructions and Devotions* (Liverpool, 1915), 36–51.

11. See Gerard Manley Hopkins, *The Poetical Works of Gerard Manley Hopkins,* ed. Norman H. Mackenzie (Oxford: Clarendon Press, 1990), 400.

12. Gerard Manley Hopkins, *The Letters of Gerard Manley Hopkins to Robert Bridges,* rev ed., ed. Claude Colleer Abbot (London: Oxford University Press, 1955), 46, 89. Hereafter cited as *LHB.*

13. Gerard Manley Hopkins, *Further Letters of Gerard Manley Hopkins Including His Correspondence with Coventry Patmore,* rev ed., ed. Claude Colleer Abbot (London: Oxford University Press, 1955), 41–42.

14. *MD* 256.

15. *MD* 1–78.

16. Hopkins, *Poetical Works,* 400 (editor's note).

17. *MD* 227–28.

18. *MD* 238.

19. Evelyn Waugh, *The Diaries of Evelyn Waugh,* ed. Michael Davie (London: Phoenix, 1995), 792.

20. Hopkins, *Poetical Works,* 266 (editor's note).

21. Hopkins, *Poetical Works,* 419 (editor's notes).

22. Virginia Ridley Ellis, *Gerard Manley Hopkins and the Language of Mystery* (Columbia: University of Missouri Press, 1991), 178.

23. John Henry Newman, *Certain Difficulties Felt by Anglicans in Catholic Teaching,* 1:290.

24. *LHB* 86.

25. Gerard Manley Hopkins, *The Sermons and Devotional Writings of Gerard Manley Hopkins,* ed. Christopher Devlin, S.J. (London: Oxford University Press, 1959), 19.

26. Michael Wheeler, *Death and the Future Life in Victorian Literature and Thought* (Cambridge: Cambridge University Press, 1990), 304.

27. Eamon Duffy, *The Stripping of the Altars: Traditional Religion in England c. 1400–c. 1580* (New Haven, Conn. and London: Yale University Press, 1992), 475.

28. See Hopkins, *Poetical Works,* 343–44 (editor's note).

29. Wheeler, *Death,* 303.

CHAPTER 3. *Hilaire Belloc and the Catholic "Thing"*

1. Hilaire Belloc, *The Cruise of the "Nona"* (1925; London: Constable, 1928), 54–55. Hereafter cited as *CN*.

2. A. N. Wilson, *Hilaire Belloc* (London: Hamish Hamilton, 1984), 4–5.

3. *CN* 20, 55, 56, 259.

4. Hilaire Belloc, *Survivals and New Arrivals: The Old and New Enemies of the Catholic Church* (1929; Rockford, Ill.: Tan, 1992), 3–4. Hereafter cited as *SNA*.

5. Hilaire Belloc, *The Great Heresies* (1938; Rockford, Ill.: Tan, 1991), 5, 18, 28, 76, 132, 147. Hereafter cited as *GH*.

6. Hilaire Belloc, *Europe and the Faith* (1920; Rockford, Ill.: Tan, 1992), 154. Hereafter cited as *EF*.

7. *EF* 2, 72.

8. *GH* 12, 97, 66.

9. *EF* 96, 165–67.

10. *EF* 170.

11. *GH* 120.

12. *SNA* 81–82.

13. Hilaire Belloc, *Essays of a Catholic* (1931; Freeport, N.Y.: 1967), 21–22. Hereafter cited as *EC*.

14. *GH* 115.

15. *CN* 126.

16. *GH* 115.

17. *SNA* 4.

18. *GH* 139.

19. *EC* 34–35, 67–68.

20. Hilaire Belloc, *The Servile State* (1912; London: Constable, 1927), 50, 75, 58. Hereafter cited as SS.

21. *SNA* 5.

22. Hilaire Belloc, *The Four Men: A Farrago* (1912; London: Nelson, n.d.), 100. Hereafter cited as *FM*.

23. Hilaire Belloc, *Hills and the Sea* (1906; London: 1941), 61. Hereafter cited as *HS*.

24. *CN* 88.

25. *EC* 95.

26. *EF* 10–11, 97, 171, 173, 191; *EC* 144.

27. *CN* 173–74.

28. *EF* 183, 186, 187, 190.

29. *EF* 187; *GH* 53.

30. A. N. Wilson, introduction (unpaginated) to *Complete Verse*, by Hilaire Belloc (1954; London: Pimlico, 1991). Hereafter cited as *CV*.

31. Wilson, introduction to *CV*.

32. *CV* 164.

33. Wilson, introduction to *CV*.

34. *GH* 144, 160.

35. *EF* 39, 41.

36. *SNA* 153.

37. *CN* 119.

38. *EC* 155.

39. *EF* 151.

40. *HS* 230–31, 191.

41. *SNA* 41.

42. *CN* 121, 124, 341, 346–47.

43. *EC* 56, 60, 121–22, 240, 305, 309.

44. *EF* 171.

45. *EC* 148, 56, 76, 78, 288.

46. *EF* 150, 185, 187.

47. *GH* 140, 154.

48. *HS* 143, 231–32, 249.

49. *CV* 25, 55, 95.

50. *HS* 6.

51. *FM* 321.

52. *HS* 182.

53. Wilson, *Hilaire Belloc*, 215.

54. Hilaire Belloc, *The Path to Rome* (1902; Washington, D.C.: Regnery Gateway, 1987), 130–31. Hereafter cited as *PR*.

55. *PR* 96.

56. *PR* 416–17.

57. *PR* 67.

58. *PR* 153–55.

59. *PR* 86.

60. *PR* 46–49.

61. *PR* 386.

62. *PR* xviii.

63. *PR* 142.

64. *PR* 223.

65. *PR* xiv; Wilson, *Hilaire Belloc,* 105–6.

66. *PR* 157.

67. Hilaire Belloc, *Letters from Hilaire Belloc,* ed. Robert Speight (London: Hollis and Carter, 1958), 151, 192, 209, 248.

68. *PR* 158.

69. *PR* 161.

CHAPTER 4. *The Dickensian Catholicism of G. K. Chesterton*

1. G. K. Chesterton, *Autobiography* (Sevenoaks, England: Fisher Press, 1992), 298. Hereafter cited as *A*.

2. F. W. Newman, *Contributions Chiefly to the Early History of the Late Cardinal Newman,* 2d ed. (London: Kegan Paul, 1891), 44.

3. Alzina Stone Dale, *The Outline of Sanity: A Biography of G. K. Chesterton* (Grand Rapids, Mich.: Erdmans, 1982), 203, 218.

4. *A.* 251. See Maisie Ward, *Gilbert Keith Chesterton* (London: Sheed and Ward, 1944), 384, for Chesterton's view of Anglo-Catholicism as "only a Porch" to the main building. See 390 for Chesterton's view of the Roman Catholic Church as "a much vaster arsenal, full of arms against countless . . . potential enemies."

5. *A* 77–78.

6. *A* 351–52.

7. G. K. Chesterton, *The Collected Works of G. K. Chesterton* (San Francisco: Ignatius Press, 1986–), 1:282. Except where otherwise stated, all references are to this edition, which is hereafter cited as *W*.

8. *A* 340–42, 345–46.

9. *W* 15:127–28.

10. *W* 15:292.

11. *W* 15:64–65.

12. *W* 15:62.

13. *W* 15:66–67.

14. *W* 15:46–49.

15. *W* 15:137.

16. *W* 15:178, 89, 187.

17. *W* 15:89, 96.

18. *W* 15:147, 184.

19. *W* 15:187–88.

20. *W* 15:326.
21. *W* 15:336–37.
22. *W* 15:106.
23. *W* 15:203.
24. *W* 15:203.
25. *W* 15:100–01.
26. *W* 15:50.
27. *W* 15:176.
28. *W* 15:201.
29. *W* 15:107.
30. *W* 15:111–12.
31. *W* 15:150, 167, 179.
32. *W* 15:188–89.
33. *W* 15:145–47.
34. *W* 15:181.
35. *W* 15:185.
36. *W* 15:131–32.
37. *W* 15:92–93.
38. *W* 15:263–64.
39. *W* 15:162.
40. *W* 15:209.
41. *W* 1:212–13.
42. *W* 2:378, 150–51. There is a serious omission of one paragraph and two half-paragraphs at 150–51 in the Ignatius Press *Collected Works,* although the words quoted here are unaffected.
43. *W* 2:185, 226.
44. *W* 1:217, 363.
45. *W* 15:193–94.
46. *W* 1:275, 277–78, 282–84, 310–15.
47. *W* 1:320.
48. John Henry Newman, *Essay on the Development of Christian Doctrine,* 40.
49. *W* 1:330–32.
50. *W* 1:330–32.
51. *W* 1:337, 301, 340–42.
52. *W* 1:293, 295, 318, 297, 299, 319, 300, 303–6.
53. *W* 1:342–43.
54. *W* 1:345.
55. *W* 1:350.
56. *W* 1:250–51, 355.
57. *W* 1:364.
58. *W* 1:317.

59. *W* 1:325–26.
60. *W* 1:307.
61. *W* 1:366.
62. *W* 1:328.
63. *W* 15:112–13, 148, 155.
64. *W* 1:230–31.
65. *W* 1:243–45, 264–65, 267.
66. *W* 1:287.
67. *W* 2:256, 309, 401.
68. *W* 2:401–2.
69. *W* 2:301.
70. *W* 2:346–47.
71. *W* 2:376.
72. *W* 2:267.
73. *W* 2:322.
74. *W* 2:360–61.
75. *W* 2:310, 312.
76. *W* 2:373–74.
77. *W* 18:171, 369.
78. *W* 18:285–88.
79. W 18:260, 309–11, 371, 359, 362, 368, 370, 330, 334, 374.
80. *W* 18:173.
81. *W* 2:131.
82. *W* 2:74–78.
83. *W* 2:88–89.
84. *W* 2:132.
85. Ward, *Gilbert Keith Chesterton,* 525–26.
86. *W* 2:483–84, 489, 494.
87. *W* 2:505, 531, 536, 538, 540–42.
88. *W* 2:429, 458, 467, 513, 517, 522, 529.
89. *W* 2:487, 483, 550–51.
90. *W* 2:430–31, 433, 435–36.

CHAPTER 5. *The Catholicism of Greeneland*

1. Marie-Françoise Allain, *The Other Man: Conversations with Graham Greene,* trans. Guido Waldman (London: Bodley Head, 1983), 21, 157; cf. 78, 161.
2. Graham Greene, *Collected Essays* (1970), 17. Hereafter cited as *CE.* All references to Greene's works are to the Penguin editions.
3. Graham Greene, *The Lawless Roads* (1947), 14–15. Hereafter cited as *LR.*

4. John Henry Newman, *Apologia pro Vita Sua,* ed. Martin J. Svaglic (Oxford: Clarendon Press, 1967), 217–18.

5. Graham Greene, *Fragments of Autobiography* (1972), 214, 120, 212. Hereafter cited as *FA.*

6. Graham Greene, *Journey without Maps* (1971), 213. Hereafter cited as *JWM.*

7. *LR* 34, 184.

8. *JWM* 17.

9. Norman Sherry, *The Life of Graham Greene,* vol. 1, 1904–1939 (Harmondsworth, England: Penguin, 1990), 260.

10. Allain, *The Other Man,* 168–69, 158.

11. *FA,* 118–20; cf. Allain, *The Other Man,* 154.

12. Allain, *The Other Man,* 160.

13. *FA,* 336; cf. 213.

14. Evelyn Waugh, *The Letters of Evelyn Waugh,* ed. Mark Amory (London: Phoenix, 1995), 2.

15. *FA* 179.

16. Graham Greene, *Stamboul Train* (1963), 103–4. Hereafter cited as *ST.*

17. Samuel Hynes, ed., *Graham Greene: A Collection of Critical Essays* (Englewood Cliffs, N.J.: Prentice Hall, 1973), 3–4.

18. Graham Greene, *The Third Man* (1971), 104, 106. Hereafter cited as *TM.*

19. *CE* 16–17.

20. Allain, *The Other Man,* 62, 37.

21. *CE* 17.

22. *CE* 21, 154, 31, 36, 40, 43. Cf. Allain, *The Other Man,* 161.

23. *CE* 123, 137–38.

24. *CE* 131, 133, 137.

25. *CE* 92, 98.

26. Allain, *The Other Man,* 82.

27. *FA* 212. Cf. Allain, *The Other Man,* 159: "I don't see why people insist on labelling me a Catholic writer. I'm simply a Catholic who happens to write."

28. Allain, *The Other Man,* 160.

29. John Henry Newman, *The Idea of a University,* ed. I. T. Ker (Oxford: Clarendon Press, 1976), 246, 259, 261, 270.

30. John Henry Newman, *The Letters and Diaries of John Henry Newman,* ed. Charles Stephen Dessain et al. (Oxford: Clarendon Press, 1978–95), 18:319.

31. Allain, *The Other Man,* 132–33.

32. *FA* 212–13.

33. *FA* 216, 214. Cf. Allain, *The Other Man,* 148: "Brighton Rock . . . started in my mind as a thriller."

34. *ST* 116–17.

35. Graham Greene, *It's a Battlefield* (1940), 140, 148.

36. *FA* 138.

37. Sherry, *Life of Graham Greene*, 256.

38. Graham Greene, *Brighton Rock* (1943), 35. Hereafter cited as *BR*.

39. *BR* 52, 91, 97, 228.

40. *BR* 36, 113, 126–27, 198–99.

41. *BR* 167, 169, 182, 189, 194, 228, 230, 241–42.

42. *BR* 246. See Roger Sharrock, *Saints, Sinners and Comedians: The Novels of Graham Greene* (Tunbridge Wells, England: Burns and Oates, 1984), 98–99.

43. *FA* 85.

44. Allain, *The Other Man*, 19.

45. *FA* 86.

46. *BR* 246.

47. See, e.g., Paul O'Prey, *A Reader's Guide to Graham Greene* (London: Thames and Hudson, 1988), 72, 75.

48. *BR* 91, 107–9, 179, 227–28.

49. Allain, *The Other Man*, 157–59.

50. *The Catechism of the Catholic Church*, Eng. trans. (London: Geoffrey Chapman, 1994), art. 1861.

51. *BR* 246.

52. *BR* 21.

53. *BR* 98.

54. *BR* 104.

55. *BR* 120.

56. *BR* 239–40.

57. For the idea of the "holy sinner" in nineteenth- and twentieth-century literature, see Sharrock, *Saints, Sinners*, 88–89.

58. Graham Greene, *The Power and the Glory* (1962), 68, 60. Hereafter cited as *PG*.

59. *PG* 61–62, 66, 118, 124, 128. The kind of hamfisted approach to matters requiring only a modicum of religious discrimination and knowledge which is so characteristic of the post-Christian literary critic is well exemplified by this crass comment on the priest in *The Power and the Glory*: "It is Greene's triumph to create a character who, while he may break every rule of Catholic dogma and some of secular morality also, is revealed to us from the inside as overflowing with a loving concern for mankind. If the rules take precedence over that, so much the worse for the rules is surely Greene's implication." Grahame Smith, *The Achievement of Graham Greene* (Brighton, England: Harvester Press, 1986), 88.

60. *PG* 22, 71, 82, 93, 167.

61. *PG* 45, 70, 82–83, 208.

62. *PG* 208, 139, 82.

63. *PG* 67, 81, 127.

64. *PG* 100, 99, 95, 196, 200.

65. *PG* 128, 131–32.

66. *PG* 135, 70.

67. *PG* 79, 126–27, 196, 208, 210.

68. See Ian Ker, *John Henry Newman: A Biography* (Oxford: Clarendon Press, 1988) 722.

69. *PG* 216, 219.

70. *PG* 176.

71. *PG* 161, 163, 173.

72. Terry Eagleton, *Exiles and Émigrés: Studies in Modern Literature* (London: Chatto and Windus, 1970), 109, 112.

73. *PG* 139.

74. Eagleton, *Exiles,* 113.

75. See Allain, *The Other Man,* 167–68.

76. *PG* 195.

77. Eagleton, *Exiles,* 117, 113.

78. Eagleton, *Exiles,* 113.

79. Eagleton, *Exiles,* 114.

80. *PG* 10.

81. Eagleton, *Exiles,* 114.

82. *PG* 193.

83. *PG* 51.

84. *LR* 123, 40–41, 44, 48–49, 50, 155, 122, 208–9, 116.

85. Allain, *The Other Man,* 155.

86. Graham Greene, *The Heart of the Matter* (1962), 35–36. Hereafter cited as *HM.*

87. *HM* 60, 89, 210–11, 217, 219; cf. 257.

88. *HM* 210.

89. Donat O'Donnell, *Maria Cross: Imaginative Patterns in a Group of Modern Catholic Writers* (London: Chatto and Windus, 1954), 76.

90. *HM* 219, 60, 210, 159, 223–24, 206, 178.

91. *HM* 189.

92. *FA* 247–48; Allain, *The Other Man,* 26.

93. *HM* 213, 224, 225.

94. *HM* 244, 232, 258.

95. *HM* 229, 265, 272.

96. Graham Green, *The End of the Affair* (1962), 123. Hereafter cited as *EA.*

97. *EA* 136–37, 191, 138, 190, 59.

98. *EA* 101–2, 106, 109, 111–12.

99. *EA* 152–54, 176.

100. *FA* 308.

101. See, e.g., Graham Greene's *Our Man in Havana* (1962), 217; *The Comedians* (1967), 162–63, 225, 235, 286; *The Honorary Consul* (1974), 210, 218; *The Human Factor* (1978), 163.

102. Graham Greene, *A Burnt-Out Case* (1963), 158.

103. Leopoldo Duran, *Graham Greene: Friend and Brother,* trans. Euan Cameron (London: HarperCollins, 1984), 289; *FA* 121.

104. *FA* 382; Allain, *The Other Man,* 136.

105. Graham Greene, *The Honorary Consul,* 206, 219, 225–26. Hereafter cited as *HC.*

106. *HC* 223, 115, 198, 217, 243, 224, 240.

107. Duran, *Graham Greene,* 239–40, 289, 315.

108. Quoted in Norman Sherry, *The Life of Graham Greene,* vol. 2, 1939–1955 (Harmondsworth, England: Penguin, 1996), 437.

109. Allain, *The Other Man,* 71.

CHAPTER 6. *Evelyn Waugh*

1. C. S. Lewis, "Kipling's World," *Selected Literary Essays,* ed. Walter Hooper (Cambridge: Cambridge University Press, 1969), 235.

2. Evelyn Waugh, *A Little Learning* (1983), 190. Hereafter cited as *LL.* Except where otherwise stated, all references to Waugh's writings are to the Penguin edition, and, in the case of *Men at Arms, Officers and Gentlemen,* and *Unconditional Surrender,* to the one-volume *Sword of Honour* trilogy.

3. See Martin Stannard, *Evelyn Waugh: The Early Years 1903–1939* (London: Dent, 1986), 37, 40, 61–65.

4. Evelyn Waugh, "The Hand of the Master," *Spectator,* 1959, reprinted in *The Essays, Articles and Reviews of Evelyn Waugh,* ed. Donat Gallagher (London: Methuen, 1983), 536–37. Hereafter cited as *EAR.*

5. See Stannard, *Evelyn Waugh,* 56–60.

6. Evelyn Waugh, preface to Francis Crease, *Thirty-Four Decorative Designs* (1927), reprinted in *EAR* 23.

7. Evelyn Waugh, *Work Suspended and Other Stories* (1951), 295–97, 303, 307–9, 314. Hereafter cited as *WS.*

8. See Stannard, *Evelyn Waugh,* 78, 82, 85, 87, 91.

9. See Stannard, *Evelyn Waugh,* 87–89.

10. Evelyn Waugh, "General Conversation: Myself," *Nash's Pall Mall Magazine,* March 1937, reprinted in *EAR* 190–91.

11. *LL* 225, 190.

12. Christopher Sykes, *Evelyn Waugh: A Biography* (London: Collins, 1975), 59–61; Stannard, *Evelyn Waugh*, 108–9.

13. *LL* 228.

14. Evelyn Waugh, *The Diaries of Evelyn Waugh*, ed. Michael Davie (London: Weidenfeld and Nicolson, 1976), 213. Hereafter cited as *D*.

15. *LL* 229–30.

16. See Stannard, *Evelyn Waugh*, 115–19, 127–28, 132–33.

17. *D* 281.

18. *D* 282.

19. *D* 289–90.

20. Stannard, *Evelyn Waugh*, 140–41.

21. Evelyn Waugh, *Rossetti: His Life and Works* (London: Methuen, 1991), 219.

22. Evelyn Waugh, *The Letters of Evelyn Waugh*, ed. Mark Amory (London: Phoenix, 1995), 27. Hereafter cited as *L*.

23. *D* 292–93.

24. *EAR* 190–92.

25. *D* 289.

26. Evelyn Waugh, *Decline and Fall* (1937), 14. Hereafter cited as *DF*.

27. *DF* 17–18.

28. *DF* 36–38.

29. *LL* 222. But cf. Sykes, *Evelyn Waugh*, 60.

30. *DF* 35, 61–63.

31. *DF* 75, 96.

32. *DF* 202, 204.

33. *DF* 141.

34. *DF* 162, 176, 175.

35. *DF* 134, 143–44.

36. *DF* 32–33.

37. *DF* 141.

38. *DF* 165.

39. *DF* 177, 181.

40. *DF* 28–30.

41. *DF* 101.

42. *DF* 58.

43. *DF* 140.

44. DF 198–99.

45. *DF* 124.

46. *DF* 128.

47. *DF* 115, 119, 142–43.

48. Evelyn Waugh, *Vile Bodies* (1938), 104. Hereafter cited as *VB*.

49. *VB* 7–8, 11, 12, 80.

50. *VB* 21.

51. See Stannard, *Evelyn Waugh,* 93–94.

52. See Stannard, *Evelyn Waugh,* 201.

53. *VB* 82–83, 86.

54. *VB* 111,

55. See Sykes, *Evelyn Waugh,* 99.

56. *VB* 111, 50.

57. Evelyn Waugh, *Labels: A Mediterranean Journal* (1985), 13, 16. Hereafter cited as LMJ.

58. *LMJ* 22.

59. *LMJ* 53–54.

60. Evelyn Waugh, *Remote People* (1985), 11, 41. Hereafter cited as *RP.*

61. *RP* 67–68.

62. *D* 335; *RP* 66–67.

63. See Stannard, *Evelyn Waugh,* 3; Robert R. Garnett, *From Grimes to Brideshead: The Early Novels of Evelyn Waugh* (Lewisburg, Pa.: Bucknell University Press, 1990), 23–24; Ian Littlewood, *The Writings of Evelyn Waugh* (Oxford: Basil Blackwell, 1983), 157.

64. *RP* 49.

65. *RP* 184.

66. *RP* 159.

67. Evelyn Waugh, *Black Mischief* (1938), 38–39. Hereafter cited as *BM.*

68. *BM* 49–50.

69. Evelyn Waugh, *Ninety-Two Days* (1986), 74. Hereafter cited as *ND.*

70. Martin D'Arcy, S.J., "The Religion of Evelyn Waugh," *Evelyn Waugh and His World,* ed. David Pryce-Jones (London: Weidenfeld and Nicolson, 1973), 64.

71. *ND* 77.

72. *L* 55.

73. *L* 267.

74. *EAR* 630.

75. *ND* 74–75.

76. *ND* 86–87, 102.

77. *D* 361.

78. Evelyn Waugh, *A Handful of Dust* (1951), 208, 210, 214. Hereafter cited as *HD.*

79. *HD* 137–38, 151.

80. Evelyn Waugh, "The War and the Younger Generation," *Spectator, 1929,* in *EAR* 62.

81. *HD* 160, 203.

82. *HD* 30.

83. Stannard, *Evelyn Waugh*, 380; Douglas Lane Patey, *The Life of Evelyn Waugh: A Critical Biography* (Oxford: Basil Blackwell, 1998), 119.

84. *HD* 14, 32, 115.

85. *HD* 97, 110–11.

86. *HD* 78–79, 84.

87. Evelyn Waugh, *Waugh in Abyssinia* (1986), 40. Hereafter cited as *WA*.

88. *WA* 56, 89, 143, 83–84, 109.

89. *WA* 49, 97–98, 65, 113, 142, 163–64, 169.

90. Evelyn Waugh, *Scoop: A Novel about Journalists* (1943), 17–18. Hereafter cited as *S*.

91. *S* 25, 179, 220.

92. *S* 149.

93. *S* 64–66, 84, 146, 92.

94. *WS* 107.

95. Evelyn Waugh, *The Ordeal of Gilbert Pinfold* (1962), 9.

96. *WS* 115–16.

97. Evelyn Waugh, *Mr. Loveday's Little Outing and Other Sad Stories* (London: Chapman and Hall, 1936), 136–37.

98. Evelyn Waugh, *Put Out More Flags*, 62, 68, 63. Hereafter cited as *POMF*.

99. *POMF* 48, 50, 49, 139, 143, 189.

100. Evelyn Waugh, *The Loved One: An Anglo-American Tragedy* (1951), 55–56, 62, 79.

101. *L* 247.

102. Evelyn Waugh, *Brideshead Revisited: The Sacred and Profane Memories of Captain Charles Ryder* (1962), 12, 213, 215–16. Hereafter cited as *BR*.

103. *BR* 167, 106–7.

104. *BR* 83–84.

105. Evelyn Waugh, "Converted to Rome: Why It Has Happened to Me," *EAR* 105.

106. *BR* 87–91.

107. *BR* 90.

108. *BR* 90.

109. *L* 215, 308, 242, 318, 267.

110. *BR* 213, 266–67, 133, 140, 314.

111. *BR* 86–87, 212–13.

112. *BR* 204–7, 293, 288, 291, 293–94.

113. *BR* 86, 316, 318, 311–12, 320–23.

114. *BR* 82.

115. *BR* 87, 175, 182, 212, 247, 273, 276–77, 324.

116. *BR* 220.

117. John Henry Newman, *Essay on the Development of Christian Doctrine,* 40; *BR* 324; John Henry Newman, *Verses on Various Ocasions,* 156.

118. *BR* 322, 330–31.

119. *BR* 22, 40, 212.

120. Evelyn Waugh, *Edmund Campion* (London: Hollis and Carter, 1947), 127.

121. *BR* 326.

122. *L* 102.

123. *EAR* 104.

124. Evelyn Waugh, *Helena* (1963), 39.

125. *EAR* 103–4.

126. *Helena,* 66, 83–84, 87, 128, 155–56.

127. *L* 339–40.

128. *D* 438.

129. Evelyn Waugh, *The Sword of Honour Trilogy* (1984), 43, 288–89. Hereafter cited as *SH.*

130. *SH* 155, 304, 246, 350.

131. *SH* 285, 311, 364, 366, 362, 408, 407.

132. *SH* 281, 368.

133. *SH* 16, 442.

134. SH 13, 26, 29.

135. *SH* 89, 99, 125, 223.

136. SH 284–85, 197.

137. *SH* 519.

138. *SH* 519, 104.

139. *SH* 149, 417, 404, 413, 11.

140. *SH* 61, 12.

141. *SH* 504, 535, 566.

142. *D* 790, 548, 164.

143. *LL* 41, 141.

144. *D* 792.

145. *SH* 159.

146. *SH* 297, 29, 312, 485, 400.

147. *SH* 437, 221, 399, 441.

148. *L* 633.

INDEX

Acton, Harold, 152
Alabaster, William, 4, 203
Alfonso Liguori, Saint, 14
Allain, Marie-Francoise, 109, 111, 115, 124, 134, 137, 140
Arnold, Matthew, 2, 75, 107
Austen, Jane, 149

Baring, Maurice, 11
Belloc, Hilaire: and Chesterton, 12, 57; status of as writer, 57, 205; *The Path to Rome*, 57, 69–74; and Newman, 57, 64–65, 67; on all questions as ultimately religious, 57–58; Manning's influence on, 57, 64; *The Cruise of the "Nonna,"* 58, 62, 66; *Survivals and New Arrivals*, 58; on Arianism, 58; on effect of secularisation of Europe, 58–59; on effects of Reformation, 59–63, 67, 69, 70; *Europe and the Faith*, 58, 62–63; on Catholic making of Europe, 59; on denial of unity of Church as essential principle of Protestantism, 59; on apostasy of Britain from the Church, 60; on individualism and isolation of Protestantism, 60–61, 62–63, 67, 204; on Catholic doctrine of equality, 61; on Protestantism as cause of capitalism, 61–63; *The Servile State,* 61; on distributism, 61–62, 70; sense of isolation of, 63–64, 72, 73–74; on Church as opposed to Christianity or Catholicism, 64–65, 204; on concrete objective reality of Church, 64–65, 73–74, 204; on realism and common sense of Catholicism, 65–67, 73; *Hills and the Sea,* 65; *Essays of a Catholic,* 66; on Protestantism's abandonment of reason, 67; on earthiness of Catholicism, 67; and Hopkins, 67; on importance of pilgrimages, 67, 69; on Protestantism's separation of sacred from secular unlike Catholic view of religion as part of life, 67–69, 70–72, 74, 204; delight of in shocking Protestants, 68–69, 71–73; "Upon God the Wine-Giver," 68; *The Four Men,* 69; powers of observation of, 69; on European Catholic unity, 70; on definitions and legalism of Catholicism, 71, 204; on matter-of-factness of Catholicism, 71–72, 204
Benson, Robert Hugh, 10
Bentham Jeremy, 29, 159
Bernanos, Georges, 115
Betjeman, John, 184, 192
Boswell, James, 6–7

IAN KER is a member of the theology faculty at Oxford University. His many works include *Newman on Being a Christian, The Achievement of John Henry Newman, Newman the Theologian,* and *Newman and Conversion,* all published by the University of Notre Dame Press.